CURRICULUM MATTERS IN IRELAND

CURRICULUM MATTERS
IN IRELAND

ANTON TRANT

BLACKHALL
Publishing

This book was typeset by Ark Imaging for

Blackhall Publishing
33 Carysfort Avenue
Blackrock
Co. Dublin
Ireland

e-mail: info@blackhallpublishing.com
www.blackhallpublishing.com

© Anton Trant, 2007

ISBN: 978-1-84218-136-2

Printed in the UK by the Athenaeum Press Ltd.

For Kathy,
Maurice, Mary-Liz, Nicholas and Barbara,
and the next generation of learners –
Michael, Heather and Luke

About the Author

Anton Trant was the founder of the CDVEC Curriculum Development Unit and, for twenty-six years, was its first director. Previously, he was a teacher in London and Malta before joining the City of Dublin VEC. In 1966, he was appointed principal of Ballyfermot Vocational School with a brief to develop a comprehensive curriculum in a community context. In 1973, he became a research fellow in education in Trinity College Dublin, where he subsequently lectured in Curriculum Studies on the M.Ed. programme. He also directed two environmental education networks, the first comprising sixty schools from ten European countries, the second with twenty-six schools in Ireland, North and South. In 1985 he received the Lorado Taft Award from the University of Illinois for his contribution to outdoor education. From 1987 to 2004 he acted as evaluator of the Wider Horizons Programme of the International Fund for Ireland.

Foreword

Two things fill the mind with ever new and increasing admiration and awe the more often and steadily we reflect upon them; the starry heavens above me and the moral law within me.

Immanuel Kant, *Critique of Practical Reason*

When considering Anton Trant and his life in curriculum development and as a teacher, I am drawn to the concluding passage of Kant's *Critique of Practical Reason*, stated above. Anton's vision of education, which explores what it means to be human, is deeply informed by Christian thought, and influenced by the desire for change and the radical ideas that emerged in the 1960s, combined with a somewhat sceptical outlook on the views of established authorities. This vision or theory of education, which asserts the central role of the teacher in curriculum development, has had very practical benefits.

Anton, while suggesting the need to walk lightly on the earth and leave few footprints behind, has paradoxically left an impressive footprint in the sphere of education in Ireland. As a founder and first director of the CDVEC Curriculum Development Unit (CDU) he initiated a number of pilot projects, many of which have developed into national programmes, and, at local level, have left a legacy of teacher capacity and confidence to initiate new developments, including those in the emerging Further Education sector.

This publication, which is part history, part philosophy, part politics and part biography, tells a story of curriculum and the influences and theories that have swayed debate around the subject. *Curriculum Matters in Ireland* asks the reader to reconsider the curriculum, particularly in an education climate deluged by legislation, external imperatives and demands for accountability, and peppered with terms such as 'performance indicators', 'risk management', 'compliance measures', 'contractual responsibilities' and 'quality assurance'. By emphasising the engineering dimension and not considering education also as a science and an art, we are at risk of fulfilling Lee Cronbach's prophecy of accountability becoming 'a sign of pathology in the political system'. Although accountability in education is necessary in a democratic and global society, it should never be the cause of inequality or damage teacher and student morale. Accountability, if it is to be meaningful, should be realistic and accompanied by a significant amount of trust. Given its nascent level in Ireland, Anton's analysis of values and evaluation opens our eyes to the task ahead of us.

Reading the book has brought home to me the importance of the ongoing endeavour of relating the curriculum to the fundamental personal and social challenges facing us today. Foremost among these challenges is the need to foster trust in human relationships. Trust is an essential part of the social fabric and must be earned, renewed and not assumed. In order to build trust in the community, educators will continually need to articulate the meaning of education and contextualise, adapt and negotiate the curriculum with different communities of learners. The degree of trust is linked to the quality of relationships formed.

I believe that, since we are social beings, education is about the nature and quality of the relationship we have with ourselves and others and with the natural and constructed world. It is through the expression of these three inter-connecting relationships that meanings are formed. The quality of the relationships profoundly affects learning and deeply influences the development of meaning. A balance between all three elements should be promoted in educational settings. We have had some success in the primary curriculum but, as we progress through secondary and onto further and higher level, there is, with rare exceptions, less focus on personal and social development and expression.

Anton's book prompts me to mention a second major challenge facing educators today. It is generally accepted that education should explore what it means to be human, and realise human potential. The question, however, is how schools, colleges and centres can realise these far from finite aims. While the concerns of the formal and examined curriculum are important, it is the development of values and the capacity for lifelong learning that will be of enduring worth to the student. One area which has the capacity to set out a new agenda and provide the basis for a renewal of the moral and social purpose of schools is in the emerging field of education for sustainable development.

Education for sustainable development (ESD) extends from the local to the global, includes the natural and humanly constructed environment and embraces the social justice values of care, respect, interdependence, human rights, peace, inclusion, equality, and citizenship. ESD questions how we use our resources, the ethics of production and consumption of goods and services, and the use and impact of technologies on the natural environment and on society. ESD challenges the values underpinning our society, and posits the creation of a global economic climate that places a high value on renewable and sustainable activities within a social justice context. In responding to these challenges, we need to develop our capacity for imaginative, creative and entrepreneurial engagement in identifying and implementing new solutions.

Education for sustainable development, like other aspects of education, is not the exclusive domain of schools, colleges and centres. The contribution by the non-formal and informal areas of education within the wider community and with various state bodies will play an important and vital role. The educational task for all learners is to deepen our understanding and develop a capacity to enhance the quality of all life without using assets that more appropriately belong to future generations.

The UN decade of education for sustainable development (2005–2015) has the potential to be a catalyst for curriculum development at all levels and sectors. In particular, it could add further impetus to the introduction of citizenship studies, politics, sociology, philosophy, and psychology at upper secondary level. Aside from the requirement to reformulate subject areas, new opportunities should be found for students to engage critically with the different forms of knowledge and find a basis to enable them to integrate their learning. Teachers will need to develop new approaches to teaching and learning that will allow for greater democratic engagement, ownership and responsibility in the quest for knowledge and the improvement of our capacity for taking action.

Anton refers to Alasdair MacIntyre's remarks that teachers are the forlorn hope of the culture of western modernity. This is a sentiment recently echoed by Garret FitzGerald when he argued that we must now look to teachers in particular to address the profound problems brought about by a changing society. The overriding concern of both authors is the collapse of a consensus on values and, although they may have an overly pessimistic view of the future, the important point is the central role teachers are being called upon to play. Given this vital role, teacher development should be the core of curriculum development

Such are the thoughts prompted by reading *Curriculum Matters in Ireland*. The opportunity to witness the development of early drafts has allowed me to engage in many a long discussion with Anton on curriculum matters in general and their relevance to the CDU in particular. Through this engagement my own understanding of the curriculum has been deepened and for this I am eternally grateful. It has allowed me, with renewed strength, to take up the baton on behalf of the CDU which is always fragile in need of nurturing and protection.

Finally, through this publication, Anton continues to exercise a leadership role. His advocacy of the teacher as learner and researcher is timely. How enriched we would be if other teachers had the time and support to tell their own curriculum story in the context of their own research and learning theory. How more engaged and less alienated our community of learners would be if the democratic values of voice, deliberation and listening were more common.

In an era where there is greater consciousness of our interdependence and the necessity for sustainable activities, there is a new urgency to reconsider the underlying values of the emerging curriculum. *Curriculum Matters in Ireland* will inspire and stimulate discussion on what is at the heart of education and hopefully will help to create the basis for informed debate, decision making and action.

Aidan Clifford
Director of the CDVEC Curriculum Development Unit, Dublin

Acknowledgements

I wish to thank the following:

- The teachers I worked with over the years, especially in the City of Dublin VEC schools. In a real sense, my book is theirs as well; it is based on good teaching practice, which is always a communal affair. I also owe a debt of gratitude to my own teachers. I realise now that one of the greatest of God's gifts is a good teacher.
- The staff members of the Curriculum Development Unit, who were my colleagues during the 26 years I spent in that unique educational community. In particular, I would like to thank Director Aidan Clifford without whose constant interest and support the book would not have been possible; the senior administrator Alma Hobson, who gave me unfailing and outstanding help; and librarians Eva Hornung and Trish Quigley who assisted with background research and references.
- The academic institutions that enabled me to think out my curriculum rationale, notably the staff of the School of Education, Trinity College, Dublin under the late Professor J.V. Rice, and Dr Paddy Walsh of the London University Institute of Education.
- The many educational administrators, inspectors and politicians with whom I came in contact in the perennial struggle of developing the curriculum. Some I disagreed with, others I greatly admired, but from all I learnt the value of always trying to work towards a consensus of minds and hearts. For me that was one of the most important discoveries in writing the book.

- My publisher, Blackhall Publishing, especially Gerard O'Connor and Elizabeth Brennan for believing in the worth of the venture and the professional manner with which they carried it through.
- Finally, my family, especially Nicholas who designed the cover, Mary-Liz who commented on innumerable drafts and shared with me her own insights on the curriculum, and my wife Kathy who prepared the text and walked every step of the journey with me.

Contents

Contents

Grey is all theory,
Green grows the golden tree of life.

Johann Wolfgang von Geothe

Introduction

Today we have a plethora of curriculum programmes and projects, many on a national scale. This is in marked contrast to the state of affairs thirty-five years ago, when a few pioneers were launching the first curriculum projects in the country. These intrepid warriors had great difficulty in making themselves understood and often met with opposition from the guardians of the system, who were outraged that anybody could have the temerity to interfere with the established order. All that has changed; the state is now investing large sums of money in curriculum development and several third-level institutions have introduced the study of the curriculum into their diploma and degree courses.

Originally, a curriculum was a running track for athletes, which reminds us of features still associated with the word – starting and finishing lines, inner and outer tracks, sorting out the competitors, drawing up a programme of events and deciding who are the winners and losers. The term came into prominence in education nearly four hundred years ago with the reorganisation of learning that followed the Reformation and Counter-Reformation. In the medieval universities, there was little structure or sequence in the way courses were given. In Glasgow, we are told the teachers met on the opening day of the academic year to decide the texts from which they would give public readings and commentaries, but there was no generally agreed order in which the texts were to be read or studied. By the sixteenth century, this haphazard approach had become more formalised, and words like *ordo* (order or sequence) and *modus* (method) had come into use. In Paris, for instance, a major revision of the university's teaching practices was called the *Modus et Ordo Parisiensis*, while in the records of the universities of Leiden and Glasgow the term curriculum, denoting an ordered and disciplined course of studies, made one of its first appearances (Hamilton 1990).

In 1599, the Jesuits published their influential *Ratio Studiorum*, or programme of studies, which is probably one of the first recorded exercises in curriculum development. A draft document had been drawn up fifteen years earlier by a committee of six, representing over 160 Jesuit colleges throughout Europe. It was sent out for comment and in 1591 a new document was issued. This in turn was revised before the final version was agreed. The following extract from the *Ratio Studiorum* is still a sound piece of advice for would-be curriculum developers:

> They shall not bring forward any views that are useless, anti-quated, absurd, or patently false, nor shall they use too much time in mentioning and refuting such views. They shall strive to prove their conclusions not by the number of their arguments but by their effectiveness.... They shall not cite the authorities of learned people too often, but if they have the evidence of outstanding writers to confirm their views, they shall faithfully quote the other's own words if possible, but briefly. (Ulich 1965: 277)

In the seventeenth century, with the growing interest in astronomy, the curriculum acquired a new dimension. The idea of a solar system with interacting parts had attractive implications for education. Just as the sun and planets were perceived to be in harmony with each other, a comparable harmony was sought in the various elements of the curriculum. But the subsequent history of education paid only partial attention to ideas of unity and harmony. As we moved into modern times, the curriculum became fragmented into subjects, modules and lessons, and the ideal of making the whole-ness of the human experience available to the learner became increasingly difficult to attain. The process of fragmentation was greatly accelerated by the industrialisation of western society and the organisation of learning tended to follow the industrial model of the conveyor belt and the division of labour.

In our own day, although we have abandoned the cruder versions of the industrial model, we still retain a fairly mechanistic mind-set about how the curriculum works. The general view seems to be that the curriculum is a means–end operation; if we spell out our objectives, inputs, methods and outputs, everything will be fine. The alternative view, that the curriculum should be the script for a learning encounter between human beings, is seldom heeded. The modern curriculum has become refined, pre-digested, packaged and marketed. It has no rivals for there are no alternatives, a situation that brings its own dangers, as David Hamilton points out:

> As the curriculum is refined, so the possibilities of intervention by teachers and learners are reduced. In the extreme, teachers are envisaged as little more than curriculum minders. They are no longer encouraged to enter into, or comment upon, the curriculum storehouse. They are relocated in a subordinate position, as curriculum doorkeepers, curriculum customs officers and curriculum security guards. (1990: 45)

What should our understanding of curriculum be today? My answer – which I deal with in this book – is coloured by my own experience. I was an accidental teacher, but in the Ireland of the 1950s probably not the only one. It was a destitute time, when jobs were scarce and emigration was high. When eras are in decline, Goethe once said, all tendencies are subjective, but when matters are ripening for a new epoch, all tendencies are objective. The mood of the 1950s was subjective, inward-looking and lacking in hope and confidence. I had left college with an arts degree and for five long months looked for a job, any job. I was offered nothing except advice – one head-teacher suggested emigrating to Australia. I followed his advice and took the emigrant trail, not to Australia but to London, where I was offered a teaching job within a day of my arrival. I vowed I would never come back.

London in the mid-1950s was enjoying a post-war boom and teachers were in short supply. Although I had no professional teaching qualification, I was accepted as a probationer on the strength of my Irish degree and put into the care of one of Her Majesty's Inspectors, who visited me once a term. At the end of the year the inspector was sufficiently happy to recommend that I be made permanent. I had become a qualified member of the teaching profession.

I think at the time I was pleased but not elated. It was not something I would have chosen for myself but now that I had a secure job I tried to interest myself in the new world I was entering. The first thing I noticed was the loneliness and how uncertain and vulnerable I often felt. For all the hustle and bustle of school life, teachers are essentially on their own and get very little affirmation. I remember asking my first school principal, a formidable but not unkindly lady, if I were any good as a teacher. She replied like the Delphic oracle: 'Only you yourself can discover the answer.' It took me many years of doubt and needless mistakes to make that discovery. Sometimes in the staff-room colleagues would jokingly refer to the tricks of the teaching trade, but at the end of the day I was on my own to survive as best I could. It was only when I became a principal myself that I realised the importance of teachers coming together to work in small teams. I also learnt that ending the isolation of teachers is very difficult to achieve because almost everything in the culture of schooling conspires against it.

This book puts forward a view of curriculum that has the teachers at the centre of the stage. It is where they deserve to be. The views expressed are based on my own work as a teacher at first, second and third level in Ireland and abroad. What I have to say is not radically new and has been said before, but I have come to realise the importance of repeating some of the old refrains. After nearly fifty years of teaching and research, I find myself concluding that, although much has been said about curriculum, little enough has been achieved. It is all the more important that the struggle for curriculum reform continues and those who now bear the brunt of the battle should be encouraged by those who, like myself, have retired from the fray.

Part I of the book begins with a chapter on values because values underlie the entire curriculum. We inherit many of our values from the past, others we shape to meet the demands of the present. Chapter 1 looks at both kinds and the value systems or ideologies on which they are based. Chapters 2 and 3 examine a particular ideology – equality of educational opportunity – from my own view point. Two experiences had a marked influence on my career: being in charge of a school and founder of a curriculum development centre. Both taught me a lot about the meaning of equality.

Part II of the book describes my curriculum rationale. It owes much to others who have gone before me, scholars like Ralph Tyler, Jerome Bruner, Paul Hirst, Lawrence Stenhouse, Malcolm Skilbeck, Denis Lawton, A.V. Kelly and Paddy Walsh, several of whom I was fortunate to have known personally. A broad view of curriculum is presented, encompassing four different elements. The first puts the emphasis on formulating and implementing aims and objectives (Chapter 4). This is primarily an instrumental approach because it views the curriculum mainly as a means towards achieving a particular purpose, sometimes broadly defined and at other times broken down into identifiable ready-made tasks. For instance, if your principal concern is to prepare young people for a certain occupation in life, then you will devise a curriculum based on the competencies and attitudes that will be needed.

The second element of the rationale views the curriculum primarily in terms of transmitting knowledge (Chapters 5 and 6). This can be called the product or content approach because it sees the curriculum as a way of packaging and passing on the different types of knowledge that young people need to lead a useful and full life. It is probably the most common and longstanding approach and still not a bad starting point in the practical job of curriculum building. The third element sees the curriculum, not as a product, but as a process or series of interactions between teachers and students. These interactions are dynamic and variable, and therefore difficult to prespecify in detail. From this point of view, the curriculum is like painting a picture that results from the interaction of colour, form and creativity

(Chapters 7 and 8). The fourth element emphasises the appraisal of curriculum outputs; this comprises the evaluation of programmes and projects (Chapter 9) and student assessment (Chapter 10).

I offer the above curriculum rationale tentatively, more as a hypothesis than a formula. The four approaches should not be rigidly separated from one another but seen as interrelated and overlapping elements in an organic whole. Nor do I believe that there should be a strict hierarchy among them, that aims and objectives should always come first and evaluation and assessment last. The curriculum is a dynamic entity and should be looked at in a holistic way. A good curriculum should always be balanced and integrated; if any one element is unduly emphasised, the entire curriculum will suffer. I believe that in this country the third approach, curriculum as process and interaction, is neglected, while the fourth, curriculum as appraisal of outputs, is emphasised to the point of distortion. I hope that the rationale will be of interest to teachers at all levels of education and also to students and parents and indeed anyone who believes the curriculum should not be treated as sacrosanct but something to be explored and constantly questioned. It is too important to be regarded otherwise.

Part III of the book describes three case studies of curriculum in action, educational disadvantage (Chapter 11), saving the environment (Chapter 12), and peace and reconciliation (Chapter 13). The studies are based on my work in these areas over the years. They do not give a detailed educational history of the period they relate to, but are meant to illustrate the different elements of the rationale described in Part II.

No curriculum rationale is complete without an overall educational vision and, in the concluding chapter, I give mine. It is based on three fundamental values which sum up what the book is about – a regard for truth, the ability to live together and leadership in the service of others. A vision should also give some hope for the future; in my own case, the hope stems from a Christian standpoint.

The methodology underlying the book is theoretical analysis illumined by narrative; each complements the other and both are equally important. I once read a lovely definition of curriculum: it is the story we tell about the good life. It is a story told from one generation to the next and is an immensely important one – a break in the telling between two generations could mean the end of much of our culture. Storytelling is sometimes regarded as unscientific and simplistic, but this view underestimates the complexity and significance of the story, both as a literary form and as a mode of understanding reality. We might be disposed to take stories more seriously, Harold Rosen observes, if we perceived them first and foremost as efforts to transform our experience into meaningful patterns that we can share and compare with those of others. Nor should the story be considered as something different from non-narrative forms of discourse such as analysis and generalisation. Inside every discourse, Rosen remarks, there stalk the ghosts of a story, while inside every narrative there stalk the ghosts of discourse. There are always stories crying to be let out and meanings crying to be let in (Rosen n.d.: 12–3).

We dream in stories and we remember, hope, despair, learn and love through stories. Narrative is our primary means of making sense of what would otherwise be a chaotic world. If we are to comprehend reality at all, we have to place it between the covers of a story that has a beginning and an end. As Rosen reminds us 'even so stark an ending as death is only an ending when we have made a story out of a life' (Rosen n.d.: 13).

All of us have our own curriculum story to tell and many of the examples in this book are part of my story. I would like to acknowledge the great debt I owe to those who have helped me along the way. I have been fortunate in being able to play a part in what I now see as a very creative movement in the history of Irish education, the school-based and teacher-led curriculum development movement that began at the end of the 1960s and lasted for nearly two decades. It was a movement characterised by flair, energy and freedom, in which a number of very talented teachers ventured into exciting areas of curriculum innovation. The movement was eventually replaced by a more centralised model of curriculum development, which, although far better resourced, was much more tightly controlled. This book cannot do justice to those pioneering teachers by telling their story as it deserves to be told. All I can hope to do is raise in passing a few flags of recognition and tribute.

I would also like to acknowledge those people who for one reason or another have disagreed with me. T.S. Eliot once remarked that you can call yourself happy if at the right time in your life you meet the right enemy, someone who challenges your ideas and changes or confirms your purpose. But some challenges are painful and the act of recalling them equally so. It is important to remember without bitterness, either towards oneself or others. In this context I would like to make my own the words of R.G. Collingwood:

> I have written candidly, at times disapprovingly, about people whom I admire and love. If any of these should resent what I have written, I wish them to know that my rule in writing books is never to name a person except *honoris causa*, and that naming anyone personally known to me is my way of thanking them for what I owe to their friendship or teaching or example, or all three. (1939: vii)

PART I

Values and the Curriculum

CHAPTER 1

Values and Ideologies

VALUES OF THE MARKETPLACE

Values underpin everything in the curriculum. Sometimes they are obvious, at other times they are hidden but nonetheless real. Examine any school timetable and you will discover interesting things about the school's value system, for instance the basis on which the students are grouped, how the good and the not so good teachers are allocated, and which subjects are given preference. The curriculum is saturated with values; teachers want their students to learn and also to care about what they learn. What are the values that are worth passing on?

In Ireland today, marketplace values are prominent to the point where they overshadow everything else. In a way this is understandable. We have waited a long time to taste the fruits of prosperity and now that it is here who but a doomsday prophet would refuse to rejoice at the good fortune that has so unexpectedly and belatedly come our way. It is often said that our prosperity is due in large part to what we claim is one of the best educational systems in the world, but we should be wary about linking education too closely to economic growth. The relationship between the two is not a simple one and some economists point out that education can be a consequence as well as a cause of growth. But whatever the causes of our new-found wealth, we are finding that we have to pay a price for it. Many people today have the choice between 'working to live' or 'living to work'. Maev-Ann Wren puts this very well:

> Despite the headline-grabbing, instant fortunes, the glossy new cars on the roads and the dynamism of today's Ireland, the pervading sense is not that we have never had it so good but that we have never worked for it so hard. (*Irish Times*, 18 May 2000)

While our official average working week has been reduced, it has to be adjusted upwards when overtime and commuting are taken into account. Journey times in and out of our cities and towns have increased in recent years and many people now spend long hours in their cars travelling to and from work. In families where both partners are working, children have to be dropped off at school in the mornings and collected in the evenings. Essential household tasks have to be done during spare hours or at the weekend. The stress of our frantic lifestyle is taking an inevitable toll on relationships and health, and has serious implications for the education of our young people.

Marketplace values are primarily economic; they are about the creation of wealth and possessions. They are not always bad and earning money for ourselves can benefit other people as well. And, although the rising tide of prosperity may not raise all the boats, it keeps quite a few afloat. But if marketplace values lead to nothing beyond the accumulation of wealth, status and power, they are limiting and self-centred. As they relate chiefly to possessions, they do not sit easily with the idea of sharing, for to share with others is to diminish our own store.

There are two prominent values associated with the marketplace – individualism and competition. When these are given unbridled scope and not balanced by more caring and less egocentric values, danger signals begin to appear, such as substance abuse, depressive illnesses and suicides. The latter is now a worrying phenomenon in Ireland and is on the increase, especially among young males. In his last article on the subject, the late Dr Michael Kelleher, founder of the National Suicide Research Foundation, made the following point:

> Ireland is becoming an increasingly materialistic society. Our spiritual values are eroded and these are what gave us our depth in the past. We have a preoccupation with achievement in sport, academia and industry, which place unnecessary pressure on our youth. In turn, drink and drugs preoccupy many of these young people. Without substance abuse much suicide would be prevented. (1998: 110)

The influence of individualism and competition can be seen in the working of our Leaving Certificate points system, which governs the allocation of student places at third level. It was described by one Minister for Education Micheál Martin as 'brutally fair', but the fact that he used the term when announcing a review of the system indicated his unease at the way it operates in practice. The minister had good reason for being uneasy because there is little doubt that the points system dominates Irish education. Its influence is felt not only at second and third level but in the upper classes of primary schools. As Joseph Dunne observes, the system is the 'focus of huge media attention, with a great public ritual of pre-examination speculation and post-examination analysis'. It is enacted twice yearly, followed by the appearance of results and the labyrinthine process of assigning a whole generation of young adults their most tangible life chances (Dunne 1995: 66–7).

The life chances that Dunne refers to are measured in terms of jobs, wealth and status, all typical expressions of marketplace values. As educators we may feel flattered that society is letting us play such a prominent role in distributing these rewards. We even claim that our schools are the gateway to success, provided the students are prepared to abide by the rules we lay down and accept the kind of knowledge we offer. But everything depends on our definition of success: if it is understood solely in economic terms to the exclusion of all other values, then Dunne is right when he says that 'education has in a sense gained the whole world but in doing so has lost its own soul' (1995: 68).

The triumph of marketplace values is reflected in the way the language of the marketplace has invaded the world of education. The work of schools is now described in terms of inputs and outputs, business plans, cost control and quality assurance, with considerations of profit and entrepreneurship dominating our educational thinking. The ideal of the school as a caring community is in danger of disappearing and aspirations towards social solidarity and the common good are regarded as utopian. Even our universities have succumbed to the blandishments of the marketplace. We would have expected them above all to have articulated what is best and noblest in our educational tradition. Instead we find university presidents describing their institutions as the engines that drive the economy in the competitive race for markets and profits.

We educators should know better. We should know instinctively that education stands for much more than the concerns of the marketplace, but we have grown timid about proclaiming this aloud. Values, we are tempted to argue, are becoming relative and individualistic, and so we are slow to show a preference for a particular value system. Why not let people make up their own minds and work out their own salvation? I think if we follow this line, we are in danger of forgetting what our western education tradition has always cherished – regard for truth, respect for persons, a sense of fair play, a willingness to co-operate with others in a worthy cause, an appreciation of beauty and goodness and an eagerness to lend a helping hand, especially to those less fortunate than ourselves.

Our current preoccupation with the marketplace is in reality an ideology – an ideology disguised as an economic system. The word 'ideology' is often taken to be pejorative; it is perceived as being aggressively defensive about our views, and even as a distortion of the truth. An ideology, however, can be more neutrally defined as a system of values held by social groups, which helps to bind those groups together and further their own interests (Reynolds and Skilbeck 1976). All ideologies are based on a belief about the nature of human beings and their place in the world, and the social and political structures in which people wish to live. Ideologies are of many kinds: religious, aesthetic, metaphysical, economic or political (for example, capitalism, communism, religious fundamentalism or democracy). Ideologies can characterise whole societies and periods of history, or they may be short-lived and specific to groups within a society.

Education has always been influenced by ideologies and any consideration of the curriculum has to take this into account. Malcolm Skilbeck (1976) distinguishes three great ideologies or value traditions in the history of western education – classical humanism, the progressive movement and reconstructionism. All three are more idealistic in their thinking and generous in their practice than the ideology of the marketplace. We shall consider each in turn.

CLASSICAL HUMANISM

Classical humanism originated in the Greek city-states of the fifth and fourth centuries BC and is associated with two of the most famous of the ancient Greek philosophers, Plato and Aristotle. Classical humanism is usually equated with the notion of liberal education, which is a contested term with different meanings attributed to it. Originally it referred to the kind of education that was worthy of free men as opposed to the slaves who formed a considerable section of the population of the Greek city-states. This gave liberal education an elitist character that, despite changing times and circumstances, it has never lost.

Plato's ideas on classical humanism are found in his two celebrated treatises, *The Republic* and *The Laws*. He believed that education should be a process of enlightenment, a turning away from ignorance and prejudice to face the light of truth. People who live in ignorance, however, see their condition as normal and resent any attempt to persuade them to change. They are, according to Plato, like prisoners chained in a dark cave with only a fire to give them light. What they see are the shadows thrown by the fire on the wall of the cave, and these they take to be real objects. They have no idea of the world of sunshine and colour that exists elsewhere. If they are suddenly freed from their chains and led outside, they will be dazzled by the light and will only gradually and painfully learn to adjust their sight. The task of education is to liberate people from the darkness of their cave and lead them to the real world of light and shade in a manner that eases their confusion and helps them adjust to their new knowledge.

Plato's ideas on liberal education were developed by his disciple, Aristotle. All human actions, Aristotle argues, can be divided into two kinds – those that are useful and those that are fine. Our preference for one or the other is determined by our upbringing and education. Aristotle was in no doubt as to where that preference should lie:

> We ought to choose war for the sake of peace, business for the sake of leisure, and what is useful for the sake of what is fine . . . these are the aims that we should keep in view in the education of children and people of any age who need education. (Politics VII: 14)

Classical humanism, as we shall later see in Chapter 5, has lasted down through the centuries, from ancient Greece through the Middle Ages and the Renaissance until it was reformulated in the nineteenth and twentieth centuries by writers like John Henry Newman, Matthew Arnold, Jacques Maritain, T.S. Eliot and A.N. Whitehead. The classical humanist curriculum concentrates on our cultural heritage – the forms of knowledge that have been worked out over time and give us access to the best in literature, art, music, history and science. It is a knowledge-based curriculum oriented towards high culture rather than that of ordinary folk. Its values have traditionally been a clear and firm discipline, high attainment in examinations, continuity between past and present, a cohesive and orderly development of institutions and a regard for the myths and rituals engendered by them (Skilbeck 1976). Up to recent times, classical humanism found its purest expression in the study of the Greek and Latin classics, an approach described by one of its exponents, Jaime Castiello, as follows:

> It is because the Greek ideal of science and art and of life was 'humane'; because the Greeks, with a peculiar instinct of their own, did not aspire to this or that specific type of beauty or of art or of style or of law, but sought in all things that which is independent of time and space, and hence cannot be tied to this or that nation or historical period: that is the ultimate reason why we study the classics. (1962: 191)

Modern educationalists have tended to expand the scope of classical humanism well beyond the study of the Greek and Latin classics. Richard Peters, for instance, identified three possible ways of interpreting liberal education. The first emphasises the acquisition of knowledge for its own sake and is not influenced by vocational or utilitarian considerations; in Chapter 5, we shall examine the ideas of Paul Hirst and Jane Roland Martin, two modern exponents of this approach. The second interpretation stresses a broad and balanced curriculum, avoiding specialisation of any kind. The third concentrates on an approach that is not constrained by dogmatic or authoritarian teaching methods but is characterised by freedom, flexibility and autonomy. Jacques Maritain, another advocate of classical humanism, described the liberal ideal as 'education directed towards wisdom, centred on the humanities, aiming to develop in people a capacity to think correctly and to enjoy truth and beauty'(Maritain 1960).

Put like this, we have to admit that classical humanism is a fine ideal, but the capacity to think correctly and enjoy truth and beauty is surely every person's birthright. Sadly, however, the way classical humanism has been interpreted in practice has been to focus on an elite and to exclude the majority, who are not considered suitable for such a finely tuned education. This has brought a reaction, which in

17

many cases has led to the rejection of classical humanism. Its ideology, as Richard Pring notes, writes off too many people:

> They fail the initiation test. Their voices are not allowed into the conversation, and the voices they listen to are not considered to be worth hearing. It is as though liberal education is but for the few. Furthermore, the liberal tradition, in focusing upon the world of ideas, ignores the world of practice – the world of industry, of commerce, of earning a living. There has been a disdain for the practical intelligence – indeed, for the technological and the useful. (1995: 186)

The reaction against classical humanism also led to a polarisation between the liberal and vocational curriculum. In Ireland the polarisation was sharpened by the fact that the liberal curriculum was largely in the hands of church sponsored secondary schools while the vocational curriculum was left to non-denominational schools in the public sector. This confessional divide was exacerbated by academic and social factors; vocational students were considered academically and socially inferior to their secondary school counterparts. There existed a kind of educational apartheid which for many years was consolidated by a blatant selection system operated by many secondary schools.

Whatever the rights and wrongs of the liberal-vocational division, what we need now is a synthesis of the two. Our guiding principle should be an understanding of the dynamic of the human personality, how every human being, no matter what course of study he or she undertakes, needs to be affirmed as a person and at the same time helped to become a useful member of society. Our notion of the humanities, which were always considered to be at the core of liberal studies, should be widened and our criterion for including any subject on the curriculum should be the following: is the content of our teaching and the way we teach it a stimulus for the personal growth of our students, something that helps them appreciate what is true, beautiful and good? To put it another way, does our teaching help our students develop their potential to live a full, happy and useful life? If we are honest in our answers, we will realise that traditional notions of liberal and vocational education will have to be re-examined and new meanings within the two terms discovered. What we need now is a liberal vocationalism.

Early in my own teaching career, I was fortunate to work in a school that embodied such an ideal. I had just returned home after teaching abroad for five years. Things were looking up in Ireland, the country was recovering from the depression of the 1950s and there was even talk of preparing to enter the European Economic Community. I was looking for a teaching job, part-time if possible, to enable me to return to university and take a teaching diploma. As luck would have it, I met a vocational head-teacher, Tom Carney, who invited me to join his school in Ringsend, on the mouth of the Liffey.

Ringsend Technical Institute was an old red-brick building, dating back to the last quarter of the nineteenth century, with lofty ceilings, spacious halls and a grand stairway connecting its two storeys. It was impossible to heat and on rainy days the floors in the annex tended to flood. But for all that, remarkable things were happening in the classrooms. Not long before I went there, the school had been threatened with closure because of falling numbers. Carney's answer was to open Ringsend to the country at large. Acting on his own initiative, he offered classes in core subjects like English, maths and science leading to a UK qualification, the General Certificate of Education (GCE). The immediate aim was to gain entry to one or other of the two Dublin Colleges of Technology, Kevin Street and Bolton Street, where the students could qualify in a range of professional courses like engineering, architecture and science.

The response to Carney's new programme was immediate. Many eager young people from secondary schools in the Dublin area, who were dissatisfied with the existing Leaving Certificate fare, applied for admission. They were joined by other students from around the country who had completed their vocational school programme and were awarded scholarships by their local VECs to study at

Ringsend. By the time I arrived, there were two GCE classes in full swing and no shortage of applicants. Carney asked me to teach English and Irish and when I pointed out that Irish was not a recognised GCE subject he bade me write a syllabus and make an application. Both were accepted without fuss. I was then told to teach French, on the supposition that when we joined the EEC we would all be speaking the language.

What struck me most during my time in Ringsend was the easy informality and dynamism of the place, especially in the GCE classes. The young people were eager to learn, they knew that they were going somewhere in their lives and were impatient with the ritualistic formalism of traditional schooling. In Ringsend they were being offered an alternative highway through the educational system and some eventually reached the upper levels of Masters and Ph.D. degrees. The school was also fortunate in a lively staff that combined a range of academic and technical disciplines. Ringsend on first sight might not have seemed the most likely venue for a liberal vocational curriculum, but I once heard Carney himself sum up its ethos: 'If you run a good school, even a hedge-school, people will beat a pathway to your door.'

PROGRESSIVE EDUCATION

Progressive education, though not as long-established as classical humanism, has nonetheless a venerable pedigree. Its prophet is Jean Jacques Rousseau and its bible is his celebrated book *Emile*, written in the middle of the eighteenth century and a bestseller of its time. It is said of the first edition that booksellers found it more profitable to rent out copies by the hour than to sell the book (Darling 1994). The progressive movement turns classical humanism on its head: where classical humanism is knowledge-based and reveres the heritage of the past, progressivism is child-centred, rebels against past traditions and puts great store on the freedom of the individual. Society is seen as a prison, from which human beings can escape through their education. Men and women are born free, Rousseau declared, but are everywhere found in chains.

Rousseau's ideas found an enthusiastic response among the many people who were already influenced by the Romantic Movement of the time and were reacting against the rationalism of the Enlightenment that had preceded it. According to the tenets of Romanticism, true knowledge is not an abstraction but should be based on experience, intuition and direct contact with people and things. One of the romantic poets of the era, William Wordsworth, believed a person's natural habitat to be the remote, the wild and the elemental, and that all learning should be free and instinctive:

> One impulse from the vernal wood
> May teach you more of man
> Of moral evil and of good
> Then all the sages can.

After Rousseau, the progressive torch was carried by educators like Pestalozzi, Froebel and Montessori, and here in Ireland we could add the name of Patrick Pearse. A new dimension was added of which probably Rousseau would not have approved – the importance of having a creative and happy community environment to complement the child's individual education. Thus was born the notion of the progressive school, like A.S. Neill's Summerhill in England and Pearse's St. Enda's in Ireland. The progressive schools were never very numerous but they exerted a considerable influence on educational thinking and practice. They resisted systemisation, each school jealously guarding its own independence. Their general ethos has been described by Malcolm Skilbeck as follows:

> A form of life grows in these communities. It is a complex whole, not reducible to a pedagogical regime, a regime of order, of control, and so forth. It blends academic, social and emotional elements; hence, the 'curriculum' of the communitarian institutions is much broader and much more complex than the activities of the

classrooms or the subjects listed in the time-table. The major tasks of the communitarian school are to nourish the sub-culture it has itself created, to induct newcomers, foster the values it professes, and to build up a secure base from which its members can challenge and confront the wider society. (1976: 32–3)

The progressive ideology is particularly relevant to pre-primary and primary education and has influenced important documents like the Plowden Report in England and the teacher handbooks of the 1971 primary curriculum in Ireland. In America, progressive education was in vogue from the last quarter of the nineteenth until the middle of the twentieth century; it led to some stirring debates between progressivists and traditionalists and raised issues that are still relevant today, such as freedom versus discipline, the individual versus society and interest-based learning versus didactic teaching. Modern curriculum theory was itself a product of the progressive movement and came into prominence in America in the 1920s among a number of educationalists who were trying in various ways to transform the curriculum of the American school. Although small in numbers, the progressive movement was highly influential and included many different shades of opinion. Two modern American educationalists summed it up as follows:

While we sometimes speak of the progressive education movement as if it were a single entity, progressive educators actually held quite varied views. Some of them were scientists and advocates of a more scientific approach to educational practice. Others were social reformers, primarily interested in improving the lot of the poor and downtrodden. Still others believed in the beauty and goodness of childhood and wanted schools that would not do violence to the child's tender feelings, as they believed the rigidly regimented schools of the day did. And some were pedagogical innovators who had studied the latest theories and practices of the renowned pedagogues of Europe and wanted American schools to become pedagogical pioneers too. (Walker and Soltis 1997: 18)

The Irish progressive movement was a more modest affair and hopefully has not yet died out. The most important thing it stands for is the freedom of teachers and schools to develop their own curriculum, and it has made its greatest mark on the primary curriculum. The story is worth telling.

In the years that followed independence, the new state was concerned with ensuring that its ideals were mirrored in the educational system. We find this view clearly expressed by Eoin MacNeill, the first minister for education: 'The chief function of Irish educational policy is to conserve and develop Irish nationality. Education, then, is either nationality in its making or its undoing' (cited in Akenson 1975: 39). This is an understandable aspiration but what is difficult to accept is the equating of nationality with the government's language policy and the burdening of the schools with the political ideal of the restoration of Irish. The emphasis on language restoration resulted in the primary curriculum becoming narrow in focus and restricted in its range of interests.

This state of affairs was not without its critics, especially the teachers themselves. They expressed their concerns through their union, the Irish National Teachers' Organisation (INTO), on two notable occasions – in 1941, on teaching through the medium of Irish, and in 1947, on the need for a more child-centred approach and a wider range of subjects. Their criticisms, however, went unheeded, the Government of the day preferring to concentrate on the 'three Rs', backed by a compulsory test at the end of sixth standard, known as the Primary Certificate Examination. In defence of this approach, Eamon de Valera declared in the Dáil: 'I do not care that teachers are offended by it . . . I am less interested in the teachers' method of teaching than I am in the results they achieve, and the test I would apply would be the test of an examination' (cited in Coolahan 1981: 43).

The 1960s, which were to prove a watershed for Irish society in general, brought a new approach to primary schooling and, as happened with other aspects of life in the country, an important stimulus for change came from outside – in this case from the report of the

Plowden Committee in England in 1967, which made a very persuasive case for progressive education in the primary sector. A teachers' study group of the INTO organised an evaluation of the report and invited Lady Plowden to Dublin to participate in a seminar (Hurley 1977: 16). Shortly afterwards, in 1967, the Primary Certificate Examination was replaced by pupil record cards. The greatest change of all came in 1971 when the Department of Education introduced a new curriculum, attractively presented in two teacher handbooks and launched amidst general approval. The curriculum was based on a child-centred ideology, which was influenced by the developmental psychology of Jean Piaget, who himself was influenced by the progressive movement. The aim of the curriculum was 'to enable the child to live a full life as a child and to equip him or her to avail of further education and go on to live a full and useful life as an adult in society' (Department of Education 1971, Part I: 12).

In keeping with its child-centred ideology, the new curriculum advocated the integration of subject matter. The argument for doing so was put in compelling terms: 'As the child is one, however complex his or her nature, so also must education be one, however complex its nature' (Department of Education 1971 Part I: 19). The fragmentation of knowledge into separate compartments was to be avoided and instead of the traditional subjects, seven broad curriculum areas were recommended: religion, language, mathematics, social and environmental studies, art and craft, music and physical education. The seven areas themselves were to be integrated with each other as far as possible.

In more recent times, the Irish primary curriculum was again revised; in 1999, after a lengthy process of consultation, a new set of teacher and pupil hand-books was jointly issued by the Department of Education and Science and the National Council for Curriculum and Assessment (NCCA). The introduction of the revised curriculum was more carefully orchestrated than that of its predecessor nearly thirty years earlier and was accompanied by a widespread teacher in-service scheme. The progressive tenets of the 1971 curriculum were reaffirmed, despite the cooling of enthusiasm for progressivism that had become noticeable in Britain and America. The authors of the 1999 curriculum nailed their colours to the mast by declaring that the first aim of primary education is to celebrate 'the uniqueness of the child, as it is expressed in each child's personality, intelligence and potential for development'. The child should be nurtured 'in all dimensions of his or her life, spiritual, moral, cognitive, emotional, imaginative, aesthetic, social and physical' (Ireland 1999: 6). The seven broad areas of the 1971 curriculum were more or less retained, but an explicit recognition of the importance of the parents' role was added, with schools being urged 'to reach out to help some parents overcome any inhibiting attitudes they may have'. This outgoing spirit was to be extended to the local community: 'It should be a general aspiration that the school would be seen as a key resource in improving the quality of life in the community and would in turn regard the community as a rich resource from which to draw educational assistance' (Ireland 1999: 22).

Today, the challenge facing the Irish primary curriculum is to ensure that its rationale will continue into the post-primary sector. I remember how, in the early 1970s, the aim of the curriculum development pioneers in this country was to build a bridge between the primary and the post-primary curriculum. That was 35 years ago but the need for bridge building is still as great. The primary curriculum has important implications for the post-primary sector: if the latter remains unresponsive to the progressive rationale in the primary schools, the gap between the two sectors will widen and the transfer of pupils from primary to secondary will be more difficult. If post-primary teachers ignore the child-centred methodology and integrated approach of their primary colleagues, we may end up with two different systems of education.

RECONSTRUCTIONISM

Reconstructionism is more socially-oriented than either classical humanism or progressivism; it views education as a major force for improving and reconstructing society. Ironically, it was Plato who first expressed the reconstructionist ideal, just as he was also the founder of classical humanism, against which reconstructionism has frequently directed its sharpest criticism (Skilbeck 1976: 6). Plato believed the Athenian city-state was going through a grave crisis and proposed to reform it by radically restructuring its educational system. What was needed, he felt, was a more just society, with harmony between the main social groups, the rulers, guardians and workers. In such a society, the rulers would be the most intelligent citizens and would be identified and trained through a rigorous educational process. Those citizens who were naturally brave and strong would be educated as soldiers and guardians. The ordinary people would only be given a rudimentary education suitable to their station in life, providing goods and services.

Modern ideas on reconstructionism are more egalitarian and their ablest exponent is John Dewey. The school, Dewey once said, should be a miniature of the ideal society where each young person learns to become a social being. Dewey was both a philosopher and a practising educator. In 1894, while still in his mid-thirties, he became the head of the Department of Philosophy at the University of Chicago, where he was later appointed the director of the School of Education. Two years later, he founded the university's Laboratory School, which catered for pupils from four to fourteen years old. His school owed much to the ideas of Comenius, Rousseau, Froebel, Pentalozzi and Herbart, which is not surprising because, of all the great educational theorists, Dewey was by far the best read in the history of educational thought. However, he was not uncritical of his precursors, and the methods he developed in his experimental school were his own.

Dewey took to heart the advice of Pestalozzi a century earlier, that the school should do for children what their parents were failing to do. By the end of the nineteenth century, many American homes had been transformed by the impact of industrialisation. In earlier times, especially in rural areas, both parents had worked at home, on the farm or at various home crafts. The children had taken part in this work but, by 1900, the scene had changed and home industries were becoming a thing of the past. Dewey wanted to compensate for what he saw as an impoverishment of the children's experience and so he introduced into his school a range of practical activities like carpentry, cooking, gardening, music, painting, science, sewing and textile work. He wanted the school not just to prepare young people for the future but to provide a dynamic and satisfying experience of the present: 'We always live at the time we live and not at some other time, and only by extracting at each present time the full meaning of each present experience are we prepared for doing the same thing in the future' (Dewey 1963: 49). The school should exemplify daily living and its activites should grow out of home life and deepen and extend home values. One of Dewey's past-pupils described her school experience as follows:

> We were a large family, anxious to put forth our kindest manners, happy to help the child who was slower to grasp the problem at hand, knowing that when we needed help it would be as gladly given. A most remarkable spirit of normal co-operation existed, the kindliest tolerance, an inspiring pride in work and play. There, every child felt as much released, as happy and as unselfconsciously contented and at ease as in his or her own home. (Martin 1992: 127)

Dewey believed the curriculum should continually reconstruct for the child the fundamental aspects of the growth of civilisation. The emphasis on the child's own activity should lead naturally to the study of the various subjects or disciplines. These should be introduced, not as completely new material, but as a way of ordering, deepening and extending the existing experience of the pupils. Expressive and constructive activities should be at the heart of the curriculum and be the avenues to the more formal subjects. There should be no hierarchy of subjects – science, art and communication are all fundamental aspects of living and are equally important. Progress does not lie in a hierarchy but in the development of new attitudes towards and interactions with experience. The curriculum should be a continuous reconstruction of experience and, in practice, the process and the goal of education should be the same (Dewey 1965: 633–5).

Dewey had a high regard for teachers. Education, he argued, is the most perfect and intimate union of science and art conceivable in human existence, and the teacher is engaged not only in the formation of people but in shaping society. Teachers should realise the dignity of their calling; they are public servants set apart for the maintenance of proper social order and the securing of the right kind of social growth. 'In this way the teacher is the prophet of the true God and the usher of the true kingdom of God' (Dewey 1965: 638).

It was part of Dewey's genius to connect his educational philosophy with the wider political and social ideology of democracy. For democracy to flourish, he argued, it was essential that people be educated in a democratic way of thinking and acting, because democracy was not just a form of government but a way of life. For Dewey, education and democracy are inseparable, as one of his disciples, Mortimer Adler tells us:

> The two, universal suffrage and universal schooling, are inextricably bound together. The one without the other is a perilous delusion. Suffrage without schooling produces mobocracy, not democracy, not rule of law, not constitutional government by the people as well as for them. The great American educator, John Dewey, recognised this early in this century. In *Democracy and Education*, written in 1916, he first tied these two words together and let each shine light upon the other. A revolutionary message of that book was that a democratic society must provide equal educational opportunity not only by giving to all its children the same quantity of public education, the same number of years in school, but also by making sure to give to all of them, all with no exceptions, the same quality of education. (1982: 3–4)

Democratic government is now regarded in the western world as the norm but its educational implications are far from being fully realised. They include equality of educational opportunity, avoidance of unfair selection and segregation, mixed ability teaching and student participation in curriculum matters. How should we implement democracy in our schools and colleges? There are two ways – teaching about and teaching for democracy. The first usually takes the form of courses in subjects like history and citizenship; the second, which is far more challenging, tries to bring about a teaching and learning environment that conforms to the democratic way of doing things. The difficulty about the latter approach is the uncomfortable fact that the majority of schools and colleges are not democratic places – we could go further and say that educational systems in general are undemocratic. This may sound unduly harsh, and we could equally question the democratic status of the rest of our socio-political structure. The truth is perhaps that democracy itself is an unrealised ideal and has never been fully achieved.

Despite our democratic deficit, democracy remains a worthwhile social, political and educational ideal. In this country, we are committed to democratic norms both as a sovereign state and as a member of the European Union. Education for democracy then should not only be a national priority, it is also crucial to our vision of what it means to be European. European citizenship is essentially a humanistic idea designed to construct a democratic Europe that is respectful of the balance between economic, technological, ecological and cultural considerations. The European vision is about nations learning to live together and to settle their disputes peacefully:

> Yesterday's European nightmare was the Holocaust, today's is ethnic cleansing . . . So the mission is to muster the people of Europe to take on one of the greatest challenges of all time: to construct a greater Europe, within a continent that is characterised by cultural differences, differing economic approaches and varying natural environments, but which is also united by a feeling of belonging to a common civilisation. For the first time, European integration will not be the result of political or military hegemony imposed by a dominating power. Rather, it will be the outcome of the steady

progress of democratic decision-making processes. (European
Commission 1997: 51)

In this chapter, we looked at the importance of values in the curriculum and the need to be explicit about them. We noted the negative influence of marketplace values on current educational thinking
and saw how our preoccupation with the marketplace is in reality
an ideology. We identified three ideologies that have shaped western education: classical humanism, the progressive movement and
reconstructionism. Although there are points of conflict among the
three, we should beware of regarding them as completely separate
from each other. All three have made important contributions to our
common education tradition and have influenced in particular the
shaping of modern thinking on equal educational opportunities for
everyone. In the following chapter, we shall examine the rise of the
equality ideal in Irish education; it was sometimes taken seriously
but many people only gave it lip service. In my own case, equality
of opportunity was an ideal that profoundly affected my life as a
teacher.

CHAPTER 2

Equality of Educational Opportunity

CHERISHING ALL THE NATION'S CHILDREN

The Irish state has had two written constitutions to guide it on its way and the present one, which dates from 1937, has important things to say about education. Some people would argue that the real foundation stone of the state is not the constitution at all but the Proclamation of the 1916 Rising, a short emotive document drawn up by the rebel leaders and proclaimed from the steps of the General Post Office in Dublin, the headquarters of the rebellion. The 1916 Proclamation had little enough to say about education but in that little space it made a key statement:

> The Republic guarantees religious and civil liberty, equal rights and equal opportunities to all its citizens, and declares its resolve to pursue the happiness and prosperity of the whole nation and of all its parts, cherishing all the children of the nation equally ... (Edwards 1977: 281)

Thus was equality of educational opportunity enshrined in the ideals of the founding fathers of the state. Three years later the Democratic Programme adopted by Dáil Éireann, the newly elected national parliament, reaffirmed the commitment:

> It shall be the first duty of the Government of the Republic to make provision for the physical, mental and spiritual well-being of the

31

children, to secure that no child shall suffer hunger or cold from lack of food, clothing or shelter, but that all shall be provided with the means and facilities requisite for their proper education and training as citizens of a free and Gaelic Ireland. (Lyons 1973: 402)

The achievement of equality of educational opportunity in the new state was disappointingly slow. Despite the assurance of the first Minister for Education Eoin MacNeill that there would be 'an educational highway' for all pupils, the educational system during the four decades following independence remained basically elitist. Only a fraction of the age cohort received post-primary education while higher education remained the preserve of a minority. 'For 90 per cent of the people', de Valera had to admit in 1940, 'the primary school is the only education' (cited in Ó Buachalla 1988: 358). A cautious government combined with a conservative church made for minimal intervention, not only in educational matters but in the entire social sphere. The state, now that independence had been achieved, seemed content with the status quo, and the social revolution implied in the ideals of the founding fathers was forgotten in the preoccupation with stability and continuity. In the Ireland after independence, Professor Patrick Lynch observed, 'there was little use for idealism and less scope for utopianism' (Lynch 1966: 53).

Equality of educational opportunity, in so far as it existed at all, was put into practice through an educational system that leant heavily on structures that had been laid down well before independence. The country possessed a national system of primary schools which had been founded in the first half of the nineteenth century, and a denominational system of private secondary schools which, on the Catholic side, had been largely developed by religious congregations of men and women founded in the eighteenth and nineteenth centuries. In the early years of the state, the majority of Irish people had modest incomes and were largely dependent on the land. They had a traditional regard for education and saw it as a means of bettering their lot, the door that opened the way to respectable white-collar jobs, such as the civil service, the banks and the teaching profession.

The system in general had a pronounced academic bias, which was only partially corrected by the establishment of a vocational sector in 1930. Even today, nearly eighty years after building the first vocational schools, the majority of Irish second-level students attend the academically oriented secondary schools. Within its own limitations the system was generally reckoned to be meritocratic. It guaranteed a straightforward no-nonsense type of education, which enabled a considerable number of young people, no matter what their background, to advance in the world, provided of course they were clever and prepared to work hard.

Up to the beginning of the 1960s, the Irish educational system looked as if it would last forever. One minister for education compared it to a plumbing system in which he himself was 'a kind of dungaree man', the plumber who 'will take the knock out of the pipes and will link up everything' (O'Connor 1986: 1). In 1962 the Council of Education, which represented the major educational interests, drew up a report on the Irish system (Department of Education: 1962). Such a body, one would have thought, should have foreseen whatever changes were necessary and have been capable of recommending new policies. The Council did nothing of the kind. It reviewed the status quo with unconcealed satisfaction and saw no need for major change. Yet, within a year of the report, the Minister for Education Dr P.J. Hillery announced a package of reforms that were to herald the arrival of one of the most exciting periods of change in the educational history of the state until then (Hillery 1963: 119–26).

Looking back today over nearly half a century, we are inclined to wonder why it was that the Hillery reforms took the Irish educational world by surprise. Perhaps educationalists are the last people to notice when the winds of change begin to blow and, in the 1960s, as we clearly see now, a strong wind was blowing. At the time it was easier to see the signs in trade, tourism, television and even religion than in the conservative world of education. In the late 1950s the Government had adopted the First Programme for Economic Expansion, which laid the basis for a resurgence in economic activity in the years that followed. Irish people were leaving the land and moving into the towns and cities to take up jobs in the growing industrial and service areas. Irish values were also changing under the impact of television, the relaxation of book and film censorship and increased contact with the outside world in trade and tourism. Traditional religious attitudes were being shaken by the events of the Second Vatican Council (1962–65) and Irish Catholicism, celebrated for its conservatism, began to discover that religion could be contingent as well as absolute.

The underlying rationale of the Hillery reforms was more pragmatic than ideological and, as such, was inspired by the practical leadership of Seán Lemass, who had succeeded de Valera as Taoiseach in 1959. Lemass is generally credited with spear-heading the economic revival of the 1960s and is usually portrayed as a hard-headed realist, the man who led the country into the modern world. 'The historic task of this generation', he once remarked, 'is to secure the economic foundation of independence' (cited in Lee 1979: 22). He was the first taoiseach to see the vital connection between education and social and economic advance, which led him to appoint some of his ablest ministers to the Department of Education. Lemass believed in giving his ministers freedom and scope, and encouraged them to take initiatives that fitted with his own overall aim – 'the building of a modern state based on the principles of social justice and with a system of equitable taxation to finance social and economic advances' (Craft 1973: 72).

Thus it was that in May 1963, Hillery, Lemass's first minister for education, launched a new era of government educational planning. It was significant that he did this at a press conference and not in the Dáil, where his predecessors usually made their pronouncements. In the typically direct style cultivated by Lemass, Hillery chose to give his message straight to the people, not bothering to consult beforehand with the various interest groups involved. 'I am launching the plan now,' he said, 'and the talking I am sure will come afterwards' (cited in Randles 1975: 119). Much has been written about the Hillery reforms, and not all of it has been complimentary. Nobody, however, has ever questioned the significance of the measures for the future development of Irish education.

The basis of the proposals was essentially two-fold: post-primary education would now be made available to all pupils and the curriculum would be comprehensive in character. The first proposal was already being put into practice and in this regard the minister was able to announce that participation rates at post-primary level had increased to two-thirds of the age cohort. He was concerned, however, at the plight of the remaining third – 'today's Third Estate whose voice, amid the babble of competing claims from the more privileged, has hitherto been scarcely heard' (Hillery 1963: 122). To provide for the needs of these pupils, who lived mostly in areas that had neither a secondary or vocational education, he proposed building a new type of institution – state comprehensive schools. This in itself was a considerable innovation and, although the schools would be few in number, they were to be the pathfinders of a new approach; they would provide a wide curriculum for all pupils with equal emphasis on the practical as well as the academic.

Hillery's second proposal, the provision of a comprehensive curriculum for all, was the most significant aspect of his plan – it was certainly his own view of the matter, as he later revealed in one of his Dáil speeches. He was strongly critical of the dual system of secondary and vocational schools which he said were 'being conducted as separate and distinct entities with no connecting link whatsoever between them' (Hillery 1963: 122). He could have added what was commonly accepted by the public at large – not only were the two systems operating in water-tight compartments but one of them, the vocational sector, was regarded as socially and academically inferior. Evidence for this, if evidence was needed, came to light two years later with the publication of an OECD report, *Investment in Education*, which illustrated convincingly the nature and extent of the inequality between the two systems (Department of Education 1965). This was why Hillery now proposed to close the gap between them by ensuring that all pupils, irrespective of the kind of school they attended, could follow the same curriculum leading to a common examination at about fifteen years of age.

George Colley, Hillery's successor, reaffirmed the Government's allegiance to the comprehensive plan. If anything, his stance was even more committed than Hillery's. He was keenly interested in education and, from the time of his first election to the Dáil, had made no secret of his ambition to become minister for education (O'Connor 1986). He wanted to raise the public consciousness of education so that it became a common talking point in people's lives. 'More than anything else', he said, 'I want parents, all parents, to take an active interest in the education of their children. I want education to be a live and important topic, not just on the rare occasions when clerical and political figures clash, or when a minister for education comes to give an address, but in the daily communications and intercourse of society' (Colley 1966: 7).

Colley's interest in the comprehensive ideal was evident from the many occasions he talked about it in public. He was also the first minister to define it: 'a system of post-primary education combining academic and technical subjects in a wide curriculum and offering to each pupil an education structured to his or her needs and interests and providing specialist guidance and advice on the pupil's abilities and attitudes' (Colley 1966*a*). It was Colley's ambition to inaugurate such a system in Ireland by persuading the secondary and vocational sectors to co-operate on a local basis in order to make available 'a curriculum broad enough to serve the individual needs of all their students and thereby to provide the basis of a comprehensive system in each locality' (Colley 1966*b*: 129). To accomplish this, he wrote directly to the various school authorities throughout the country, asking them to come together to find common areas of co-operation.

Colley's request was in general well received. The time was propitious, being early in 1966 when the country was preparing to celebrate the fiftieth anniversary of the 1916 Rising. Cherishing all the nation's children was at last, it seemed, becoming a realisable aspiration. Colley regarded his own effort to bring about an integrated second-level curriculum as the concrete realisation of Pearse's dream that, in a free Ireland, an Irish minister for education would succeed in uniting the conflicting elements of the system into a harmonious whole (Colley 1966c).

Despite the general goodwill, there were obstacles in the way of implementing the plan. Longstanding barriers still existed between the secondary and vocational schools. However, these might well have come down because the spirit of the mid-1960s was one of dialogue and ecumenism. Unfortunately, the minister who had initiated the dialogue did not remain long enough in office to pursue it effectively. In July 1966, after only a year and three months in office, Colley was transferred to another ministry.

Colley was succeeded by Donogh O'Malley, who has become something of a folk hero in the history of Irish education. A senior official in the Department of Education at the time of O'Malley's arrival left us the following description of the new minister:

> He had a reputation as a hell-raiser, as being impetuous and as having little respect for convention, which blinded many to his ability and his deep concern and sympathy for the underdog. Senior civil servants are generally apprehensive when ministerial changes are announced. They know the outgoing minister's policies and priorities and have adjusted to his pace; the new man may not have the same interests as his predecessor. From O'Malley we expected fast and furious action (O'Connor 1986: 139).

O'Malley's advisers in the Department of Education had expected him to pursue Colley's policies on comprehensive education according to a staged plan of action that would culminate with the raising of the statutory school leaving age in 1970, by which time a measure of free post-primary education for all would be introduced. The new minister, however, opted to go his own way and, although only a few months in office, announced to a startled but largely delighted public that, from 1967 onwards, free post-primary education would be available for all, accompanied by a scheme for free transport and free books.

The free education scheme precipitated a sharp debate between the Department of Education and the secondary schools but, despite the accusation of one unfriendly critic that the minister had gone on 'an egalitarian spree', most of the schools eventually opted to join the scheme. O'Malley, who saw the scheme as the culminating point of the efforts of his two predecessors to secure equality of educational opportunity, reiterated his loyalty to Colley's plan for the 'dovetailing of the activities of the secondary and vocational school systems'. But he was not as patient as Colley in wooing the support of the religious authorities, and sometimes freely expressed his exasperation. On a famous occasion in the Senate, he hit back at his critics:

> I know I am up against opposition and serious organised opposition, but they are not going to defeat me on this. I shall tell you further that I shall expose them and I shall expose their tactics on every available occasion whoever they are ... Maybe some day I shall tell the tale and there is no better man to tell it. I shall pull no punches. Christian charity how are you. (Randles 1975: 262)

Personalities apart, there was another and perhaps more fundamental reason for the clash between O'Malley and the Irish educational establishment. This was the issue of control: who was really in charge of the system? Up to the end of the 1950s, ministers for education had been content to take a back seat but, from the 1960s onwards, the situation began to change as the state sought to take initiatives that entailed the exercise of central power and the assertion of ministerial supremacy. As early as March 1964, Hillery had given a clear signal: 'It is of course the function and duty of a minister for education to be captain of the ship and so have the vessel in good trim and see that all hands are at work' (cited in O'Connor 1986: 80).

It was in the context of growing central control that the comprehensive idea was introduced into Ireland and, although the actual number of comprehensive schools was never intended to be large, it was assumed that in a centralised system their influence would spread rapidly. Similarly, the desire of the Department of Education to bring about a comprehensive curriculum through a unified secondary and vocational system seemed a feasible proposition in a country where financial control was increasingly in the minister's hands. Later events, however, were to test the hypothesis.

An Experiment in Comprehensive Education

The Irish system of education is not completely centralised; its most significant concession to local involvement lies in the structure of vocational education committees (VECs) which, under an Act of the Oireachtas in 1930, were given authority to organise vocational and technical education for areas within the remit of the local county councils and county boroughs. However, the power of the VECs under the Act was seriously curtailed because most of their major decisions were subject to ministerial approval. Nonetheless, they had a measure of freedom in which to manoeuvre and this freedom could sometimes be exercised by a VEC that felt itself sufficiently confident to go its own way.

In the 1960s, a notable example of an independent-minded local education authority was the City of Dublin VEC (CDVEC). Throughout those years, the leadership of the CDVEC was in the hands of one of its ablest chief executive officers, Martin Gleeson, who was then at the height of his career. Gleeson was a forceful, Churchillian personality, with influential connections in Church and State; he was reputed to be on friendly terms with Seán Lemass and also the Catholic Archbishop of Dublin John Charles McQuaid, one of the most powerful members of the Irish Catholic hierarchy. Gleeson had travelled widely and admired some of his counterparts in the English educational scene at the time – CEOs like William Houghton in London, Alec Clegg in Yorkshire and John Newsom in Hertfordshire. Gleeson was determined to give a similar lead as CEO of Dublin City and in this he was highly successful. Under his direction, the CDVEC's remit expanded to include over twenty second-level schools, five colleges of technology, a youth and adult education service, and a school psychological and guidance service developed by Tom McCarthy and Brede Foy, the first of its kind in the country.

In 1966, the year the Department of Education opened its first comprehensive schools, the CDVEC launched its own initiative in comprehensive education. Whether the permission of the Department was ever obtained for the venture is open to question – at best there was an informal agreement between the two parties. At any rate the CDVEC was determined to show it was not going to be outdone in its own commitment to the comprehensive ideal. Two areas were chosen, Ballyfermot and Clogher Road, both working-class suburbs on the west side of the city. In each, a new vocational school was designated as a pilot comprehensive school. The term 'comprehensive school', however, was never officially used, probably in deference to the Department of Education, which reserved the title for its own three newly built comprehensive schools. The two Dublin schools were known instead as major regional schools. The term was significant because, in comparison with the other Dublin vocational schools at the time or indeed with Irish post-primary schools in general, the new schools were intended to be large. It was expected that they would have an annual intake of 240 pupils with a junior cycle enrolment of 720, and their senior cycle, it was hoped, would increase this figure to around 1,000, a big number by Irish standards. Two principals were appointed, Séamus Rossiter in Clogher Road and myself in Ballyfermot. We were each given two vice-principals which, although unusual at the time, was a recognition of the projected size and complexity of the two schools.

The most important thing about the CDVEC initiative in Ballyfermot and Clogher Road was the curriculum the two schools intended to offer. Up to this time the traditional curriculum in Irish vocational schools had been quite narrow with a strong emphasis on the practical subjects. The accepted goal of the schools was to place their students in apprenticeships and in service and secretarial jobs, which meant that the students could never aspire to entering the universities or the professions. The Hillery reforms changed all that and so, in the second half of the 1960s, for the first time in their history, the vocational schools were preparing students for the Intermediate and Leaving Certificate examinations, which hitherto had been reserved for the secondary schools. Ballyfermot and Clogher Road went further; they offered a wide choice from a curriculum that included up to seventeen subjects. They were able to do so because of the size and variety of their teaching staffs, their generous teacher-pupil ratio and their wide range of facilities and equipment. The two schools were the pride of the CDVEC and were launched like flagships to lead the rest of the metropolitan schools into the exciting years that appeared to lie ahead.

There was one area in which both Ballyfermot and Clogher Road fell short of what purists would have regarded as the full comprehensive ideal: each was a boys' school only. Attitudes to co-education in Ireland had been greatly influenced by the teaching of the Catholic Church on the subject, as exemplified in the encyclical of Pius XI, *The Christian Education of Youth*, where the practice had been roundly condemned as 'a confusion of mind which cannot distinguish between a legitimate association of human beings and a promiscuous herding together of males and females on a completely equal footing' (Pius XI 1929: 32). Co-education was only tolerated in Irish post-primary education where the size of a particular catchment area made it difficult to build separate schools for boys and girls. Nonetheless, the building of a number of co-educational vocational schools in rural areas in the 1930s drew a sharp clerical reproof: 'No economic reason could justify the close association of boys and girls in schools during the period of adolescence. It is a form of naturalism that is not tolerated even in Nazi Germany' (Brenan 1941: 127).

By the 1960s, some of the opposition to co-education had abated and the Department of Education had succeeded, albeit with some difficulty, in persuading the Catholic bishops to support the building of the state comprehensive schools which were also intended to be co-educational (O'Connor 1986: 95–6). Dublin, however, was different and Archbishop McQuaid's strong line on the matter gave the practice of single sex education the force of an unwritten law. In 1946 the CDVEC had prudently resolved to adopt a policy of building separate schools for boys and girls – a resolution which had been rewarded by a strong measure of episcopal approval. 'I do not praise that resolution merely for reasons of moral discipline', the Archbishop told the CDVEC, 'I consider it a marked advance in your educational practice and I feel sure that the years will amply justify the wisdom of respecting the differentiation that is grounded in the diverse but complementary natures of the boy and the girl' (McQuaid 1946).

The Ballyfermot and Clogher Road schools interpreted their comprehensive brief primarily in terms of the concept of the neighbourhood school. Both neighbourhoods lacked many of the facilities found in middle-class areas in other parts of the city, and the two schools tried to compensate by offering as many extra-curricular activities as possible – dance, drama, music, hobbies, debates and study facilities in the evening. This placed a considerable burden on the teachers but, during the first year of the experiment, the staff of both schools were enthusiastic and fired with a missionary zeal. This spirit is evident in a school brochure produced by Ballyfermot at the time:

> To make the comprehensive idea a success calls for a spirit of adventure and a willingness to work, sometimes far beyond the normal call of duty. There is no room in an enterprise of this kind for the cynic or the sceptic. What is needed is the pioneering spirit and teachers who are ready to give of their best, to try and go on trying until success crowns their efforts. Success when it does come cannot be claimed for one individual more than another; all the staff are involved. All must work together as a team and stay as a team through success and failure alike. (Trant 1967: 10)

The second year of the comprehensive experiment was to bring a different story. Unfavourable comparisons regarding salary and status were now being made with the Department's official comprehensive schools. The fact that the two Dublin schools were denied official recognition by the Department was a cause of rancour. What rankled even more was the payment of a special allowance to teachers in the state comprehensive schools. Matters came to a head when the CDVEC teachers began a 'work-to-rule', which meant that all extra-curricular activities ceased. It also meant, as often happens in work-to-rule situations, that less work was in fact done than would be expected in normal circumstances. Morale in both schools rapidly deteriorated, so much so that the CDVEC experiment in comprehensive education showed every sign of disintegrating within less than two years of being inaugurated.

Throughout the school year 1967–68, both Ballyfermot and Clogher Road were in a state of crisis. The reason for the crisis, afterwards stated by the two principals, was largely a difficulty in communication:

> As events turned out the problems exceeded the progress but this was probably due to the fact that the basic concept underlying the function of the two schools – the idea of their being experimental and pilot ventures – was not sufficiently spelt out. Consequently the two principals concerned often found themselves in equivocal situations vis-à-vis their own staffs and sometimes vis-à-vis the Department's officials. The question was often asked and not always answered – what is a major regional school and what is so special about it to make it different from other vocational schools? (Rossiter and Trant 1971: 2)

This view is an oversimplification. It was not just a question of spelling out the concept of the CDVEC's comprehensive experiment, there was also a fundamental ambivalence in the nature of the experiment itself. Were Ballyfermot and Clogher Road really comprehensive schools, comparable to those officially launched by the Department of Education? According to the CDVEC the answer was 'yes' but the Department, because it chose to ignore the very existence of the experiment, seemed to take the opposite view.

The school year 1968–69, the third year of the experiment, was to prove crucial. Séamus Rossiter and I decided on a policy of retrenchment. All overt allusions to implementing a comprehensive plan were abandoned and instead a policy of 'normalisation' was followed; henceforth the two schools were to be regarded as no different from any other vocational school in Dublin City. No special privileges were sought and the schools were to work out their salvation as ordinary run-of-the-mill vocational schools trying to serve the needs of their respective areas. As a result, from then on there was less contact between the two schools. Originally they had been launched as a joint experiment with a brief to maintain close liaison with one another. In the future, however, each school was to travel its own road.

BALLYFERMOT VOCATIONAL SCHOOL

In Ballyfermot, the school year 1969–70 marked a fresh beginning. By now I realised that the comprehensive experiment was heading for failure. The major difficulty was that it lacked official status and compared unfavourably with the prestige enjoyed by the state comprehensive schools. I resolved, therefore, that Ballyfermot should not rely on any designation, official or otherwise; it would generate its own ethos and rationale, based on its own assessment of the needs it should serve and the role it should play. I had in my own mind a broad aim for the school, adapted from the Second Vatican Council's *Declaration on Christian Education*. The purpose should be to develop the whole person, provide an introduction into the cultural heritage won by past generations, promote a sense of values, prepare for working life, create friendly contacts between students of diverse temperament and background, foster among them a willingness to understand one another and, finally, to be a centre of activity that would engage the participation of the various cultural and civic groups in the local area. In order to put this aim into practice, I set about attracting teachers who were talented, imaginative and ready to experiment. In my staffing policy I was helped by two factors. Firstly, the school was rapidly expanding, which provided the opportunity to recruit new staff. The second factor was crucial. The CDVEC fully endorsed my staffing policy by allowing me wide scope in recruiting teachers of my own choice and permitting a generous teacher-pupil ratio. Ballyfermot quickly acquired the reputation of being a liberal and progressive school and attracted many innovative teachers, several of whom came from abroad.

The staff mix in Ballyfermot was unusual and sometimes explosive, but it produced striking results, especially in the short period from 1969 to 1973. The school pioneered adventure education in Ireland. It had a purpose-built educational drama unit with a teacher who explored the possibilities of drama to a point unheard of in Irish schools. The school also had remedial and enrichment groups and a pastoral care system well before these things became the practice in Ireland. The physical education department was one of the largest and most comprehensive in the country and catered not only for games, athletics and gymnastics but also for music and movement. Creative work in art and craft flourished, and language teaching in English, Irish, French and German was fresh and imaginative.

The management structure was also unusual. At the time of my appointment, I was thirty-two years old and had never before held a senior administrative post in a school. I was fortunate that my deputy, Jim Shortall, was an older man and more versed in the politics and complexities of school administration. We were to become close friends and succeeded in forming a partnership in which we complemented each other. Thus the school became a place where ideas flourished within a strong framework of good order and traditional discipline.

Ballyfermot was notable for the on-going debate on educational innovation it fostered among the staff. Each new school year began with an entire week devoted to inservice planning and discussion and the process continued throughout the year. In this way, a consensus began to emerge about what the school stood for which in turn influenced the students and parents. By the early 1970s we were in a position to promulgate a clear and simple statement of where we were going:

> The educational policy of the school may be summed up thus: it is comprehensive in organisation and community in orientation. When

we say we are a comprehensive school we mean we do not select our intake, we provide a wide variety of subjects on the curriculum, we maintain a balance between the academic and the practical and we do not stream the students. By streaming we mean the grouping of students into permanent classes according to general ability. A policy of non-streaming forces us to experiment with other methods of grouping such as mixed ability or setting by subjects. (Trant 1972: 4–5)

We were also trying to make the school a caring community, not merely a place of instruction. This was an idealistic stance and laid a heavy burden on the teachers:

It implies the recognition of a basic fact that education can be meaningless unless the school takes into account all the factors in the environment of the students. If there are factors which militate against their education, the school must seek to redress the balance; for instance there is little point in a teacher setting homework where students have neither the capacity to study on their own nor the facilities to do so even if they wished. The caring school must undertake to teach the students how to study and provide them with a room in which to do it. A caring school, because of its concern for the student as a person, inevitably becomes involved in problems that reach deep into the life of the family. If the family is under stress, the school will seek in every way possible to create within itself an atmosphere where the student will feel secure and respected as a person. (Rossiter and Trant 1971: 4–5)

The ethos of the school was characterised by a fundamental respect for persons, which was enshrined in the 'Guide to Staff', a handbook distributed to all the teachers:

Our school should be above all else characterised by mutual respect for one another – students and teachers as well as the other members of the school community. If everyone is accorded the basic respect that is due to him or her as a human being, the school will face the tensions of change with equilibrium and harmony. It will be a school characterised by order, without which learning is impossible, but an order achieved with dignity and consideration. There will be no need for a multiplicity of rules. If the members of the school community are not agreed about their aims and objectives and if there is no mutual respect, then no amount of rules and regulations will mend the cracks in the edifice. (Trant 1972: 2)

One of the most notable features of the comprehensive experiment in Ballyfermot was the interest we took in student grouping. It began in 1966 when, as part of the school's brief, streaming by ability – the usual way of grouping students in Irish post-primary schools at the time – was replaced by subject setting. This was an arrangement whereby all the first year students were timetabled in units of three simultaneous classes for as many subjects as possible. After an initial period of observation, the students were then to be placed in new groups or sets for each subject. In theory it allowed for a more flexible grouping arrangement than was possible in the traditional streamed classes; for instance, in a setting arrangement, it was possible for the same student to be in an A-group for maths, a B-group for English and a C-group for science. But, in practice, the setting arrangement in Ballyfermot was a failure. Despite the skill and ingenuity exercised in drawing up a setting timetable, the teachers were not inclined to put it into effect. In hindsight it would be unfair to blame them; to have operated a setting arrangement would have required far more experience in joint planning than was the case in the 1960s. It would also have entailed a well thought-out teacher support programme, which was unheard of at the time.

During the school year 1969–70, we changed the grouping policy to that known as banding. The first year intake was divided into three broad bands – above average, average and below average, and within these bands the students were grouped into mixed ability classes. This system worked reasonably well. Its chief merit was that it sorted the students into three manageable groups with regard to examination expectations. But it had a serious drawback: it was a system that owed more to administrative convenience than the needs of the students themselves. Some of the staff believed that a fairer and more appropriate grouping system would be to arrange all the first year pupils into classes of mixed ability and maintain that arrangement for a complete year. The first year would then become a genuine observation period and no long-term decisions about the pupils' academic future would be made until the end of the year. The policy would also fit in better with the idea of comprehensive education, advocated in the Hillery reforms of 1963.

At the beginning of the school year 1970–71 the first year plan was put into practice in Ballyfermot. The underlying rationale, like much of the school's general policy, was stated in idealistic terms:

> The great challenge before us in Ballyfermot is to create a learning situation which will cater more fully for the needs of our students. Everybody knows that the students are working well below their potential, that the drop out rate is high and that motivation is low. Everybody is familiar with the environmental factors that militate against the educational progress of our students. But to say all this in no way excuses us from the obligation of finding new approaches and solutions to the problems that face us. The answer to our problems does not lie in school organisation or even curriculum change as such. We must be prepared to face something much more fundamental, a reappraisal of the learning situation itself. We must be prepared to examine traditional aims and methods and change them radically if necessary. This is a formidable task and should be undertaken first in a controlled situation by a team of teachers working closely with one another. Considerable flexibility and room to experiment will be essential to such an undertaking; essential also will be the need for continuous dialogue among the teachers. Conditions most favourable to such a venture now exist in the first-year programme. (Trant 1969: 1)

In order to demonstrate publicly that the basis of the first year grouping arrangements was genuine mixed ability and not a camouflaged streaming process, the pupils were put into classes according to alphabetical order. Strictly speaking, this was not a mixed ability arrangement at all, but was more akin to random grouping. We decided on alphabetical grouping because we were aware of the powerful influence of teacher expectations:

> Students tend to live up to the expectations of their teachers. We cannot afford to have many assumptions about the capabilities and talents of the young students who are coming to us for the first time. Attempts, however well intentioned, to sort them into prearranged categories often have sad and lasting effects on their morale and self-respect. And what of the categories we use? Whatever labels are given to them, they always amount to the same two-fold distinction: students who will pass their external exams and those who will not. If we make the touchstone of our students' success in school coincide with their examination prospects, small wonder that many of them get discouraged quite early in their courses and eventually drop out altogether. Many have poor examination prospects from the outset and to categorise them accordingly is the equivalent of branding them publicly as failures. (Trant 1969: 1–2)

Besides the grouping arrangement, there were two other factors worth mentioning about the new first year plan in Ballyfermot. Firstly, all the students were housed separately from the rest of the school, which was possible because the school was built on two sites separated by a main road. Secondly and more significantly, the students for the most part were taught by teachers whose sole commitment was to the first year programme. For practical purposes the first year students now had their own school, their own staff and an assistant principal, Noel Halpin, charged with their special care.

The plan lasted for three years, from 1970 to 1973. It has to be said that there were many things about it that made for tension and even dissension in the overall running of the school. Its most obvious fault was that it tended to polarise the staff. The first year teachers, all of whom had volunteered for the assignment, were in favour of a liberal, child-centred approach in line with the new primary school curriculum which had been adopted nationally. The teachers in the main part of the school, however, wanted a more institutional, examination-oriented and, in their view, realistic approach. Tension between both groups was inevitable and sometimes acute.

The plan had other aspects which were more positive and rewarding. It made for an atmosphere in which all pupils entering the school for the first time were accepted for what they were and not for their potential in terms of examination success. It created a climate of freedom and experiment where the teachers were not afraid to try new approaches and afterwards to discuss frankly among themselves the reasons for success or failure as the case might be. It generated, too, a momentum for innovation: on occasion the normal timetable was suspended entirely and a project week inaugurated instead, when the pupils went to special interest groups such as toy-making for a local children's hospital, publishing a school bulletin, or making a radio programme for live transmission.

The testing point for the plan came at the end of its first year, when the teachers were torn between repeating the programme with a new intake or remaining with their pupils throughout the ensuing second and third years. They opted eventually for the former but the choice was a painful one, a testimony to the close bonds that had grown between them and the students. In my own thinking, the first year plan would have developed into a three tier arrangement – a junior, middle and senior school, each in a separate building and each with its own ethos. But, as things turned out, the senior school was not built until a decade later and, by that time, the circumstances of the school had changed and I had left the scene.

SCHOOL AND COMMUNITY

The aspect of the Ballyfermot experiment that attracted most public attention was the school's involvement with the local community; an account of this appeared in an OECD report, which described the school as 'a centre for community renewal and resurgence' (1980: 34). There were three dimensions to the school's community involvement: the extension of formal adult classes into more generalised community education activities; the forging of links with the local community association; and the development of a community-oriented curriculum.

Evening classes for adults have always been provided by vocational schools in Ireland, but the most notable feature of Ballyfermot's adult programme was not the numbers involved but the variety of the groups catered for. The traditional notion of adult education gave way to a wider concept that embraced as many aspects of community living as possible and tried to attract people into the school by creating a relaxed and informal atmosphere. Various social activities such as visits to art exhibitions, concerts and weekend hikes were organised to help the different groups meet each other. Classes were also encouraged to hold end-of-term parties. Much informal learning took place through clubs and discussion groups; for instance the aim of the ladies club, which met once a week, was recreational, a break from housework.

The school possessed two gymnasiums and both were in constant use up to 10.00 p.m., providing training facilities for various sports groups. When it was found that the period from 5.30 p.m. to 7.00 p.m. was a slack time in the gyms, arrangements were made with some of the local street committees to take young children who were not receiving any physical education in their primary schools. To cater for teenagers, an arts workshop was launched which met in the school four nights a week under the guidance of the drama teacher and eight voluntary helpers. The workshop provided for self-expression through dance, drama, art and music and was later extended into a young adults drama group and a film society. It eventually acquired premises outside the school and went on to become a successful community organisation.

The second dimension of the school's community policy was its involvement with the politics of local community development. Community politics are often volatile and confrontational and, at this period, Ballyfermot was no exception. Encouraged by professional medical and social workers in the area, the local tenants group adopted a high profile and renamed itself the Ballyfermot Community Association (BCA). Soon the BCA found itself in conflict with the officers of Dublin Corporation over a number of issues relating to planning in the area. The BCA was making a bid to be treated as an organ of local government in its own right and made astute use of the media to gain public sympathy for its cause.

I aligned myself closely with the BCA by becoming a member of its council which met regularly in the school. My position was ambiguous; as principal of a local authority school, I found myself supporting a group that sometimes openly opposed the officers of the same authority. The dilemma eased when I succeeded in having a member of the teaching staff appointed as community education organiser. I was then able to distance myself somewhat from the politics of community development, while at the same time being fully informed and supportive of what was going on.

The third aspect of the school's community policy, the development of a community oriented curriculum, was the most difficult of the three to achieve. The difficulty was expressed by Liam Healy, the community education organiser on the school staff:

> Here we have a paradox; by venturing out into the community and making contact with youth work, adult education and industry, the school is eventually forced to look at itself, its objectives and its curriculum. Close integration with the community generally leads to a realisation that the very hub of school activity, the curriculum, should become community oriented. By this is meant a curriculum relevant to the needs of the students in their local environment. The idea is that the students and the school should study the local area in greater and greater depth, see its problems and attempt to formulate solutions – the student perhaps through social work as part of the school curriculum, the school through greater commitment to community development. Thus closer school-community relations lead to the school becoming a resource centre for the community while

the local neighbourhood is increasingly being regarded as part of the educational facilities of the school. (1972: 17–8)

Healy put his theory to the test by developing a social and environmental studies course for first-year students, entitled 'Dublin Today and Tomorrow'. The underlying theme was change, which was reflected in the introduction to the course:

Look out the classroom window. Ballyfermot is changing. We can see a new road being built, new factories and an extension to a school. Look towards town. We can see new skyscraper blocks. Dublin is changing. We are caught up in the change. It affects us; can we also affect it? We shall study three areas of particular importance: where people live, where they work, and where they take their leisure. (Healy 1972: 17–8)

The course was activity-based, with opportunities for the students to go into their neighbourhood and into the nearby city to look at things, meet people and ask questions. Why were municipal housing estates being built in one part of the city rather than another? Why not move Dublin airport to let the city expand to the north? Why were 80 per cent of the parents working in town rather than in the local area? The enquiries the students conducted were disciplined, their contacts with public officials were positive and friendly and the comparisons they drew between their own and other areas both neighbouring and distant made them keenly aware of the amenities they themselves possessed or lacked. They became aware too of what could and could not be changed and, most significantly, they acquired an inkling of the part they themselves could play in bringing about change.

Healy was a key figure in articulating the idea of a community-oriented curriculum, but practically all the teachers had a hand in the development of the concept in so far as they all tried to understand the background of their students and reflect this understanding in the way they taught their respective subjects. The staff also supported the effort to make the school a cultural centre in the area. Tony Breen and Terry Doyle produced an accomplished and daring performance of *Hamlet*, the national youth orchestra played to a full house, so too did the young pianist John O'Connor, while Vincent Sammon took groups of adults on sketching trips in the Wicklow hills and Frank Lee-Cooper organised an exciting art exhibition – to mention but a few examples.

The school's commitment to community education was well ahead of official thinking at the time. The Department of Education's policy on the subject was first revealed in October 1970 in a document that also marked the latest stage in the official effort to create a unified post-primary system. The document proposed that in certain areas throughout the country the existing post-primary schools, secondary and vocational, would be amalgamated into a new purpose-built school (Department of Education 1970). The newcomers would be knows as 'community schools' and would be similar in size, purpose and ethos to the state controlled comprehensive schools opened four years earlier. The title was a distraction because, as the editor of one of the national newspapers pointed out, the politics involved had little to do with any of the basic ideas underlying community education:

> Before discussion on the Department of Education's latest document gets under way it might be wise to remind ourselves that there are other issues in Irish education besides that of the control and ownership of schools.... For a country which sets so much store by education, in fact we have done surprisingly little to work out a coherent philosophy of the subject. (*Irish Times,* 12 November 1970)

The Department of Education's document on community schools plunged the Irish educational world into controversy. One historian of the period, Eileen Randles, saw in the document the emergence of a new pattern, a state system of community and comprehensive schools aimed at eventually replacing the existing secondary and vocational schools (Randles 1975: 303). But this probably argues too much for the extent of the Department's ambitions. A later study by Noel Barber described the document as 'a modest proposal' because the policy of amalgamation that it proposed was only intended to apply to schools with an enrolment of less than 400. Where schools had a higher enrolment, they were deemed to be able to offer a comprehensive curriculum and so could remain as they were, either secondary or vocational (Barber 1989: 60).

As the 1970s progressed the positions taken on the community schools proposal became more entrenched and the original ideal of a unified post-primary comprehensive system was lost in the conflict over the control of the new schools. There were other factors too which served to weaken the impact of the comprehensive initiative. In 1973 the Fianna Fáil Government, which had held office for sixteen years, fell from power and was replaced by an inter-party coalition. The new Minister for Education Richard Burke was less enthusiastic about the comprehensive ideal than were his predecessors and, in the Department of Education itself, support for comprehensive education began to weaken, especially when Seán O'Connor, who was one of its chief advocates, retired from the office of secretary in 1975. The universities were silent on the issue while among the religious and clerical authorities 'there was little enthusiasm and much hostility' (Barber 1989: 101).

The CDVEC's comprehensive education experiment cannot be said to have been any more successful than that of the Department of Education. It started in virtual isolation from the Department's scheme, went its own way and was always confined to the efforts of two schools. The 1970s saw the departure of key CDVEC figures associated with the experiment: Martin Gleeson retired from the CEO's post and Tom McCarthy, one of his chief advisers and the architect of the comprehensive plan, left the service. The CDVEC in general was now preoccupied with the Intermediate and Leaving Certificate courses, which had been introduced in the 1960s to give the VEC system parity of esteem with the secondary schools. In these circumstances, the intentions and expectations surrounding the comprehensive initiative were largely forgotten.

I spent six years in Ballyfermot and, although there were ups and downs, I can say in retrospect that the years were filled with all kinds of interesting experiences. Our brief was to experiment, and experiment we certainly did – in grouping procedures, integrated curriculum, home-school liaison, remedial and enrichment classes, outdoor education, school industry links and community education. I was lucky to have had the help of gifted and imaginative teachers. I can now see that there were several things we should have done differently and taken more care and time in the doing. I was a young man in a hurry and often impatient of obstacles and opposition. James Connolly, the 1916 revolutionary, once said he had made two mistakes in his life: the first was to emigrate to America, the second was to come back. I sometimes feel the same about my time in Ballyfermot: it was too short to have accomplished much in the way of lasting results but long enough to learn that genuine innovation is a slow, complex and often painful affair.

At the end of six years, I had come to realise that there were limits to what any school could accomplish on its own, no matter how progressive its policy or talented its staff. The need for support structures for innovative teachers and schools was one of the chief lessons I learnt. By 1972 I had also become aware of curriculum development projects in the United States, Sweden and Britain and was looking for an opportunity to launch a similar project in Dublin that would build on the Ballyfermot experience and involve a network of other interested schools. This idea was the genesis of what eventually became the Curriculum Development Unit, which is the subject of our next chapter.

CHAPTER 3

Launching a New Initiative

CONCEPTION OF AN IDEA

'Precisely the same textbooks are being read tonight in every secondary school and college in Ireland.' These words were spoken by Patrick Pearse in 1912 about the rigid curriculum and examination system in the Ireland of his time. Pearse had hard things to say about the system, which he described as a murder machine:

> It is cold and mechanical, like the ruthlessness of an immensely powerful engine. A machine vast, complicated, with a multitude of far-reaching arms, with many ponderous presses, carrying out mysterious and long-drawn processes of shaping and moulding, is the true image of the Irish education system. It grinds night and day; it obeys immutable and predetermined laws; it is as devoid of understanding, of sympathy, of imagination, as is any other piece of machinery that performs an appointed task. (Ó Buachalla 1980: 356–7)

Half a century after independence, some of Pearse's strictures could still be applied to the Irish educational system. In the early years of the state, the Department of Education had tried to open up the curriculum by discontinuing set texts, but this practice had to be abandoned by 1940. Prescribed syllabi and predictable examinations were to dominate the Irish system for the following thirty years. In 1954 the Report of the Council of Education stated that in a democratic country examinations were absolutely essential and, in 1966, T.J. McElligott, in his study of education in Ireland, concluded that, 'the triumph of examinations would seem to be complete' (1966: 69).

In September 1970, an event took place which showed that the examination system, if not beginning to crack, was at least showing signs of strain. A committee was established by Padraig Faulkner, the Minister for Education, 'to evaluate the present form and function of the Intermediate Certificate Examination and to advise on new types of public examinations' (ICE Report 1975). The committee contained representatives from the major powers in Irish education and was chaired by an assistant secretary from the Department of Education, Seán O'Connor, who was fast making a name for himself as an unconventional and charismatic civil servant. (The chairmanship was later taken by Fr Paul Andrews, a notable Jesuit educationalist.) The committee's terms of reference were wide: the aims, role and effects of the public examinations at the end of the junior cycle were to be scrutinised. Clearly the traditional system was about to undergo a thorough review.

The setting up of the Intermediate Certificate Examination Committee, or the ICE Committee as it came to be called, was noted with interest by many educational bodies in the country and one of these was the Board of Studies of the CDVEC. The Board, which had been established as far back as February 1932, comprised the principals of the Dublin vocational schools and colleges, along with senior members of the CDVEC's administrative and advisory services. The Intermediate and Group Certificate were of great importance for the CDVEC because for most of the students in the vocational schools, these examinations marked the terminal point of their educational careers. Any change in the examinations would bring corresponding changes in the curriculum and could not be viewed lightly by the principals of the Dublin schools. Furthermore, the Intermediate Certificate Examination itself was a comparative novelty in the vocational schools and the practice of allowing vocational school pupils to enter for it was a bare four years old. It would not have been surprising had the principals reacted cautiously to the possibility of changing the examination structure. For many of them, the Intermediate Certificate had long been a coveted prestige symbol, hitherto reserved for secondary schools; now that parity of esteem at last looked possible it would seem wise not to tamper with the examination mechanism.

The Board of Studies did a surprising thing. In November 1970 it appointed a sub-committee of six principals to look at the operation of the Intermediate and Group Certificate in vocational schools in Dublin City. Appointing a sub-committee was not surprising – the Board usually came to grips with most of the problems that confronted it in that way. What was surprising was the radical nature of the conclusions reached by this particular sub-committee. More surprising still was the fact that the conclusions were accepted by the Board, when they were presented to it the following May.

In the opening sentences of its report, the subcommittee nailed its colours to the mast by declaring that a radical change in the Irish examination system was needed:

> Any consideration of the Group Certificate or Intermediate Certificate examination cannot be divorced from a consideration of the curriculum which these examinations purport to assess. The influence of Group and Intermediate on the junior cycle curriculum of our schools is preponderant. Indeed, before any significant curriculum change can be brought about, the present mode of examining would have to be altered (CDVEC Board of Studies 1971: 1).

This did not mean that the sub-committee members were hostile to the idea of public examinations. They recognised that examinations had their uses provided they were kept firmly in their place. They could be powerful allies in the battle to improve the curriculum but they should never be allowed to dominate it. The curriculum came first and the examinations second and if the curriculum needed changing it should not be beyond the bounds of ingenuity to devise a mode of examination appropriate to that change.

The subcommittee next asked the question: why attempt to change the curriculum in the first place? This question was seen as largely academic since there were forces for change already at work:

> We are no longer in a position to define the limits of any body of human knowledge. Still less are we in a position to impose upon our students with any degree of sureness the task of acquiring any specific body of subject matter. The disturbing thing is that much of what children learn in school today will be irrelevant before they reach adulthood. (1971: 1)

Curriculum change was not an option but a necessity and it would happen whether educators wanted it or not. More learning was taking place outside the classroom than inside and schools could no longer claim to be the sole providers of education. An enormous challenge now confronted teachers, which in the words of Marshall McLuhan, 'has destroyed the monopoly of the book as a teaching aid and cracked the very walls of the classroom so suddenly, we're confused, baffled' (Stearn 1968: 137).

In terms of curriculum rhetoric, there was nothing noteworthy about any of these statements. They were arguments that had been rehearsed many times by reformers in other countries, and it is obvious that the subcommittee used them to set the scene for a more pointed attack on certain aspects of the curriculum in Irish post-primary schools. 'The present junior cycle curriculum has a deceptive and naive uniformity. It does not follow that because all children study the same things for the same examinations that all in fact enjoy equality of educational opportunity' (CDVEC Board of Studies 1971: 2). Here was the nub of the matter: the curriculum contained built-in biases which favoured some children at the expense of others. It also placed an undue emphasis on cognitive and literary skills as if these were the only means through which children could be educated.

These were strong words and were written particularly with a view to the needs of the pupils who attended the Dublin vocational schools, the majority of whom came from a working-class background. Many of the pupils were put at a disadvantage by the traditional curriculum because of its undue emphasis on literary skills. The report was at pains not to devalue the merit of such skills, but argued that they had been over-emphasised to the point of being accepted as the only valid pattern of education in Irish schools. There was a need to explore the potential of other approaches in education, such as music, drama, mime, dance, art, craft, film-making, photography and tape recording. The subcommittee was also conscious of two related problems in the Dublin vocational schools: the remedial and the drop-out problems. Many pupils were judged remedial because, from the primary school onwards, they had never enjoyed a curriculum suited to their needs; for the same reason many left school at the first available opportunity.

In recommending a new approach to the curriculum and examinations, the report was plainly influenced by the work of the Schools Council for England and Wales and by the development of flexible modes of examining in the Certificate of Secondary Education (CSE) which had been introduced there. The subcommittee was impressed by the underlying principle of the Schools Council: that each school should have the fullest possible measure of responsibility for its own work, with its own curriculum and teaching methods, based on the needs of its own students and evolved by its own staff (Ministry of Education 1964). Mode 3 of the CSE, which allowed a school under external moderation to devise and assess its own curriculum, was particularly welcome. A similar examination mode could be developed in Ireland if the Department of Education supported it.

The major recommendation of the report was that the CDVEC should establish a curriculum planning group comprising representatives from the Dublin vocational schools and also from the universities, the Department of Education and business and industry. The function of the group would be to initiate curriculum development projects at different levels and over varying lengths of time. The group would facilitate, co-ordinate and evaluate these projects, and relate them to the structure of the examination system.

We have given prominence to the report of the CDVEC subcommittee because it had far-reaching results. It was duly endorsed by the Board of Studies and, like many similar reports, could have languished on some official's dusty shelf and then been quietly forgotten. But this was not its fate. It started a train of events that culminated in the establishment of a curriculum development unit, committed to implementing the recommendations it had made.

SPONSORS

The Irish theologian Enda Lyons argues that for any community to come into being three things are necessary. The first is interest, without which there can never be a community of any kind. The second is association; people who have a strong interest in something, naturally and spontaneously seek out and associate with others who are of the same mind. The third is organisation: 'When people who share a common interest associate with one another for the purpose of sharing and pursuing their interest, they automatically set up, or avail of, whatever structures or institutions they think will help them to pursue their interest' (1987: 7). Lyon's model aptly describes how the Curriculum Development Unit (CDU) came into being. Three sponsors assisted at its birth: the CDVEC, Trinity College Dublin and the Department of Education. The three were very different from each other and had correspondingly different expectations of what a curriculum unit should be. It is worth examining these expectations because they were to have important implications for the subsequent development of the CDU's work.

The expectations of the CDVEC, the CDU's principal sponsor, derived from the nature of the education it was obliged to provide under the terms of its founding charter, the 1930 Vocational Education Act. The hallmark of the VEC system has always been a practical approach to learning which is never far removed from the realities of the workplace. Side by side with the emphasis on preparing for work, vocational schools have traditionally cultivated an active methodology which stresses initiative and autonomy. The

Report of the Commission on Technical Education, which laid the basis for the 1930 Act, envisaged the future vocational school as 'a school, not for vocational training, as the name would seem to imply, but as a secondary school with a very strong practical bias.' The Commission was specific about the educational climate it envisaged for vocational schools:

> The school atmosphere should be quite different from that of the primary school. The teaching should be on lines suited to adults rather than school children, the pupils being made conscious that it is in their interest to avail themselves of the services of the teacher and the responsibility for doing so rests on them rather than on the teacher. They should feel that they are passing into a new educational environment where they are invited to begin to study afresh, with the idea of fitting themselves to earn their livelihood. The main object of the teacher should be to encourage observation, initiative and self-reliance rather than to impart information and to enforce rules. (1928: 46)

As well as having a practical approach to learning, vocational schools were also expected to enshrine in their curriculum the traditional values of liberal education. In a letter to the chairman of the Commission, the then Minister for Education John Marcus O'Sullivan laid down a guiding principle for the future development of vocational education in Ireland:

> In dealing with these and other problems of technical instruction, I feel confident that your Commission will handle them on the fundamental principle that technical instruction can have and should have as profound an educational and civic value as other forms of education, and that no matter how effective a system of technical education may be in the narrower vocational sense of the word, it will fail in one of its chief purposes if it does not uplift every person not merely as members of their particular trade, but as a member of the community and as a member of the state. (1928: 46)

This at least was the theory: the reality in vocational schools turned out to be different. From the outset, they were refused parity of esteem with the secondary schools and were not allowed to teach the Intermediate or Leaving Certificate courses, which meant that vocational students were debarred from entering the universities, professions, civil service or the Church ministry. This remained the case for forty years until eventually in the 1960s, as we saw in Chapter 2, the Hillery reforms and the dawning of the comprehensive ideal changed things and the vocational sector began to find a new confidence. This confidence was expressed by the CDVEC's eagerness to be part of one of the first curriculum development initiatives in the country.

The CDU's second sponsor, Trinity College, presents a very different picture. Established by royal charter in 1592, Trinity was to remain Ireland's only university until the mid-nineteenth century. Throughout most of its history, Trinity was identified with English rule in Ireland and became a symbol of Protestant domination and foreign presence in the country. The image persisted even after the founding of the new state. The custom of singing *God Save the King* at high table in Trinity remained until 1939, while the practice of drinking the King's health was only discontinued in 1945.

It is scarcely surprising that Trinity's position in the new Ireland was for many years an ambivalent one. As one unfriendly critic remarked: 'Trinity was widely disliked: many people coming into their own in the new state saw the college as an alien institution, making much of its Elizabethan charter, its silver plate and its Protestant tradition' (Donoghue 1986: 171). To add to Trinity's discomfort, the Catholic bishops were reluctant to allow their flock to attend a university that they regarded as unsympathetic to the Catholic ethos. Their view was articulated in unambiguous terms by John Charles McQuaid, Archbishop of Dublin: 'Trinity College Dublin, as a non-Catholic university, has never been acceptable and is not now acceptable to Catholics' (Ó Buachalla 1988: 217).

Trinity, however, learned to accommodate the realities of the new state, if for no other reason than the economics of survival.

Ironically, it was de Valera, the standard bearer of republican sepa-
ratism, who came to Trinity's assistance after the College's plea
for money had been brusquely dismissed by the first coalition
Government (McDowell and Webb 1982). By 1970, the attitude of
the Catholic bishops had softened to the point of rescinding the ban
on Catholic students attending the university. The change of heart,
however, owed more to the pressure of events than any consideration of principle, as a historian of the period points out: 'During the
sixties, as access to higher education grew, many urban Catholics
were unwilling to forego the convenience of a centre city campus. It
was probably their rebellion rather than any actual or contemplated
change in Trinity College which prompted the removal of the ban'
(Ó Buachalla 1988: 218). In other words, it was not a question of
Trinity going native as the natives coming to Trinity.

The CDU's third sponsor, the Department of Education, dates
from June 1924, when it was established under the provisions of the
Ministers and Secretaries Act of the new state, which brought the
hitherto separate sectors of primary, secondary and technical education under the control of a single department. But, apart from this
act of administrative rationalisation, little else in the nature of radical reform was attempted. The new Government was largely con-
tented with the structures it had inherited, so much so, according to
one observer, that 'next to our pillar boxes, probably the most distinctive monument recalling English rule in Ireland is the system of
education' (McElligott 1955: 27).

The most significant characteristic of the Department of
Education is the degree of control it exercises over the entire system. The basis for this was laid down in the early years of independence when the chief preoccupation was survival; the new state
had first to negotiate a transfer of government from Britain and then
suffer the trauma of a civil war. In such circumstances it is not surprising that government ministers relied heavily on their senior civil
servants, most of whom had been retained from the imperial regime.
These officials were critical to the process of continuity, and in this
regard the Department of Education was fortunate in the stability of

tenure of its departmental heads, the first two having served thirty years in office between them (Ó Buachalla 1988: 251). The emphasis on stability leant itself readily to a policy of conservatism, especially when the new Government allied itself closely with the Catholic hierarchy, which was equally disposed towards maintaining the status quo (Akenson 1975: 28).

The basic conservatism of the Department of Education is underwritten in the terms of its founding charter, the Ministers and Secretaries Act. Under the Act, the Minister is responsible to the Dáil for all the actions of his civil servants, which considerably inhibits the amount of initiative or risk that individual officials may wish to take upon themselves. John Harris, who served as special adviser to two ministers in the 1980s, painted the following picture of the decision-making process in the Department:

> It can often happen that a complex and problematic issue may emerge at a relatively low level in the chain of command. The normal procedure is to refer that issue to a higher level for decision. In fact, if the issue is particularly sensitive or difficult, or has political implications, it is likely to pass up the hierarchical ladder, perhaps as far as the Minister's desk. There is a danger that, somewhere along the line, creative thinking about the issue may become stifled, fears may be voiced about creating a precedent, or anxiety expressed about being accused of taking risks or making mistakes. This may result in the soft or safe option being taken, regardless of the merits of the case for the alternative. One hopes that, when files come finally to rest on desks where decisions are actually taken, the decision makers will not be unduly confused by the fog which may have been created around the issue on the way up. (Harris 1989: 11)

We have briefly described the three institutions that agreed to sponsor the CDU. That three such different bodies should have come together at all to launch an educational innovation may be considered something of a minor miracle. But we should beware of regarding institutions solely as impersonal entities; every institution has a human dimension within which can be found on occasion people prepared to take risks. The initiative that led to the founding of the CDU was taken by a group of five people – two from the CDVEC and three from Trinity College. The two from the CDVEC were the CEO Jerry Sheehan and myself. The original idea was born in my Ballyfermot years. Chapter 2 examined the background, and in this chapter we have seen how the report of the Board of Studies' subcommittee helped to set the scene. It was Sheehan, however, who took the first steps in making the idea a reality because, for practical purposes, the key decisions lay in his hands.

In 1971 Sheehan had succeeded Gleeson as CEO of the CDVEC. He had formerly been an inspector in the Department of Education where he had played a prominent part in establishing a network of regional technical colleges throughout the country. He had the reputation of being an able and energetic administrator but, for some people in the CDVEC, his appointment had come as somewhat of a shock. The fact that the new CEO had been a former official of the Department raised some doubts as to his willingness to take an independent line in the tradition that Gleeson had established.

Sheehan, however, was to show that in many ways he was his own man. Since much of the impetus for physical expansion in the CDVEC had finished with Gleeson, the new CEO had to be prepared to invest much of his considerable energy in the development of ideas. Thus, when he was presented with a plan for a curriculum unit in Dublin City, he responded immediately with enthusiasm. His previous experience as inspector had brought him into contact with the OECD curriculum initiatives and he was happy to see something similar take root under his own aegis in Dublin.

Trinity's part in founding the CDU was shared by three people, the first of whom was Val Rice, director of the university's School of Education. Rice had been appointed to the chair of education while still in his early thirties and was the first Catholic to occupy the post in Trinity's history. The appointment for many people was taken as a sign of the College's changing ethos: a Catholic and an outsider was being admitted to the sensitive position of professor of education. Rice had impressive qualifications, among which was a doctoral degree from Harvard. His appointment seemed a daring and imaginative stroke on the part of the Trinity authorities and promised to open up an exciting era in education in Dublin, if not nationally.

On 28 March 1969, within three years of his appointment, Rice addressed the CDVEC Board of Studies. He spoke of his desire for closer contacts between Trinity and the CDVEC schools and said he thought it was wrong that university departments of education in Ireland were more involved with secondary than vocational schools. It was clear from the reaction to his remarks that he had made a favourable impression on the CDVEC principals although, as a philosopher of education, he possibly would not have agreed with the wording of the vote of thanks, which complimented him on 'the replacing of the accent on the technology of education rather than on its philosophy' (CDVEC Board of Studies 1969).

In the following year, Rice and I became acquainted. He was interested in my idea of launching a curriculum initiative and encouraged me to consider basing it in Trinity. With this in view he introduced me to Bryan Powell, a key member of his staff who, as well as being registrar of the School of Education, was also lecturer in curriculum theory and science methodology. Powell was a dynamic and personable Welshman, who had achieved a reputation throughout the country for his inservice work with teachers of biology. In 1969 he had spent a year in the West Indies where he had directed an international team that introduced an integrated science curriculum into the schools. Therefore, Powell's previous curriculum experience made him something of an authority in the area in Ireland.

The third Trinity person was Tony Crooks, a Ph.D. student in the School of Education. Crooks was a Trinity graduate who had recently returned to Dublin after four years teaching in Ontario. While there he had taken a postgraduate degree in Curriculum Studies with the Ontario Institute for Studies in Education. This had given him a thorough grasp of the theory of the subject which he now wished to apply in a practical situation in Ireland as the basis of his doctoral research.

When Rice, who was his professor, suggested that he work with me on the new curriculum initiative, Crooks readily agreed. We met for the first time in 1971 and began to work together in a partnership that was to last for twenty years.

The role of the Department of Education in the founding of the CDU was more restricted than that of the CDVEC or Trinity and nobody from the Department was involved to the same degree as the five founder members from the other two institutions. The Department's principal contribution as a sponsor could be expressed more in negative than positive terms: it did not make any major objection to the CDU's foundation. Although the initiative came in the first instance from the CDVEC and Trinity, the final word lay with the Department; it alone, as the ultimate authority in a highly centralised system, had the power to give or withhold final permission. In the case of the CDU, the Department chose to be generous but, as we shall later see, not without reservations.

BIRTH OF THE CURRICULUM DEVELOPMENT UNIT

On the 11 January 1972, I wrote to Jerry Sheehan, enclosing a document entitled 'Memorandum on Curriculum Development in the City of Dublin VEC'. I had intended the memorandum as a working document for a meeting the following day with Sheehan and Powell. The purpose of the document was to prepare the ground for a further meeting some weeks later with the Department of Education when we would make the case for initiating a curriculum project. Sheehan and Powell declared themselves happy with the text of the memorandum and so it was decided to send it virtually unchanged to the Department.

The central argument in the memorandum was that a curriculum unit should be established under the joint auspices of the CDVEC and the Trinity School of Education, with the approval of the Department of Education. On 4 February 1972, the Department responded by calling a meeting chaired by Seán O'Connor who was at the time the assistant secretary responsible for post-primary education. Two other officials were present: Torlach O'Connor, an educational psychologist and William Hyland, a statistician. Both were close advisers to the assistant secretary and the former was later to play an important role in the CDU's development. The meeting was also attended by Sheehan and myself from the CDVEC, Powell from Trinity, and Diarmaid Ó Donnabháin, the principal of Shannon Comprehensive School, who was trying to initiate a similar curriculum project in the southwest of the country. This meeting had a historic significance for curriculum innovation in Ireland. O'Connor signified his willingness to allow the two projects to proceed, adding the laconic comment that the worst that could happen was that they might fail.

The meeting, however, was unofficial and its conclusions, no matter how favourable, could not be taken as a basis for action. To remedy this, Sheehan immediately started to put the wheels of official machinery into motion. His first task was to secure the permission of his local education authority, the CDVEC, which was successfully negotiated by the end of February 1972. Following normal procedure, the recommendation of the CDVEC was then sent to the Department of Education for sanction. But the Department was not to be rushed in such matters and two months later Sheehan had to remind O'Connor that no word had yet come back from Marlborough Street. Departmental delay of this kind, however, was nothing unusual and Sheehan would have had no cause for feeling unduly worried.

In the meantime, negotiations between the CDVEC and the Trinity School of Education were proceeding apace and the agreement reached by the two bodies was formalised in a document drawn up by Sheehan on 7 April entitled 'Proposal for Joint Curriculum Development Project for Junior Cycle Post-Primary Courses'. The document contained six major points:

- A steering committee was to be appointed comprising Sheehan, as chairman, Rice, Powell, myself and a representative from the Department of Education.
- I was to be seconded from my post as principal of Ballyfermot to be the first director of the project.

- Powell was to be given half-time release from the School of Education to work on the project.
- Crooks was to be engaged on the project on a majority time basis.
- The project was to be based in premises owned by Trinity in Westland Row, on the periphery of the main college campus.
- The CDVEC would meet the costs of the project over a period of four years, from 1972 to 1976. (Sheehan 1972*a*)

On 7 April 1972 the steering committee held its first meeting and formally adopted the provisions of Sheehan's document. The following month, when it held its second meeting, Rice was able to report that the Board and Council of Trinity had approved the project. But the Department of Education had not yet replied to Sheehan's letter of the previous February requesting sanction for the project, nor had a representative from the Department come to any of the steering committee meetings. In September 1972, with the beginning of the new school year, the project began to operate with a group of seven pilot schools but still there was no official word from the Department. Not surprisingly, Sheehan was now becoming concerned and, on 25 September, sent a reminder to O'Connor. By this time the project had made substantial commitments in staffing and accommodation and, more importantly, in terms of what it was promising to deliver to teachers, pupils and parents. It was vital, therefore, that the Department gave its official approval.

Eventually, on 13 December, O'Connor's belated response came:

The Department's agreement in principle to the project was on your undertaking to finance it from your committee's resources and the only direct finance agreed by the Department was that Mr A. Trant would be released to act as director of the project and that his salary would be paid by the Department. It was made clear to you that no money would be available for the project from the Department's research funds. This is still the position. (Sheehan 1972*b*)

O'Connor's response was enigmatic. The most that Sheehan had hoped for was that the CDVEC would be allowed to finance the project from its own resources, and he had never expected the Department to pay my salary from its research account. But he was not the kind to look a gift horse in the mouth and so he was quick to interpret the letter as a written approval for the project. On 24 January 1973, he wrote to O'Connor telling him as much and offering to relieve the Department of the burden of paying my salary. 'I feel', he said, 'that, because of the relatively long-term nature of the project, it is not desirable to tie up Department research allocations even to the extent of Mr. Trant's salary, but rather that all project costs be made from one source, i.e. the VEC budget' (Sheehan 1972*b*). In Sheehan's view, this would be the more sensible arrangement and would moreover fit in better with the role the CDVEC intended to play in the new project. He was also careful to give the Department full credit for allowing the project to proceed:

> I regard it as a very welcome and significant development, that your Department has authorised a research budget within a local authority financial scheme. Given the size of my Committee's budget, it is certainly reasonable, indeed necessary, that curriculum research should be undertaken. The modest outlay involved should yield excellent results in cost/benefit terms. I take this opportunity to thank you for the personal backing you have given our proposals for this project'. (Sheehan 1972*b*)

Six weeks later O'Connor replied, protesting that Sheehan had misinterpreted him by saying that he had authorised a research account for the CDVEC:

> What I said at our earlier discussion was that there was no money in the Department's research fund for the project but that we would agree to the secondment of Mr. Trant. My memory is that you said that you would find the other costs from your general allocation. I could not accept therefore that what was a loose arrangement

between us should be subsequently formalised into Departmental authority for a research budget. (Sheehan 1972*b*)

At this remove it is possible to detect a hint of good humoured point-scoring in the exchanges between the two men. This is not surprising since both had been colleagues in the Department of Education before Sheehan took up his post as CEO of the CDVEC, and both were sufficiently friendly to be able to write to each other on first name terms. This friendship was undoubtedly helpful in securing a basis for the CDU's existence and Sheehan was well placed to decode the messages that O'Connor was sending. The Department was not going to give a formal, explicit authorisation for the CDU; it was prepared, however, to allow 'a loose arrangement' which would permit the CDVEC to provide the necessary finance from its own general allocation. The arrangement was vague but in Sheehan's view it was the best deal he could get. He was content therefore to let the matter rest and it was on this ambiguous understanding that the CDU came into being.

The tripartite nature of the CDU's sponsorship was unusual if not unique in the history of Irish education, and in the nature of things produced its fair share of tensions and misunderstandings. But it also proved to be dynamic and creative, and was the basis for the innovative nature of much of the CDU's work. The sponsors brought their own distinctive traditions and outlook to the task of curriculum analysis and development, and they were prepared to learn from one another as the following chapters will show. The debate between them was often lively, sometimes tempestuous but never dull or unproductive. The important thing was to maintain an equitable balance in the relationships between the three, in which everybody's views and expectations were respected. This was the essential ingredient in a partnership that was to last for over three decades and is still a paradigm of meaningful co-operation between a local education authority, a university and a government ministry of education.

This chapter concludes the first part of the book which looks at the central place of values and ideologies in the curriculum.

Examples of a number of influential ideologies were given, and one in particular, equality of educational opportunity, was examined in the context of my own experience as a school principal and director of a curriculum development centre. The experience of both positions gave me the foundation on which to build a curriculum rationale. Later, I was able to articulate the rationale through contact with two universities, the London Institute of Education, where I completed a doctorate in Curriculum Studies under the guidance of Paddy Walsh, and Trinity College Dublin where I lectured on the M.Ed. programme led by Dan Murphy and Elizabeth Oldham, and the diploma in Curriculum Studies led by Ann Fitzgibbon. The rationale is described in the second half of the book, beginning with Chapter 4 which looks at the first element – the formulation and implementation of aims and objectives.

PART II
Curriculum Rationale

CHAPTER 4

Curriculum as Instrumental: Aims and Objectives

MAKING SENSE OF AIMS

In this chapter, we look at the place of aims in curriculum building and at some of their advantages and disadvantages. We examine how aims can be broken down into short-term, identifiable objectives and how this approach has led to controversy among educationalists. We also note how objectives can be used in an imaginative as well as a restrictive manner and we describe how the Objectives movement has played a part in the reawakening of interest in vocational education and training.

The word 'aim' is related to the Latin *estimare* meaning to reckon or estimate; in aiming at something, we estimate the choices and means at our disposal and the direction we must travel. Aims are considered good things to have; they focus our energies and help measure our progress. They remind us when we are falling behind and encourage us to persevere on the path we have chosen. From time to time we may have to examine our aims to see if they are realistic or need readjusting, but generally they are reckoned to be an important part of living. Nobody wants to be accused of being aimless.

The important question about aims is not how they are defined but who does the defining. If aims are handed down like commandments from on high, the chances are they will be ignored or at best given lip service. If on the other hand they are worked out in dialogue, especially with the people most affected by them, there is a better chance they will be accepted. This does not mean that there should be no arguments about aims; arguments are good, provided we end up by making the aims our own. If aims are to be effective, they must be internalised – they have to be adapted and made relevant to our lives. They should also be simple and concrete because, as John Dewey reminds us, education as such really has no aims. Only people have aims and there will always be a great variety in the way their aims are expressed. But we must be wary of treating these expressions as gospel truth:

> Even the most valid aims which can be put in words will, as words, do more harm than good unless one recognizes that they are not aims, but rather suggestions to educators as to how to observe, how to look ahead, and how to choose in liberating and directing the energies of the concrete situations in which they find themselves. (1966: 107)

Aims can also conflict with one another. For instance, should the curriculum be elitist or egalitarian, should it give priority to students with the greatest potential or cater in equal measure for everybody? There are two kinds of elitism – social and meritocratic. Social elitism has a long history and is based on land, class or money. It is still part of our society and we find it wherever people are rich enough to be able to buy the kind of curriculum they want for their children. Meritocratic elitism on the other hand claims to be based on ability, which is usually determined by selection tests. Meritocratic elitism is often defended on the basis that society needs leaders and the best way of obtaining them is through selection for a specially designed curriculum. On the other hand, people who favour an egalitarian curriculum claim that it is the educational corollary of democracy and is based on the principle of equal opportunity for all. Carried to its logical conclusion, the egalitarian ideal means that a democratic state should not only provide the same quantity of education for all but also the same quality. The comprehensive education movement, which we examined in Chapter 2, was largely a reaction against an elitist curriculum.

The academic versus the practical is another example of two conflicting aims. Basically the argument is whether knowledge should be regarded as an end in its own right or something to be pursued because of its accompanying advantages, such as helping to earn a living or winning power and esteem. The two aims of course should not be mutually exclusive, but, in practice, one is nearly always emphasised at the expense of the other. This can be seen in the perennial debate about the relative merits of a liberal versus a vocational curriculum, which we referred to in Chapter 1.

A further example of two conflicting aims is the specialist versus the general curriculum. Today, the tendency towards specialisation, with a consequent narrowing of the range of subjects studied, is justified by the necessity for high standards. If we ask who is demanding these standards, we find that the pressure usually originates from outside: the universities demand high entry requirements from second-level students, and the second-level schools make similar demands on the primary sector. These demands and the standards they impose are in fact a hidden form of selection. The argument for a general curriculum is based on the importance of a broad and balanced education for everybody. This is sometimes called the common curriculum, an idea we shall look at it in more detail in Chapter 6.

Our final example of conflicting aims is the official versus the hidden curriculum. The official curriculum is what teachers are supposed to teach while the hidden curriculum refers to the various side-effect messages, often regrettable, that a school in practice conveys to its students (Walsh 1997). Examples of such messages are that students should be passive learners, tolerate long periods of boredom, accept male dominance as natural and in some cases regard themselves as failures. Schools usually convey these messages without intending to or realising what they are doing. But once the messages have been identified the schools have a responsibility to organise counter measures, for example by introducing anti-sexist or anti-racist programmes when the necessity for these becomes apparent.

The difficulty in discussing aims is that the final word can never be said. The best we can do is conclude with some tentative remarks, which are more paradoxical than definitive. Firstly, our aims should be practicable but at the same time they should stretch our energies and ingenuity. They should make sense but also inspire and lead us beyond what we think are our limits. Secondly, we need to question our aims continually and, in attempting to fulfil them, grow to understand them better. It is reasonable to expect that aims will need modification from time to time, but we too should be prepared to change if our aims are to be fulfilled. Thirdly, aims should point upwards as well as downwards. They point upwards in the sense that the really important things in education are often beyond the scope of schools and colleges. As Jacques Maritain reminds us, we can never succeed in learning everything; there may be courses in philosophy but not in wisdom, in morality but not in courage or prudence, in painting but not in creative genius. Above all, where can we find a course that can teach us about intuition and love?

> For human beings there is indeed nothing greater than intuition and love. Not every love is right, nor every intuition well directed or conceptualised, yet if either intuition or love exists in any hidden corner, life and the flame of life are there, and a bit of heaven in a promise. Yet neither intuition nor love is a matter of training and learning, they are gift and freedom. In spite of all that, education should be primarily concerned with them. (Gallagher and Gallagher 1972: 23)

Aims should point downwards in that their implications have to be continually teased out and translated into short-term workable propositions. For instance, how are the broad aspirations of a government white paper to be translated into classroom realities? We are now in the realm of objectives, which we shall consider next.

SPECIFYING OBJECTIVES

Educational objectives have been defined by Ralph Tyler as 'the criteria by which materials are selected, content is outlined, instructional procedures are developed and texts and examinations are prepared' (Tyler 1949: 3). Tyler is often portrayed as the champion of an impersonal and technocratic approach to curriculum but the description does not do him justice. He wrote with ordinary teachers in mind and wanted them to be part of the construction as well as the implementation of objectives. In devising objectives, Tyler tells us three things we should avoid:

- Objectives should not be stated in terms of what the teacher should do, for example to present the theory of evolution or introduce the Romantic poets. The purpose of education, according to Tyler, is to bring about significant changes in the behaviour of the students, so objectives should focus on student outcomes not teacher activities.
- It is not sufficient to state objectives as elements of learning content because this does not tell us what the learner is expected to do. For instance, if we say that the objective in a science lesson is to learn the law of gravity, it is not clear what we expect of the students. Are they to memorise the law or be able to apply it to concrete situations in their daily lives, or see it as an example of a scientific explanation, or all three together?
- Objectives should not be stated solely as changes in the behaviour of the students. For instance, the objective of developing critical thinking should include a description of the kind of problems we wish the students to think about.

In this way Tyler reaches a definition of an educational objective. It should identify two things: (i) the behaviour to be developed in the student and (ii) the subject content which will help this development. In the final analysis, objectives are matters of choice and are based on value judgements. It is important then that the choices and judgements are wise and well-informed and, to guide us in this matter, Tyler offers some suggestions.

To begin with, we should know the learner's needs. An educational need is defined as the gap between the present condition of the learner and what the desirable norm should be. For instance, the literacy or numeracy levels of a particular group of students may be below the acceptable norm for the school courses they are following or the kind of occupations they are aspiring towards. We should also know something of the background of the student's daily life. Tyler is critical of many school and college courses because they have little to do with outside reality. Education, if it is to be relevant at all, should help young people to grow up and take on the responsibilities of adult and working life. They should be able to look after their health, form happy relationships with others, play their part in civic life and care for things of the spirit.

In specifying objectives we should listen to suggestions from subject specialists but not always follow them. The trouble with specialists is that they often forget the needs of the ordinary student. The specialists, according to Tyler, tend to want others to become specialists like themselves and so their advice is oriented towards further study rather than the world of living and working.

We should also have a sound theory of learning. All objectives are based on a theory of learning of one kind or other, sometimes explicit but more often implicit. It is important that such theories are discussed by both teachers and students; otherwise objectives based on them may turn out to be unrealistic.

Underlying everything, we should have a sound educational philosophy. This is the most difficult but also the most vital factor in the formulation of objectives. Since objectives are based on values, it is important to articulate these values as clearly as possible. There are two reasons for doing so. Firstly, value systems can conflict with each other; for instance a school may claim to promote democracy but may practise the very opposite of a genuine democratic way of life. Secondly, we may sometimes have so many objectives that it is impossible to implement them all in any meaningful way. Choices have to be made about which objectives are the most important and this implies an educational philosophy.

Tyler was not the first person to advocate objectives. In 1924, a fellow American, Franklin Bobbit, published a book called *How to make a Curriculum* in which he listed no fewer than 160 objectives, ranging from items such as 'ability to use language in all ways required for proper and effective participation in community life' to 'ability to make one's sleep contribute in maximum measure to the development and maintenance of a high level of physical vitality' (Eisner 1985: 17). This illustrates one of the main weaknesses of the objectives approach: it generates such a profusion of statements that teachers can feel confused and daunted at the prospect of trying to put them into practice – in other words objectives tend to collapse under their own weight. Tyler is not to blame for the proliferation and trivialisation of objectives because his own approach was reasonably broad and flexible. But some of his followers narrowed the concept of objectives by adding other elements to his two-fold definition: objectives should be identified, not only in terms of student behaviour and learning content, but also be observable and measurable.

Tyler's thinking on objectives had enormous influence and, although several aspects of his work have since been questioned, it remained for many years the accepted model for curriculum development.

OBJECTORS TO OBJECTIVES

The objectives movement did not go unchallenged. In 1966, Elliot Eisner from the University of Stanford wrote an influential paper setting out some serious objections (Eisner 1985). Eisner acknowledged the strength of the case for objectives: they provide goals for focusing the curriculum, facilitate the selection and organisation of content and make it possible to evaluate outcomes. They represent a rational approach to curriculum development and, as Eisner ruefully observes, who would choose irrationality? Nonetheless, the objectives approach has its problems: Eisner identifies four.

The first comes from the nature of teaching itself. Objectives assume that it is possible to predict what the outcomes of teaching will be. The business of teaching, however, is not as simple as that; it may have a degree of predictability, but only in some things – for example, if we are teaching algebra, there is no reason to assume that the students will learn to compose sonnets instead. But, in many other curriculum areas such as literature and art, teaching is such a complex and dynamic affair as to be largely unpredictable. Many variables enter into the teaching situation – the interaction between teacher and students and among the students themselves, and the various changes in the mood, pace and tempo of the teaching-learning process. Teaching is more kaleidoscopic than stable, a fact that all good teachers realise and use to their advantage. Often the most desirable outcome is a surprise to both student and teacher.

Secondly, Eisner takes issue with the view that objectives provide the criteria against which achievement is always to be measured. This assumption fails to distinguish adequately between the application of a standard and the making of a judgement. Applying a standard is the normal way of measuring something physically; it requires the designation of some arbitrary or socially derived quantity, such as a metre, a litre or a kilogram, by which things can be compared. Not all curriculum outcomes, perhaps not even most, are amenable to such measurement; they demand a qualitative judgement. By applying a standard, you can determine whether a student has successfully extracted a square root but it is only in a metaphorical sense that you can measure how well a student has written an expressive narrative.

Eisner's last objection is to my mind the most powerful. The objectives approach is based on a teaching model that is technocratic and mechanistic. It is assumed that the right way to teach is to formulate objectives before selecting content or learning activities. At first sight this may seem a rational way of doing things, but it is not necessarily the best way to proceed. Teachers often work from the other end: they first identify the activities that seem to them to be appropriate and rich in educational opportunities, and only afterwards do they identify the objectives and possible consequences. Specifying outcomes in advance may seem logical – it is reasonable that you should know the name of the destination before going on a journey – but in human affairs this is not always the case. There are other reasons for embarking on a journey and sometimes you only know the destination after you have reached it.

This is very true of teaching: no matter what we think we are attempting to do, very often we only know what we want to achieve when we have tried to achieve it. Instead of asking 'what am I trying to accomplish?' teachers ask, 'what am I going to do?' and out of the doing comes the accomplishment.

The implication of Eisner's argument is that the underlying model of teaching should not be technocratic but artistic and creative. The methods of a teacher are similar to those of the artist and creative scientist. The art and science of teaching requires careful blending of many elements and variables – the personalities of the individual students, the dynamics of the class group and the opportunities provided by the subject matter.

Objections to objectives were not confined to America; some of the strongest criticisms came from Britain and the person most often associated with them was Lawrence Stenhouse. Stenhouse's opposition stemmed from his ideas on the nature of knowledge and its place in schooling. In his 1975 study he pointed out that a school has four different functions:

- training students in various skills, such as typing, making a canoe, speaking a foreign language, handling apparatus or baking a cake;
- imparting different kinds of useful information, like historical dates and names of places, the table of chemical elements, a recipe for making pastry or German irregular verbs;
- initiating students into the values and norms of society;
- inducting or leading students into the thought systems of the culture. This Stenhouse considered to be the essence of education.

Objectives can be successfully applied to the first two of these functions but not to the third or fourth. It is the fourth – the knowledge-base of the curriculum – with which Stenhouse is chiefly concerned. Following Eisner, he argues that it is here that the objectives approach makes its greatest mistake by considering learning to be predictable; on the contrary, all true learning is provisional, temporary and highly unpredictable. When students are predictable in their learning, it is because their thinking is stereotyped, limited and unfree. It is the job of the teacher to liberate them by awakening their imagination and leading them towards true learning. Paradoxically, such an approach is successful only to the extent that the outcomes are unpredictable.

Stenhouse's criticism is based on his ideas of what constitutes good teaching practice. Advocates of objectives claim to improve teaching by specifying its purposes, but in reality this is not the way any practice is improved. We do not teach athletes to jump well by setting the bar higher but by helping them criticise their perform-ance in a constructive manner. Similarly, teachers become better at their job through the critical awareness of their own teaching. Improving practice rests on diagnosis more than prognosis.

Stenhouse asserts that there is often a hidden agenda in the use of objectives; they are advocated by people who wish to control or even threaten teachers. Objectives imply unspoken statements like 'we are not happy with your performance', or 'we wish to make you more accountable'. Although it is reasonable to look for accountability in teaching, the objectives route is not the only or best one to take.

TOWARDS A COMPROMISE

Is there any middle ground between the champions of objectives and their critics? Although Eisner was among the latter, he was will-ing to compromise by suggesting a distinction between instructional and expressive objectives. An instructional objective specifies a learning outcome in advance and so is predictive. An expressive objective is more like an encounter; it does not specify or predict an outcome but identifies a learning situation – a problem that students have to cope with, or a task that they have to engage with. An expressive objective, therefore, is evocative rather than prescriptive. Eisner allows for the use of both kinds of objectives but there is lit-tle doubt as where his own preference lies. Most teachers, he says, prefer to use expressive objectives, which have to do with the more important aspects of teaching and learning – what Stenhouse calls induction.

Malcolm Skilbeck (1982) also argues for a middle ground in the objectives debate. He acknowledges that the rhetoric of the objectives school has not helped matters – 'the jejune and barren language to be found in the lists of behaviour objectives' – but he points out that there is an unnecessary polarity in the debate and the antagonists are often nearer to each other's positions than they realise or care to admit. The most important aspect of objectives, according to Skilbeck, is the emphasis they place on student learning rather than on the actions of the teacher. He sees particular merit in the application of objectives to school-based curriculum development, which should begin with a review of the existing curriculum before deciding what way to change it. In the review process, the identification of current objectives and the formulation of new ones can be a very useful exercise. The role of objectives in reviewing the entire curriculum was also explored by two members of the CDU staff, Cynthia Deane Fogarty and Tony Crooks (Fogarty and Crooks 1987). Objectives, however, should always be used flexibly: they should be 'directional and dynamic, in that they must be reviewed, modified, and if necessary reformulated progressively as the teaching/learning process unfolds' (Skilbeck 1984: 235). Skilbeck also stresses the need for consensus and participation in drawing up objectives; teachers, students, parents and other relevant interests should be involved.

In his study of the objectives model, Paddy Walsh distinguishes four different assumptions that people make about objectives (1997: 64):

- Education is a planned, methodical, purposive enterprise and therefore necessarily has objectives.
- These should be stated in terms of learning outcomes rather than teaching processes.
- Student behaviour is the only sure criterion of student learning.
- Setting systematic objectives is a desirable means for achieving control of the curriculum.

Walsh likens these assumptions to stations on a train journey; not everyone would wish to make the full journey, preferring to get off at the first, second or third station before reaching the end of the line. Some people might even wish to make conditions before deciding to make the journey at all. In other words, we should be prepared to modify the objectives model to our own particular teaching and learning needs.

In Irish education, one of the most striking examples of an imaginative approach to objectives can be found at the margins of the system, in the Junior Certificate School Programme (JCSP). JCSP was first developed in 1979 to identify potential early school leavers and to design, implement and evaluate a curriculum suitable to their needs. Early school leavers at the time were defined as those students who derive little or no benefit from their schooling, who leave school at the earliest opportunity, are unfitted for the world of work, and consequently either drift from one job to another or remain more or less permanently unemployed. The new programme recognised that there were many reasons for early leaving, but one in particular stood out:

> Success in school is usually determined by the value of the public examination system. This is not necessarily a value judgement, but a simple statement of fact. Certain students, perhaps large numbers, thrive on the examination system, others lose out. These are the students who do not measure up to the demands of the examinations. For one reason or another they do badly and, what is worse, they themselves and sometimes their teachers, expect they will do badly. Hence, their natural defence is to drop out either physically or psychologically from school. This is hardly surprising since nobody likes a threat they cannot cope with. We all need status, security and a sense of achievement, and if we are in a place where these things are denied us, we will either rebel or drop out. (Trant 1982: 30)

JCSP is now a thriving, national programme catering for about 180 schools, with a full-time co-ordinating staff led by Aideen Cassidy and Bernadette Kiely. It is undoubtedly one of the CDU's most successful ventures, with impressive arrangements in place for literacy, numeracy, inservice and a school library provision. At this stage it is hard to realise that the programme had a humble and even hazardous initiation period but that is a story we shall return to in Chapter 11.

The starting point of JCSP is the belief that, in the task of educating young people towards maturity, the school should be helped, not hindered, by the examination system. The current system is sometimes praised for promoting a culture of excellence but it does this at a high cost. As Aideen Cassidy points out, excellence has value only because it is not accessible to all. 'A culture of failure is an essential part of the present system and it exists to prove the value of the successful' (1997: 157). The JCSP aims to counteract the culture of failure by emphasising what the students are able to accomplish, thereby building up their confidence and self-image. The same affirmative approach is used with parents. The usual reaction of parents on receiving a message from the school is one of anxiety; in the case of the JCSP, the message is often one of congratulations for something the student has achieved.

In a sense, the JCSP is not a new programme at all; it is a fresh way of approaching the normal Junior Certificate course in order to make it more meaningful and interesting to students who would otherwise have difficulty coping with it and, as a result, would be tempted to drop out of school. As former JCSP team member Elizabeth O'Gorman remarks, these are the students whose education is like a mystery tour in the dark: 'They have no idea where they are going, why they are going or how they are going to get there' (1998: 35).

Consequently it is important to break down their curriculum into short-term learning objectives that can be easily understood and readily achieved. For instance, the aim of a particular section of the JCSP English course is that each student can use written language to express and reflect on experiences. This aim is broken down into nine learning objectives (O'Gorman 1998: 40):

- Write a brief note or paragraph about a personal experience or interest, e.g. for a diary or journal.

- Write three paragraphs about a personal experience or interest, e.g. in a letter to a friend.
- Give a written account of specified personal likes and dislikes, e.g. favourite musicians.
- Write a note or paragraph expressing the experiences of seeing, hearing, touching or tasting.
- Write a note or paragraph expressing the emotions and experiences of a given solution.
- Write a note or paragraph expressing a preference or opinion about a given situation.
- Write a response to a letter, story, poem, book, film, newspaper or TV programme.
- Imagine the ending of story, background of a character or event and write it.
- Re-read, revise and correct your own writing.

On reading the above list, the casual reader could be forgiven for thinking that the level in question is more appropriate for Leaving Certificate than for students struggling to pass their Junior Certificate. Yet the entire JCSP curriculum is built on similar statements and related learning objectives. One of the principal reasons why the JCSP students succeed in achieving these objectives is because they themselves participate in selecting the statements they will aim at and also in recording their progress in achieving the learning objectives. In this way, they take ownership of their own curriculum as they chart their success through a series of interrelated statements and objectives that are incorporated in turn into an individual student profile – a public acknowledgement by the school of what the student has accomplished. To quote Aideen Cassidy again:

> We are evolving from a whole school to a whole system approach to education now that the Department of Education is recognising the value of such programmes and is willing to provide resources to support and train teachers in their efforts. If school authorities embrace this opportunity and actively support the intervention,

then we in the education community can proudly say that we are striving to fulfil our obligation to cherish all the children of the state equally. (1997: 161–2)

These words were written a quarter of a century after Tyler but he would have understood and approved.

REDISCOVERING VOCATIONAL EDUCATION

The objectives model is far from dead; as we have seen, it can readily be applied when imparting information and cultivating skills, aspects of curriculum that are traditionally associated with vocational education and training. There is renewed interest today in vocational education and a corresponding preoccupation with vocational qualifications, usually specified in terms of targets and outcomes. But before considering this, let us first examine in outline the evolution of the Irish vocational tradition.

'The establishment of a co-ordinated system of technical education in Ireland', notes one educational historian, 'is a twentieth-century story' (Coolahan 1981: 83). Nonetheless, it is possible to trace the origins of the story to the last quarter of the nineteenth century when several initiatives of a private philanthropic or municipal character mirrored the growing interest in linking education with business and industry. In England, the Devonshire and Samuelson Commissions were important milestones that led to the Technical Instruction Act of 1889. The Act was applicable to the United Kingdom in general but Ireland had to await another decade before technical education really got under way. When it did so, it owed much to the initiative of one man in particular, Horace Plunkett, the father of the agricultural co-operative movement in Ireland.

Plunkett had strong views on Irish education – 'a system calculated in my opinion to turn our youth into a generation of second-rate clerks, with a distinct distaste for any industrial or productive occupation in which such qualities as initiative, self-reliance or judgement are called for' (1905: 129). He was convinced that there was little hope of any solution to this problem 'unless and until those in direct contact with the specific industries of the country succeed in bringing to the notice of those engaged in the framing of our educational system the kind and degree of the defects in the industrial character of our people which debar them from success-ful competition with other people' (130). In Plunkett's view, the way forward lay in a coalition between the two forces of leadership in Irish life, 'the force with political influence and that of proved industrial and commercial capacity' (213).

Acting on his convictions, Plunkett issued an invitation to promi-nent businessmen and politicians to come together to work out a plan for the material betterment of the country through industrial enterprise linked with a practical system of education. The invita-tion, which was contained in a letter to the press dated 27 August 1895, was addressed to people on both sides of the political divide, nationalist and unionist. It should be recalled that at this time the country's political life was at a low ebb. Parnell was dead, the Irish Parliamentary Party was bitterly divided and Home Rule as a real-istic aspiration had receded. Plunkett appealed to nationalists and unionists alike to put aside their political differences, at least for the moment, and to meet informally when Parliament was in recess.

Surprisingly, the idea took hold. An informal committee, known as the Recess Committee, was established and made its report on 1 August 1896, less than a year after Plunkett's original invitation. The Government, anxious to conciliate nationalist feeling, or as the popular phrase had it, 'to kill Home Rule with kindness', was quick to respond. Two important Acts were quickly put through Parliament, the Local Government (Ireland) Act in 1898 and the Agriculture and Technical Instruction Act the following year. The two Acts were to be the basis of technical and vocational education in Ireland. The first established the machinery of local administration on which the new system was to be built; the second made provision for a department of Government to co-ordinate the system, the Department of Agriculture and Technical Instruction. In 1900, the Department came into being and Plunkett was made its responsible minister. A new spirit of optimism was beginning to manifest itself, a spirit which Plunkett described as being based on constructive thought and expressing itself in a wide range of practical activities. This spirit he celebrated in a controversial book which, looking forward to a more hopeful future, he entitled *Ireland in the New Century*.

Despite Plunkett's optimism, technical and vocational education in the new century was a slow growth. It was not until the coming of independence in the 1920s that the new Irish state, anxious to push ahead with industrial development, made it a priority. In 1926, the Government established a commission 'to enquire into and advise upon the system of technical education in Saorstát Éireann in relation to the requirements of Trade and Industry' (Commission on Technical Education 1928: vii). The Commission produced five volumes of evidence, taken from a wide range of interested parties, and succeeded in making its final report within a year of being set up. The report led to the framing of the 1930 Vocational Education Act, which laid the foundation of the modern system of vocational schools and technical colleges in Ireland.

The 1930 Vocational Education Act is rightly considered to be one of the landmarks of Irish educational legislation. It was in fact the only major piece of legislation affecting schools which was enacted by the Irish Government in the first 70 years of independence, and the system which it inaugurated can be said to be a truly native institution. The system, nonetheless, had some serious drawbacks and these were becoming painfully obvious as the country moved into the era of modernisation that began around 1960. For one thing, the typical vocational school course was decidedly limited; it lasted only two years and the students could aspire to nothing higher than apprenticeships and low level jobs. Another drawback was the low esteem accorded to the schools by the public in general, most parents preferring to send their children to the more prestigious secondary schools which opened the door to professional and clerical employment and higher education. As a consequence, the vocational schools tended to languish; they were regarded as the Cinderella of the Irish system.

In the 1960s, a change came about. As we have seen in Chapter 2, the Government of the day, fired with a new-found enthusiasm for equality of educational opportunity, resolved to upgrade the status of the vocational schools through the establishment of a comprehensive curriculum for the entire post-primary sector. The new arrangement meant that the vocational schools now had access to the same examinations taken by the secondary schools, the Intermediate and Leaving Certificates. It also meant, although nobody foresaw it at the time, that the vocational schools would eventually lose something of their original character. A decade later, the ICE Committee commented on this with regret. The attempt to broaden the curriculum had brought about a lessening of the time devoted to practical subjects with a consequent decrease in emphasis on the vocational aspect of the schools. The traditional vocational school examination, the Group Certificate, was altered radically and became devalued as a result of being subsumed into the more academic Intermediate Certificate. The overall outcome was unfortunate: 'Rigidity set in; there was little time or opportunity for innovation and the system tended to become in the main a second-year exercise in the path towards the more prestigious Intermediate' (ICE Report 1971: 45).

By the mid 1970s, the need for a more meaningful system of vocational education was becoming obvious. The flexible and work-orientated approach that the 1930 Vocational Act had inaugurated had been, in the words of the ICE Report, 'shouldered out of vocational schools' by the demands of the Intermediate and Leaving Certificate examinations. Furthermore, there was no provision for students who had completed their junior cycle education and wished to continue at school for a further year to prepare themselves for employment. These students had little interest in the traditional two-year Leaving Certificate course; what they needed was something more directly linked to their employment interests, the kind of curriculum in fact that the vocational schools had been originally set up to develop. It was now forty years since the passing of the 1930 Act and the Irish vocational education system badly needed a new stimulus.

The stimulus came from outside the country. On 13 December 1976, the Council of Ministers of the European Community passed a resolution 'concerning measures to be taken to improve the preparation of young people for work and to facilitate their transition from education to working life'(Commission of the European Communities 1976:1). The resolution, which was prompted by the increasing rate of youth unemployment throughout Europe, was a watershed in the Community's attitude to education. Education as such had not figured in the Community' s foundation charter, the Treaty of Rome; it was considered to be a highly sensitive area which was best left to the jealous care of each member state. Vocational training, however, was a different matter; it was seen as something essentially connected with the world of trade and industry and could therefore be regarded as one of the Community's legitimate concerns. The significance of the resolution was that it brought the spheres of education and training more closely together, thus heralding an awakening of interest in vocational education throughout the Community.

Ireland's response to the Community's initiative was to launch a new vocational programme at senior cycle called 'pre-employment courses'. A vital factor in their development was the financial assistance the Irish Government was able to obtain from the European Social Fund. The Fund had been originally set up to compensate workers in the European Coal and Steel Community for the difficulties caused by the economic changes resulting from the creation of a common market. By the mid-1970s the Fund had been considerably broadened and was now used as a training fund for the unemployed. The fact that the Irish Government was successful in gaining access to the Fund for the development of vocational education was a sign of the new emphasis on social policy which was becoming part of the Community's general programme.

According to the Department of Education, the pre-employment courses were 'intended for students who would ordinarily leave school to seek employment on attaining the school leaving age but, in failing to get employment, would return to school to attend a course specifically aimed at assisting them in their efforts to secure a job' (1978: 6). The description is remarkably similar to the definition of the purpose of vocational schools nearly forty years earlier – 'to prepare boys and girls who have to start early in life for the occupations which are open to them' (1942: 3). In both instances, the primary consideration was to prepare young people to take their place in a world where employment opportunities were scarce.

The stated aim of the pre-employment courses was to bridge the gap between the values and experiences of the educational system and those current in the world of work. The courses had three inter-related sections: personal development, technical studies and work experience. A novel feature was the way the course was assessed: each student, instead of taking a written examination, was given a folder which described his or her performance in the different parts of the course, including an assessment of work experience from the student's employer. The courses were introduced nationally in 1977, when about 1900 students from 80 schools participated. Five years later the figure had almost doubled and the number of schools had increased to 118, most of which were vocational schools (MacSuibhne *et al.* 1983: 19–20).

The pre-employment courses were never considered a challenge to the prestigious Leaving Certificate, but in September 1988 such a challenge was issued when the CDVEC launched a radical alternative, the Career Foundation course. The new course offered a greater degree of vocational specialisation by being oriented towards a particular career cluster, such as engineering, building construction, electronics or marketing. All the elements of the course were related as far as possible to the working environment and the methodology was practical and project-based. The course targets were ambitious – a gateway to worthwhile employment or entry into a college of technology. The course was in fact intended as the equivalent of a technical Leaving Certificate, something that had been mooted several times before in Irish education but never implemented. Sadly, however, the Career Foundation course never prospered and was only supported by a small number of CDVEC pilot schools, notably North

Strand Vocational School under Seán Ganly; Coláiste Íde, Finglas under Alex Silke; and Liberties College under Michael King.

In 1984, with the help of increased funding from Brussels, the pre-employment courses were expanded into a two-year programme entitled the Vocational Preparation and Training Programme which was now extended to secondary schools. The second year of the programme was to prove significant. It gave funding and recognition to a variety of post-Leaving Certificate courses (PLCs) which had sprung up in many vocational schools, especially in Dublin and Cork, in response to widespread unemployment and falling rolls at junior cycle. By the end of the 1980s there were over 5,000 students enrolled in a plethora of PLC courses.*

The PLCs were a spontaneous expression of school-based curriculum development in the vocational sector and, in many instances, went against the general thrust of official policy at the time. This was particularly evident in the way the courses were certified. Some were certified by the schools themselves, others used certifying agencies in the UK like City and Guilds and the Royal Society of Arts, while the CDVEC schools developed their own certification scheme, operated by the CDU under the leadership of Tony Crooks, Liam O'Dwyer and Liam Lee. It was not surprising that eventually the Department of Education felt under pressure to establish a national system of vocational certification. In 1991, such a system was inaugurated with the creation of the National Council for Vocational Awards (NCVA).

The NCVA began its work with confidence and energy. It set out its stall in forthright terms, beginning with a trenchant criticism of the traditional educational fare which, it claimed, was often irrelevant to the working world. Many school leavers lacked basic skills, positive attitudes towards enterprise, technological knowledge and the necessary qualities and attitudes to help them cope personally

---

* At the end of the 1980s too, Eurotechnet, one of the first European-sponsored IT national programmes, was established under the leadership of Aidan Clifford of the CDU.

and economically. The NCVA was clear about the remedy: what was needed was the integration of education and training, more vocational relevance in the courses provided, clear statements of the standards to be achieved, an emphasis on basic skills and personal effectiveness, an expansion of social and life skills, relevant work experience and clear pathways of progression from school to further education and employment (Annual Report 1994: 26).

To achieve all this, the NCVA divided the vocational curriculum into four distinct levels. Each level contained a number of courses and each course was made up of individual modules. The modules were the building blocks upon which the entire curriculum was built and were defined in classical objectives terminology – concise statements of the standards to be achieved in order to gain a particular result. The standards themselves were expressed as specific learning outcomes – what the learner should be able to do on successfully completing each module.

The language of an objectives-based curriculum can appear tough and uncompromising. The NCVA seemed aware of the danger and tried to soften its technocratic tone by claiming allegiance to the traditional liberal goal of fostering the personal development of each learner. But the question could be asked: how much of this was genuine and how much rhetoric? One researcher believes that the evidence to sustain the NCVA's claim is not conclusive:

> The NCVA system did exhibit some characteristics of a liberal vocationalism and to that extent it fulfilled its early goal of combining the best of both traditions [liberal and vocational]. However, the system did not succeed in other respects and it has certain illiberal features that are partly the responsibility of the organisation and partly the result of external factors that were beyond the organisation's control. (Trant 2002: 269–70)

In 2001, the NCVA which, up to this point, existed as an *ad hoc* body, was reconstituted as a statutory agency under the title of the Further Education and Training Assessment Council (FETAC). The title itself reflects the official recognition of a new chapter in the history of vocational education in Ireland – the coming into existence of the further education sector. The establishment of the new sector, however, has in effect divided the Irish vocational curriculum into two: one part is in the domain of FETAC while the other remains anchored in the schools.

Within the mainline educational system, two new vocational courses were developed during the past two decades, the Leaving Certificate Vocational Programme and the Leaving Certificate Applied. The former is a variation of the traditional Leaving Certificate, the latter, however, is radically different and gives some hope that the creative energy inherent in the vocational system has been not entirely extinguished.

The Leaving Certificate Applied is different from traditional school courses, firstly in its structure: it is modular, semesterised and cross-curricular, with internal as well as external assessment. It is also different in its curriculum approach, integrating the academic and the vocational through class activities, individual student learning tasks and work experience. The programme was piloted by Shannon Curriculum Centre and developed nationally by a combined Shannon-CDU team under the leadership of Diarmaid Ó Donnabháin from Shannon and Aidan Clifford from the CDU.*

Vocational education is now experiencing a renaissance but its scope is often narrowly defined in terms of objectives and outcomes. A note of warning may be timely. In any consideration of vocational education there is a danger of over-emphasising its practical and work-oriented dimension at the expense of its liberal potential. This is particularly true of the initiatives that are supported by European funding. The European Union is primarily interested in vocational preparation, and its official pronouncements in the area have, for the

---

* The other members of the team included Sheila O'Driscoll, Nora O'Connor, Anne Tuohy and Neil Bray from Shannon, and Miriam O'Donoghue, Marie Rooney, Sharon Phelan, Carmel McKeon, Tony Collisson and Harry Freeman from the CDU.

most part, been expressed in training rather than educational terms. This is largely because the EU officials are more at home with the former than the latter, and indeed initially had difficulty in justifying their position on any issue that could be seen as strictly cultural or educational. Thus the training paradigm has become the dominant one and educational considerations are often disguised in training terms, with the result that the distinction between education and training has become blurred. It may be unwise to make too much of the distinction but it would be equally unwise to ignore it.

For educationalists, the most important thing about the new vocational movement should be an awareness of the liberal values that are inherent in it. Vocational education, if it is to be called education at all, should provide general education through a practical mode and should be as liberalising and humanising as the traditional academic approach. In this sense there can be no educational basis for a hierarchical distinction between the academic and the vocational. 'A technical or technological education, which is to have any chance of satisfying the practical needs of the nation', A.N. Whitehead once pointed out, 'must be conceived in a liberal spirit, as a real intellectual enlightenment in regard to principles applied and services rendered. In such an education, geometry and poetry are as essential as turning laths' (1950: 70).

The liberal potential of vocational education has never been given the recognition it deserves in the Irish system. An unnecessarily rigid distinction is still made between the arts and humanities on the one hand and the technological and craft areas on the other. This distinction not only impoverishes the creative dimension of vocational education but, at a deeper level, ignores the inherent links between art and craft which were such a fundamental part of classical civilisation and which, nearer home, resulted in the masterpieces of the golden age of the early Irish monastic culture. In Chapter 1 we argued for a synthesis of liberal and vocational education. Past divisions between the two, at least in Ireland, have been more the result of institutional rivalry than of any deep-seated philosophical differences. Education in its true sense is both liberal and vocational.

The liberal dimension of vocational education is particularly evident in the great variety of adult education courses that have been developed in recent years, especially in the context of lifelong learning where people of all ages are given the opportunity to make up for the deficiencies of their earlier schooling. This idea is one of the most important and exciting that has arisen in modern times and in Ireland owes much to the imaginative work of many vocational schools and colleges. New approaches like the Vocational Training Opportunities Scheme (VTOS) and various community education programmes, pioneered by people like Jacinta Stewart and Pat Feehan in the CDVEC and Helen Keogh at national level, are reformulating the liberal ideal in modern terms.

In this chapter we described the first element in our curriculum rationale: formulating aims and objectives. We looked at the rise of the objectives movement and how its influence is reflected today in vocational education and training. Not everybody, as we have seen, agrees that this is the right way to proceed, but there is little doubt that the approach, especially when it follows the Tyler model, has found wide acceptance. I remember in the early days of the CDU, when we were taking our first tentative steps in curriculum development, how impressed we were at the way Brian Powell adapted Tyler to the needs of the newly founded science project, of which he was the director. Analysing student needs, specifying objectives to meet those needs, designing a programme to meet the objectives and, finally, evaluating the outcomes appeared to be a rational, comprehensive and scientific approach to curriculum development. And so it was, but afterwards we came to realise that there were other equally valid ways of doing the job. One of them is the time-honoured method of starting with the content of the curriculum itself, with what the classical humanists call the cultural heritage. This will be the subject of our next chapter.

CHAPTER 5

Curriculum as Content: The Transmission of Knowledge

MYSTERY OF KNOWLEDGE

The transmission of knowledge is the second element in our curriculum rationale. For many people, perhaps the majority, the curriculum primarily refers to its knowledge content and this knowledge is so important that it is considered a public affair. 'Prophets', says Lawrence Stenhouse, 'may teach private wisdom: teachers must deal in public knowledge' (1975: 6). One of the principal tasks of the school is to help students to gain entry into a commonwealth of knowledge by handing on to them a selection of society's intellectual, emotional, moral, aesthetic and technical traditions. The crucial question, however, is who should select this knowledge and what criteria should be used?

Today we often value knowledge insofar as we can put it to practical use. Knowledge, we say, is power because it opens the door to success. We want our schools and colleges to be purveyors of knowledge so that our children will go forth armed with the qualifications that enable them to make their way in the great battle of life. There may be some justification for this attitude, but only some. It is on the whole a narrow and inhibiting view which sees knowledge as a commodity that can be used and measured like coal or oil. It fails to recognise that there are other ways of looking at knowledge and other benefits to be obtained from acquiring it.

An alternative approach to knowledge is to value it for its importance in developing the mind of the learner. Knowledge only becomes worthwhile when it nourishes and strengthens our minds and becomes part of ourselves. It is like wood thrown on a fire: if the wood is dry it will burn brightly and make the fire stronger, but if it is damp it will put the fire out. Similarly, knowledge that comes to us as lifeless information will never nourish us. It must first be transformed into the very substance of our minds and we must make it completely our own. It is for this reason that choosing the right kind of intellectual diet is so important. A.N. Whitehead's warning about the danger of inert ideas are as relevant today as when he first wrote it seventy-five years ago:

> In the history of education, the most striking phenomenon is that schools of learning, which at one epoch are alive with a ferment of genius, in a succeeding generation exhibit merely pedantry and routine. The reason is that they are overlaid with inert ideas. Education with inert ideas is not only useless: it is above all things harmful. (1970: 2)

'Knowing' is a concept that we usually take for granted. Like breathing, it is an activity that we engage in continuously and is a fundamental part of our existence. Yet if we ask what is really happening when we know something, we have to admit that it is ultimately a mystery. Our thoughts appear to be boundless; they can transcend time and space and encompass the universe. As teachers, however, we must try to understand, if only a little, how we acquire this mysterious entity called knowledge. We are aware that this is a difficult task. Experts who have studied the subject talk about lateral and vertical thinking, left-brain and right-brain activity and logical and intuitive reasoning. To delve into the mystery of knowledge is like opening Pandora's box and we could almost be excused for avoiding the subject altogether. But it will not go away; students down through the ages have asked their teachers about the nature of knowledge and the best way of learning. We must take a closer look, then, at the process of knowing.

Knowing never starts with a blank sheet or *tabula rasa*, a mind completely untouched by previous learning experiences. All students bring with them a fund of ideas, beliefs, convictions and impressions that have been acquired through personal experience and interaction, or gathered from various sources of information. Much of this knowledge is found to work in everyday life and is shared with large numbers of other people. It is often called common sense knowledge and is not to be treated lightly or disregarded, as sometimes happens in the world of education. It contains much accumulated wisdom, usually expressed in homely terms, and is the very stuff of people's minds. It is this knowledge that good teachers build on, developing and refining it through a process of critical reflection with their students.

If we reflect on the way we gain knowledge, we become aware of a number of things. First of all, we realise that every act of knowing involves a subject or agent, an object and some kind of interaction between the two. In this two-way interaction, we send out feelers through our senses and we take back messages, which we co-ordinate, digest and turn into an image, perception or idea of the object in question. When we know something, we are also aware that we know it. We can reflect on the messages we receive and modify and draw conclusions from them. We can reason. We believe that what we know corresponds with the reality of what is out there. Sometimes we are wrong about this but when we realise our mistake we can correct and modify it and so continue on our endless search for the truth of things.

We are also aware that our minds not only generate knowledge but are influenced and conditioned by what we know. The mind feeds on knowledge and grows according to its diet. That is why parents consider it important that their children receive the right kind of intellectual nourishment from the books they read, the films they watch, the subjects they study and the schools they go to. It is for the same reason that there are keen arguments about what is considered worthwhile knowledge in the curriculum. It is important that young minds are given the very best nourishment available. The things we habitually think about influence the kinds of people we become.

If we reflect further on the way we think, we notice we usually make a distinction between two kinds of knowledge. For example, we believe that there are good grounds for accepting that certain statements or propositions are true, like Dublin is the capital of Ireland or that the earth is round. This is sometimes called propositional knowledge. We are also aware of another kind of knowledge that is principally a matter of skill, experience and know-how. This is procedural knowledge – knowing how to swim, ride a bicycle or make an apple tart. The relationship between the two types of knowledge is a matter of importance in the curriculum. We know instinctively that they are closely connected and should always be properly balanced in every learning activity. But this is not always the case and only too often the first kind of knowing overshadows the second. In other words, the curriculum tends to be too theoretical and academic.

Two final points can be made about the nature of knowledge. Firstly, knowing is a communal as well as an individual activity: we build our knowledge by standing so to speak on the shoulders of other people, some of whom have been giants in pushing back the frontiers of ignorance. The act of knowing is rarely a purely private affair and we often learn best in dialogue with others, whether face-to-face or through the medium of books, films or information technology. Secondly, as we have noted, we are aware that in some way our knowledge is boundless and is not subject to time or space. We can wander in the lanes of the past or contemplate the avenues of the future. Our minds seem to have a non-material dimension, but at the same time our thinking is bound up with the corporeal aspects of our being – if we think too hard or for too long, we get tired. The functioning of our minds is dependent on health, exercise and diet; we are not angels but body and spirit, mind and matter, linked together in that union we call a person. It is the person as a whole who knows and learns, and our intelligence is in our hands as well as in our heads.

ACADEMIC SUBJECTS

The traditional way of organising knowledge in schools and colleges is through academic subjects or disciplines. Subjects give the appearance of being timeless and many people hesitate to question them, believing that they have always existed. This is not so. Subjects have a history; they come and go and are continually changing, sometimes slowly, other times rapidly. Changes also occur within the boundaries of subjects or the boundaries themselves may change as the subject shrinks or expands. During the past fifty years, subjects like Latin and Greek have greatly diminished in popularity while newcomers like technology, classical studies and citizenship have appeared on the scene.

The changing nature of subjects is not without its problems. Old subjects do not die and new subjects are not born without pain. The curriculum always tends to be overcrowded and efforts to bring in a new subject may push another out – a kind of curriculum musical chairs. The result is a rivalry between subjects that in turn intensifies the politics of power within the curriculum. How a subject arrives on the curriculum can make a fascinating study in itself, as Ivor Goodson has shown in the case of geography (1983; 1985; 1994). In the last quarter of the nineteenth century, geography began to emerge as a subject in the English elementary, grammar and public schools. It was neither inspired nor enlightened, mainly comprising the memorising of dull facts – the 'capes and bays' approach, as it was called. 'Capes and bays' were in turn replaced by 'homes in many lands', as the British public began to see a place for geography in an empire on which the sun never set and more specialist teachers of geography, usually non-graduates, came on the scene.

A milestone was reached in 1893, with the founding of the Geographical Association to promote the knowledge and teaching of geography from preparatory school to university in the United

Kingdom and abroad. In 1903, H.J. McKinder, one of the founding fathers of geography, outlined a four-point strategy for giving the new subject its rightful place:

- Encourage university schools of geography, where geographers can be trained.
- Persuade secondary schools to place the geography curriculum in the hands of trained teachers of geography.
- Work out by discussion and experiment the best teaching methods, upon which the geography examinations should be based.
- Ensure that examination papers are set by practising geography teachers.

This strategy reads like a prescription for a monopoly, which in itself tells us much about the way subjects become established. As things turned out, the strategy was remarkably successful. In 1904 geography was included among the officially designated subjects in the regulations for secondary schools in England and Wales. By 1917, with the rise of external examination boards as a defining factor in the secondary school curriculum, geography became an accepted examination subject at School Certificate and Higher School Certificate levels.

The next step was to establish geography as a recognised discipline in the universities. University status was difficult to achieve but came eventually, especially from the 1960s onwards. A price, however, had to be paid – the upper reaches of the subject now began to lose touch with the lower, as the traditional regional geography and field studies were replaced by quantitative methods and abstract model building. The 'new geography' had arrived and past methods were *passé*.

The new geography opened up a gap between the schools and the universities – an ironic development when it is remembered that it was the schools in the first place that pushed geography into the universities. In their efforts to establish the subject, the schools had succeeded in colonising the universities, but they now found themselves marching to a university tune. There were of course compensations. Improved status brought resources in its train, and geography was no longer regarded as a motley collection of idiosyncratic facts but a disciplined body of knowledge that aspired to being a science.

We can see from the example of geography that a subject is much more than a body of knowledge; it is a community of people with their own rituals, ambitious hierarchies and world view. In fact, a subject is a social system in its own right and its members play different roles in what A.R. King and J.A. Brownell called a spectrum of many different talents:

> At one end [of the spectrum] a few people of extraordinary talent create the new directions; a large number, but still a minority, make masterful contributions by extending these new germinal forms, constructs, or ideas; a still larger number teach in colleges and secondary schools with little attempt at scholarship, as they are denied this opportunity by personal desire, institutional policy, or workload in teaching; and finally a band of students and teachers exist who have not yet made a contribution to community dialogue. (1966: 70)

All the members of the social system that is a subject are united in a community of scholarship, at least in theory. The practice may fall short of the ideal and there is often a gap between the creation of new knowledge at one end of the spectrum and its appearance at the other. A major task for every subject, therefore, is to narrow the gap between scholars at the frontiers of knowledge and the pupils in the classroom.

For a subject to be an effective community, it must have its own means of communication – its language and symbols, its books, journals and bulletins, and its conferences and seminars. A subject also has its own rites of initiation and testing, its preferred ways of instruction and its established pathways to promotion and preferment. The subject hierarchy exerts a discipline over the other members of the community and is suspicious of mavericks, loners and heretics. If the heretics eventually turn out to be on the side of the angels, great efforts are made to authenticate their orthodoxy, often after their demise. A subject is basically a school of thought from which individual members deviate at their peril and only within acceptable limits.

A subject is also concerned with guarding and extending its boundaries. Spatial metaphors such as 'area', 'domain', 'field', 'province', 'sphere' or even 'kingdom' describe what a subject attempts to stake out for itself in the larger territory of the intellectual life. It is often difficult to define the limits of a subject's proper domain, as King and Brownell point out:

> The domain is that which the members of the community claim it to be. No plenary body stipulates boundary lines; no discipline files deeds in academic court-houses; no intellectual tribunal tries claim-jumpers. (1966: 74)

This *laissez-faire* attitude may on occasion be taken to the point where some subjects embark on a policy of empire building by raiding the territory of other subjects. All subjects, however, try to show that they have some kind of epistemological basis to their claims, that is, they are more than an arbitrary arrangement of facts acquired at different times and in various ways, but represent an ordered and sequential pattern of knowing that can take its rightful place in the overall framework of human knowledge. To use another spatial metaphor, every subject wants to have an identifiable position in a recognised map of knowledge.

MAPS OF KNOWLEDGE

There have been many efforts to draw up maps of knowledge from classical to modern times. Plato and Aristotle, as we saw in Chapter 1, wrote about the essential things that young people should learn and how knowledge should be divided, and their ideas greatly influenced the notion of the liberal arts. The Greek concept of the liberal arts was taken up by Latin writers like Quintilian and Augustine of Hippo, and gained a prominent place in Roman thinking on education. Augustine described the liberal arts in some detail under seven broad headings: (i) grammar, the use of words as signs; (ii) dialectic, the study and practice of reasoning; (iii) rhetoric, the clear and persuasive presentation of facts and arguments; (iv) arithmetic, the study of number; (v) music, the science of metrics; (vi) geometry, the study of proportion and solidity; and (vii) philosophy, the art and practice of wisdom (Curtis and Boutwood 1965: 87–8).

Augustine did not regard his divisions as sacrosanct, but later writers like Boethius, Cassiodorus and Isidore of Seville, consolidated the practice of dividing the curriculum into seven liberal arts so that, by the Middle Ages, it had become a fixed tradition. The seven-fold division had by now become sacred and was further divided into two broad areas – the *Trivium* (grammar, rhetoric and dialectic) and the *Quadrivium* (arithmetic, music, geometry and astronomy). The *Trivium* and *Quadrivium* were themselves regarded as an introduction to the higher studies of philosophy and theology (Curtis and Boutwood 1965: 89–92).

The curriculum never stands still and that of the Middle Ages was no exception. Eventually it had to change as the Renaissance awakened a new interest in classical literature, art and philosophy as well as in the emerging vernacular cultures of Europe. The Renaissance curriculum in turn changed under the impact of the Reformation and Counter-Reformation, which stimulated the cut-and-thrust of religious argument, and generated the energy to implement institutional reform. In the eighteenth century, the Enlightment saw the introduction of scientific thinking into the curriculum, and later the Industrial Revolution brought an emphasis on vocational skills. The twentieth century witnessed an explosion of knowledge with so many things to learn that the curriculum became overburdened and efforts to map the 'essential' elements of knowledge became problematic. Nonetheless, curriculum maps continued to be made and one of the most influential of them is Paul Hirst's theory of forms.

Hirst begins by examining the classical Greek notion of liberal education which he says contains two fundamental ideas: first, that our minds are capable of grasping external reality and secondly that the knowledge that ensues from this process is the natural food of the mind. Knowledge that truly nourishes the mind is rightly called 'liberal', not simply because it is an education suitable for free people, but because it liberates the mind to function according to its true nature, free from error and illusion. Such knowledge is also our best guide to good conduct and how to lead the good life. The idea of liberal education, as we have seen, has reappeared several times in the history of education. It has an intrinsic appeal according to Hirst, because 'its definition and justification are based on the nature and significance of knowledge itself and not on the predilections of pupils, the demands of society, or the whims of politicians' (1965: 32).

The difficulty about this argument, as Hirst himself is prepared to admit, is that not everybody today would accept the philosophical basis of his idea of liberal education, that the mind is capable of grasping external reality. Does this mean that the whole notion must be rejected? Hirst does not think so and to prove his point sets about constructing a theory of knowledge based on an understanding of our experience of external reality without necessarily demanding that our minds can grasp what is essentially out there. There are seven ways, he maintains, in which we can make sense of our experience of reality, seven distinct forms of knowing and understanding.

First we have empirical knowledge, the kind of knowledge that is based on the evidence of our senses and is developed through the physical sciences. We are also aware that we are capable of abstract thinking and reasoning, and this is particularly evident in what we call logical and mathematical knowledge. A different kind of knowledge comes into play when we turn our attention to the world within, both within ourselves and others – our inner thoughts, feelings, intentions, attitudes, beliefs and aspirations. This knowledge can be labelled 'interpersonal' and is the basis of a range of disciplines like psychology, history, sociology and political science. Our sense and appreciation of the aesthetic yields another distinct form of knowledge – symbolic forms of expression, which have been developed through the centuries by painters, sculptors, musicians, singers, dancers, actors, writers and poets. Moral reasoning and ethical principles give us yet another form of knowledge, which is at the basis of many of our most important achievements, especially in education, law, politics and religion. Religious thinking can also be considered as a separate category of knowledge and is the gateway to a transcendental order of being that is universally recognised. Finally, we have philosophical understanding, the knowledge of things through their ultimate causes, which has enjoyed a special place in the pantheon of learning from ancient times to the present day.

Such are Hirst's seven forms of knowledge, each of which he describes as 'a distinct way in which our experience becomes structured around the use of accepted public symbols' (1965: 44). Every form has a number of distinguishing features:

- It involves central concepts that are peculiar to its character, for instance, gravity, oxidisation and photosynthesis in the case of the physical sciences; number, integral and matrix in the case of mathematics; God, sin and prayer in the case of religious knowledge; and responsibility, intention, and right and wrong in the case of moral knowledge. These concepts in turn make up a network of relationships in which experience can be understood and explained, and it is this network of relationships that gives to each form its distinctive logical structure. A historical explanation, for instance, is different from a religious or a scientific explanation of the same event but all three can be acceptable from their own particular viewpoint and within their own terms of reference.
- Each form of knowledge contains statements or expressions that can be tested against experience according to the particular criteria for truth that have been developed within the form itself. For instance, a statement of an historical nature must be in accordance with verifiable evidence, a statement

in mathematics must be deducible from statements that have already been proved, and a statement in the physical sciences must be based on observations either through our senses or through instruments that magnify or refine them. Each form has developed its own particular techniques for exploring and testing experience.

- The statements developed by each form are expressed publicly, sometimes in words, sometimes in non-verbal forms. For instance, within the aesthetic form, knowledge may be expressed in words as in poetry, in stone as in sculpture, in bricks and mortar as in architecture or in sound as in music. The important point is that the language or symbolic expression used is broadly agreed on so that access to any particular form of knowledge is open to anybody who is interested and takes the trouble to understand the language.

- Acquiring knowledge of any particular form is not something that can be attained through solitary study only, but 'must be learnt from a master on the job' (1965: 45). In other words the knowledge in question must be learnt through practice within a tradition that is handed on. This of course has profound implications for the way students of all ages should be taught.

- The various forms of knowledge, although essentially distinguishable from each other, are also interdependent and borrow freely from one another: the physical sciences use mathematical concepts; the moral and religious forms are closely related; so too are the interpersonal and empirical, and most contain a moral and philosophical dimension. Apart from such examples of overlapping forms, Hirst also argues for the existence of what he calls fields of knowledge, which are made up of a number of basic forms and are held together by some broad theme around which the subject matter is organised. Geography is a good example: the underlying theme is the study of people in relation to their environment and can encompass historical, sociological, economic and physical aspects.

Hirst's forms give us a logical basis for the division of knowledge into subjects or disciplines but in practice it would be rare to find any particular subject absolutely coinciding with a corresponding form. More often than not we find subjects in a 'mixed state', like in Hirst's fields of knowledge. English, for example, is a mixture of the interpersonal and aesthetic, and can include moral, religious and philosophical elements as well. Geography, as has already been pointed out, is a combination of the empirical and interpersonal, and can also contain logical-mathematical and philosophical elements. Even mathematics, which could be regarded as the closest we can get to a pure form of knowledge, can include philosophical, empirical and aesthetic elements.

Hirst distinguishes between the inherent logical structure of any particular form and the psychological principles involved in learning it. Understanding a form should never be constrained by its logical structure, nor is the best way to teach it necessarily the most logical one:

> Coming to understand a form of knowledge involves coming to think in relations that satisfy the public criteria [underlying the form]. How the mind plays round and within these is not in itself being laid down at all, there is no dragooning of psychological processes, only a marking out of the territory in which the mind can wander more or less at will. Indeed understanding a form of knowledge is far more like coming to know a country than climbing a ladder. (1965: 50)

If we wish to know a country we need an up-to-date map of the terrain. In the same way we must ensure that our map of knowledge is constantly updated if we wish to develop a good curriculum:

> Many well-established courses need to be critically re-examined both philosophically and psychologically before they can be acceptable for liberal education. Superficially at least most of them would seem to be quite inappropriate for this purpose. (Hirst 1965: 50–1)

Hirst's influence has been considerable and even one of his sever-
est critics admits that his theory has become 'one of the paradigms
in the field of philosophy of education' (Martin 1998: 171). His
ideas have been adapted by educationalists in many countries as a
basis for specifying the curriculum, not only in terms of subjects or
disciplines but also as fields of knowledge or areas of experience.
His importance for curriculum developers lies in his effort to unify
the curriculum through a theory of knowledge, based on a modern
interpretation of the essential meaning of liberal education. He
believed that the curriculum should be constructed, not simply in
terms of isolated facts and skills, but as an introduction to the inter-
related aspects of each of the basic forms of knowledge. It is in
grasping the relationships between the different forms that we come
to see the underlying unity of all knowledge, which in turn helps to
strengthen and unify our minds. 'The outcome of a liberal education', Hirst argues, 'must therefore not be thought of as producing
even greater disintegration of the mind but rather the growth of ever
clearer and finer distinctions in our experience' (1965: 52). He was
careful to point out that liberal education does not include the whole
curriculum but, without explicitly saying so, he leaves us in no
doubt as to which part of the curriculum he considered the most
important.

Hirst has not gone unchallenged, nor is his seven-fold division of
knowledge the only one possible. Jane Roland Martin considers
his notion of liberal education to be narrow, excluding many
important educational activities such as artistic performance,
learning another language and practical moral action as distinct
from moral reasoning. She accuses Hirst of being overly concerned
with the development of 'ivory tower personalities' – people who
can reason, but have no desire to solve real problems, who understand science but do not worry about the uses to which it is put,
who can grasp the concepts of biology but may not be disposed to
exercise or eat wisely and who can reach flawless moral conclusions but have neither the sensitivity nor the skill to carry them out.
Ivory tower personalities, in other words, are prone to be overly

detached and uninvolved and live in an idealised world. In Martin's view this is far from what real education should be about:

> In a society whose dominant institutions foster virtues such as caring about others, a sense of justice, honesty and benevolent action, faith in the sufficiency of an initiation into the forms of knowledge might be justified. In a society whose institutions encourage conformity of thought and action, a desire for instant riches and worship of self – that is, our society – I am afraid such faith is nothing but a pious dream. (1994: 175)

Martin's views may be somewhat overstated, but to my mind her most telling criticism is directed at the unduly restrictive nature of Hirst's notion of liberal education. She accuses him of formulating an abstract theory of knowledge, remote from the nature of human beings and the lives they lead. The issues she raises extend the debate well beyond the forms and fields of knowledge by raising questions about the integration of thought and action, intellect and feeling and the human and natural worlds. What we need, according to Martin, is a more generous understanding of liberal education, which stresses not only freedom from ignorance but also the emancipation of the human person from the constraints of habit, custom and inertia – in fact she is demanding what amounts to a curriculum revolution and a new paradigm of education.

The most fundamental criticism of the theory of forms as a basis for the curriculum came from an unexpected source, from Hirst himself. In 1991, over 25 years after he had first propounded his theory, Hirst changed his mind. He had originally argued that the curriculum should be based on the knowledge that is found in the traditional disciplines. Now he advocated an alternative view: the primacy of practice. We understand the world we live in primarily in practical terms. For instance, we learn the important things about food, not in scientific terms, but through obtaining, preparing and eating food. Similarly we learn about personal and social relationships primarily by relating to other people. We do not achieve understanding by first discovering knowledge in the formal, structured disciplines and then applying it to practical situations. Knowledge comes in an integrated way by experiencing areas of human living, not in dismembered items to be discretely mastered and then put together. Knowledge is always generated in relation to relevant skills, attitudes and values:

> I am arguing that academic subjects are secondary and indirect in their significance for human living. Important though they are for the development of sophisticated advances in living, they are directly of little use to us individually unless we are professional academics or professional generators of new possibilities for social or technical practices. On this view we will want pupils above all to master the best practices of living available in our society, not academic subjects and specialised skills. The latter are for the few and not what education is basically about. (Hirst 1993: 35)

Hirst is suggesting that, instead of the traditional subjects, the curriculum should be based on what he calls the practices of living, and in this context he proposes the following six practices:

- coping with the physical world, including practices relating to food, health, safety, domestic and environmental circumstances;
- communications, including reading, writing, conversing, numeracy and information technology;
- relationships in personal and family life;
- wider social practices, such as those relating to local, national and international institutions, work, leisure, economic matters and law;
- arts and design, such as literature, music, dance, painting, sculpture and architecture;
- religious beliefs and fundamental values.

Hirst says very little about implementing his practice-based curriculum; all he gives is a short sketch with some basic suggestions. The notion, however, is not new, as Hirst himself acknowledges. The same idea was expressed by some of the leading figures in the modern curriculum development movement, particularly between the 1960s and the 1980s, and we shall return to this point in Chapters 7 and 8. For the present, we should note that two important questions arise from what Hirst proposes. Firstly, on what basis should the curriculum be divided into practices and, secondly, why should some practices be included and not others? Both questions relate to the problem of integrating the curriculum, which is the subject of our next chapter.

CHAPTER 6

Seeing the Big Picture

INTEGRATING THE CURRICULUM

In the last chapter we saw how a subject-based approach is a convenient and universally recognised way of organising the curriculum. We find it enshrined in the traditional school timetable, especially at post-primary level where teachers, students and resources are matched with impartial efficiency. The subject-based curriculum operates on the twin principles of knowledge specialisation and division of labour, independent of the personalities of the people involved. If a particular teacher happens to leave, he or she can be replaced by another with similar qualifications in the required subjects and so curriculum continuity is safeguarded. The timetable also provides a variety of teaching styles, which is a safeguard of sorts against boredom; it ensures, at least in theory, that outstanding as well as indifferent teachers are shared across the curriculum.

The main disadvantage of the subject-centred curriculum is its fragmented nature. Specialisation and the division of labour may be efficient in a factory but are not necessarily the best way of organising learning; if emphasised too much they can lead to depersonalisation and bureaucratic control. Genuine learning must always rest on good personal relationships and a self-motivated quest for truth. The present-day curriculum with its water-tight divisions of content can sometimes be a meaningless way of organising learning.

It is to counteract the tendency towards fragmentation that the effort to integrate the curriculum finds its justification. Good examples can be seen at primary level where specialisation and fragmentation are most easily avoided. We also have examples of integration in the secondary and tertiary curriculum, although usually they are confined to collaboration among teachers at the planning stage. Rarely do we see examples of full integration, where planning, teaching and assessment are all integrated into a unified synthesis. Such an approach is obviously beset with difficulties because it cuts across existing subject boundaries. Subjects, as we have seen, are made up of communities of people, who do not like to see their boundaries transgressed, still less their kingdoms abolished.

Despite the difficulties of integration, we have to acknowledge the need for it: the curriculum should provide a unified picture of reality and help us find meaningful patterns in the vast world of knowledge and experience. Although we live for the most part in a fragmented culture, we have an inner yearning for a more complete picture of life and, in the scattered pieces of our existence, we want to find some kind of unified pattern. Often as not we fail, but we are not deterred from trying again and again. The curriculum should reflect this deep-seated human aspiration, as Jacques Maritain reminds us: 'The whole work of education and teaching must tend to unify, not spread out; it must try to foster internal unity in human beings' (1961: 45). It is not an easy task to develop a curriculum that reflects this aspiration; perhaps the best way is to proceed in stages.

Firstly, we could promote elementary co-operation among different subject teachers. Many subjects share the same ideas and cross into each other's territory. Examples are mathematics and science in the use of decimals; technology, history and geography in explaining the Industrial Revolution; and biology, history and religious studies in discussing Darwin's theory of evolution. Many similar examples could be given. Therefore, it makes sense in planning the curriculum to take account of the way one subject uses concepts and skills that are more fully developed in another. For instance, when the history teacher is dealing with the two world wars of the twentieth century, it would help if the relevant mapping skills and physical background were covered in the geography class. The fact that this elementary co-operation does not often take place reflects poorly on the degree of effective curriculum planning in our schools and colleges. It should be a basic requirement in any educational institution that the sequencing of important concepts within subjects should be correlated. A similar point could be made about making links between the primary, post-primary and tertiary curriculum.

Secondly, a popular and effective form of integration is to undertake a project or enquiry, based on a particular theme. This has the merit of being flexible with regard to the time allocated (an afternoon, a full day, a week, a term or a complete year), the number of staff involved (one teacher or several), the location (indoors or out-of-doors), and subject matter (a great variety of themes can be chosen from areas of current interest like environment, health, politics and employment).

The project approach can be traced to John Dewey's model of problem solving and reflective thinking. Dewey argued that this model should be at the basis of all educational methodology and be brought into play especially when the traditional classroom activities fail to hold the attention and interest of the students. The students are encouraged instead to focus on a particular problem in contemporary life. The students study the problem, discuss it, and are then invited to make a leap into the unknown, that is, to formulate a hypothesis that might bring about a solution. Next the hypothesis is tested; deductions, projections and predictions are made, and a certain course of action is agreed. The results are then reviewed. If a solution to the original problem seems in sight the exercise will come to an end, otherwise the entire process will be repeated. In either case, the students will have begun to think reflectively, which is the purpose of the whole exercise. As Malcolm Skilbeck remarks:

> Dewey's view is that reflective thinking is essentially a process of changing or modifying situations, beliefs and knowledge itself. Thus education founded on processes of reflective thought itself

becomes a change process, the means whereby individuals learn to take a measure of responsibility for their environment. No longer passive recipients of messages and commands, they become agents of cultural development and renewal. Dewey believed that a large part of the intellectual side of education could be best handled by organizing learning tasks around this problem-solving framework. (1976: 41)

A project may look deceptively easy but considerable care has to be exercised in carrying it out successfully. The following steps are suggested; they are based on the experience of an environmental network of 60 European schools co-ordinated by the CDU between 1977 and 1985 (see Chapter 12):

- Agreement on a problem or a meaningful theme. This is crucial as many themes turn out to be vague, irrelevant and lacking in interest or educational value. If more than one class is participating, it is important that everybody is satisfied with the theme that is chosen.
- Collaborative planning. This is essential in all multi-teacher projects where broad agreement should be reached on aims, methodologies and outcomes. Time for planning and reflection should be made available, preferably as a timetabled activity. The planning sessions will also enhance the professionalism of the teachers.
- Team teaching. Seldom do we find fully fledged team-teaching; nonetheless, there is plenty of scope for limited collaboration, particularly on field trips or other activities outside the school.
- Provision of adequate resources. Projects demand a variety of learning resources beyond the everyday text-books – worksheets, articles, reference works and various audio-visual materials. If the need for adequate resources is not taken into account, the finest project ideas can fail.
- Evaluation. This should be informal, continuous and participative; it can also of course be formal and summative and even

124

be part of the official examination structure. The evaluation should always fit the project or else it may undermine it (see Chapter 9).

- Outcomes. It is good to have long-term and short-term outcomes in mind. They help to focus the project and motivate both teachers and students. Exhibitions, competitions, open days, small-scale publications and providing some kind of service to the local community are all possible outcomes.

Good examples of the project approach can be found in curriculum areas like citizenship, environment and health education. These provide themes that excite widespread interest and even controversy. They raise problems that do not recognise national or international frontiers, social, political or academic. Hence, projects based on them have to transcend subject barriers and commit themselves to genuine interdisciplinary inquiry (see Chapter 12).

A third way of integrating the curriculum is to design and implement a unified course, based on a broad theme such as Irish, classical or environmental studies. This is similar to the project approach but takes the commitment to integration much further. Ideally the course should have parity of esteem with traditional subject courses but, in order to achieve this, the course must become part of the official examination structure. Herein lies the difficulty: it can take years for a new course to gain acceptance, especially if it has originated outside the control of the official curriculum. However, this control can be relaxed on occasion, as we shall see in Chapter 8.

CORE CURRICULUM

A fourth and very effective way of integrating the curriculum is to organise it around a group of essential subjects or learning experiences, known as the core or common curriculum. The two terms are often used interchangeably but some theorists distinguish between them. 'Core' more properly refers to the part of the curriculum that holds the whole structure together and, as such, is an instrument of unity and meaningfulness in relation to the student's life experience (Walsh 1993: 94). A good example is Hirst's attempt to give a unifying structure to the curriculum through his seven forms of knowledge (see Chapter 5). The common curriculum refers to the knowledge and areas of experience that all students should have access to (Lawton 1980: 6). For instance, in 1918, an influential American report, *Cardinal Principles of Secondary Education*, defined the curriculum in terms of seven broad areas – health, command of fundamental processes (reading, writing, arithmetic and oral expression), home membership, vocation, citizenship, use of leisure and ethical character (Walker and Soltis 1997).

During the past 25 years, there has been a renewed interest in the idea of a core curriculum, particularly by governments wishing to raise standards and orient the curriculum towards the needs of their competing economies. This has resulted in the prescription of aims and objectives, the definition of curriculum content usually in the form of subjects and the insistence on attainment targets and a means of assessing them. Examples of such centralising trends can be seen in Australia, Canada, New Zealand, the UK and the US, countries where a strong tradition of local decision-making and variety in curriculum matters had previously been the norm. In the UK, for instance, legislation was introduced to specify a core curriculum for the compulsory years of schooling in mathematics, English, science, history, geography, technology, music, art, physical education and a modern language for students at second level. In the US, several prominent reports in the 1980s such as *The Paideia Proposal, A Nation at Risk* and *A Nation Prepared*, which argued for a common core of studies, have influenced the school systems in many of the individual American states (Skilbeck 1990).

In Ireland, the pattern of curriculum organisation at second level can be described as a clustering of subjects according to the dictates of the state examinations. Despite the recommendation of an OECD report for the introduction of a sequential core curriculum throughout the years of compulsory schooling, the Irish curriculum landscape, in the words of Jim Gleeson, continues to be 'dominated by the mountains and valleys of examinations in individual subject areas' (1992: 16). Nonetheless, there are some signs of change. The National Council for Curriculum and Assessment, in a review of the junior cycle curriculum (NCCA 1999), defines the core curriculum in terms of eight broad areas: language, literature and communication; mathematical studies and applications; science and technology; social, political and environmental education; arts education; physical education; religious and moral education; and guidance counselling and pastoral care.

A similar framework had been suggested in the 1980s by the NCCA's predecessor, the Curriculum and Examinations Board, but the pressures of examinations on the traditional subject-based curriculum rendered the suggestion ineffective. It has to be said that this is still largely the case, despite the NCCA's best efforts to bolster its recommendation of a core curriculum with the promise of a range of short courses, special in-career training for teachers and a new guide which will provide alternative strategies to the subject-based approach. The structure of the curriculum remains largely unchanged, thus betraying the power of the vested interests that uphold the existing subject-based arrangement.

The NCCA's aspiration towards a core curriculum is better realised at primary level where, as we have seen in Chapter 1, the revised curriculum of 1999 largely retains the integrated approach first adopted in 1970. The revised curriculum, at least on paper, seems to satisfy the demands of the most ardent advocates of integration, but a word of caution is necessary. If the post-primary curriculum remains fixed in its present subject centred ways, the shadow of subjects will inevitably fall on the primary curriculum. This happened in the case of the 1971 primary curriculum when new areas of integrated content were easily identified in terms of their separate subject components. This time around, however, things may turn out differently. The implementation of the revised curriculum has been accompanied by extensive inservice support. So we have some grounds for hoping that one section at least of the Irish education system, perhaps the most important one, will be a genuine example of an integrated core curriculum.

The key question about core curriculum is not what elements it contains but in what way it is implemented. Malcolm Skilbeck spent five years helping to design a core curriculum in Australia, as director of the National Curriculum Development Centre in Canberra. He gives the following three definitions of core curriculum, each depicting a different approach to the way such a curriculum can be developed:

- A set of required subjects or subject matter embodied in a centrally imposed syllabus of basic information and skills to be taught to all students.
- A set of required subjects or subject matter determined by a school and embodied in required courses and activities for all students.
- A broad outline statement of required learnings for all students defined in partnership by both central and local bodies and interpreted by schools. This definition accepts central guidance but also ensures a collaborative and participatory approach by the schools. (1984: 172–3)

I remember being educated through a core curriculum very much on the lines of Skilbeck's first definition. I refer to the Intermediate and Leaving Certificate courses as specified by the Department of Education and implemented through the examination system. This curriculum made little allowance for individual interests and differences. It was enforced on all students – fine, if they fitted the mould, but too bad if they did not. Skilbeck's second definition applies to schools that can ignore the public examination because the parents feel strongly that an alternative curriculum should be provided for their children. But in our modern world such schools are increasingly difficult to find, not just in Ireland but anywhere.

Skilbeck's third definition of core curriculum, which is the kind he developed himself in Australia, allows for a dynamic partnership between the school and the central and local authority. Here in Ireland we have taken a few initial steps towards a core curriculum – for instance the Junior Certificate School Programme, the Leaving Certificate Applied, the Leaving Certificate Vocational Programme and the Transition Year Programme. Skilbeck makes a strong case for this model, but he insists that much more than a specification of content is needed. Attention must also be paid to the learning process itself and the environment in which it occurs. 'Areas of knowledge and experience', he maintains, 'are quite inert pedagogically so long as they remain unconnected with the learner's experience. How learning takes place is as significant for what is learnt as is any outline of topics or themes' (1982: 34). In other words, the key question with regard to a core curriculum is how to go about building one.

CULTURE AND THE CURRICULUM

Denis Lawton gives an alternative basis on which to build a core curriculum through what he calls cultural mapping. Culture, according to Lawton, refers to the way of life of a people, the sum total of their knowledge, skills, attitudes, values and beliefs. If a particular culture is to survive, it has to be transmitted from one generation to the next and in this process the school plays a vital role. It is society's designated agency of cultural transmission. This leads Lawton to define curriculum itself as a selection from the culture. The selection should reflect all the essential aspects of that culture and should be continually updated. We live in a fast-changing society in which there is usually a lag between what the school transmits and what people actually need. 'One of the fascinating aspects of curriculum studies', Lawton asserts, 'is that for most societies for many periods of time, schools have operated with curricula which were, in one way or another, inappropriate' (1996: 23).

The school then must continually review and revise its curriculum and, to help it in this task, Lawton outlines a strategy of cultural analysis. The culture of any society can be divided into nine overlapping systems: socio-political; economic; communication; rationality; technology; morality; belief; aesthetic and maturation. The socio-political system is about the way we relate to each other and the kind of roles we play in the social and political structure. It embraces the arrangements by which we are governed, the way we work and recreate ourselves, the kind of clubs and associations we join and how we get on with people beyond our borders. In agricultural societies, the socio-political system revolves around the ownership and use of land; in industrial societies, it is based on the ownership and use of the means of production, while in post-industrial societies it is concerned with the exchange of goods and services and the control and use of information.

In Ireland, like in many other countries today, the study of the socio-political system is now part of a national programme in citizenship education at primary and junior cycle levels. The story of how it got there is a long one. As far back as 1922, the Government of the new Irish state contemplated introducing civics into the primary curriculum but abandoned the idea because of opposition from the Catholic Church authorities (Hyland 1993). Over four decades were to pass before the idea surfaced again, and in 1966 civics became part of the post-primary curriculum as a separate subject. Five years later, it was introduced into the primary schools. However, as we saw in Chapter 5, new subjects are not born without pain and do not thrive without care and protection. No serious provision was ever made for the new arrival and so civics languished on the curriculum scene for twenty years, virtually ignored. It was not until the mid-1980s that fresh ideas and renewed energies were brought into play under the direction of Gemma Hussey, the first woman to become minister for education in the history of the state. In the early 1990s a happy combination of different interests led to the establishment of a curriculum development project in citizenship education. The principal people involved were Colm Regan, head of the education department in Trócaire, the Catholic agency for world development; John Hammond, co-ordinator of a CDU development education project funded by Trócaire; Jack Henderson, a senior inspector in the Department of Education; and Albert Kelly, the chief executive of the NCCA. The new project flourished under the leadership of John Hammond and later under Stephen McCarthy and Conor Harrison so that, by the end of the 1990s, citizenship education under the title of Civic, Social and Political Education (CSPE) had become a reality in the Irish post-primary curriculum.

The economic system in any society is closely linked with its socio-political system and is principally concerned with the control, use and exchange of resources, especially when these are scarce and in demand. Modern societies tend to have complex economic systems, which many people do not understand. The majority of young people, Lawton observes, leave school with almost no attempt having been made to provide them with an economic understanding of their own society.

If it is to survive, any society needs a communications system, hence the importance of language skills in education. But the complexities of modern living demand more than the ability to read and write. We have to interpret many kinds of symbols, some of which are a matter of life and death – think what would happen if we refused to bother about road signs or traffic lights. Add to that the intricacies of modern information technology, which touches almost every aspect of our lives, and we realise the crucial importance of communication.

Every society has a more or less acceptable way of explaining reality by agreeing on a common rationality system. This is the product of a long period of evolution in our thinking. For instance, a thunder storm or the outbreak of some disease is explained differently today than would have been the case a thousand years ago. We are proud of our rationality system and consider it superior to anything in the past. We often call it the scientific approach because it is influenced by developments in modern science and technology. But it could be argued that we rely on it too much, to the neglect of other valid ways of explaining reality, for example, interpersonal, artistic and religious modes of thinking.

Learning how to make and use tools is a characteristic of all human societies, and has always been thought important enough to hand on to the next generation. Today we have a highly developed and complicated technological system underpinning every aspect of our lives. But we wonder sometimes if we are more its victims than beneficiaries. We know that our technology system needs specialists to develop and maintain it, but is there not some general level of understanding that we all should have, otherwise we risk being overawed? There is also the danger that modern information technologies will bring about a new stratification in society, resulting in a cleavage 'between those that can interpret, those who can only use, and those who are pushed out of mainstream society – in other words between those who know and those who do not know' (European Commission 1996: 26).

All human societies need a morality system and a code of behaviour. In Ireland, this has been closely linked in the past with the practice of the Christian religion but, as we become increasingly secular and multi-cultural, the connection between morality and any particular religious faith becomes more tenuous. The need for moral education in its own right will probably become a future priority, but how do we make it a curriculum reality? This will be one of the big questions facing curriculum developers in the years ahead.

Along with our moral code, we have a belief system, a common stock of rituals, convictions and ideals. In Ireland, our belief system has been largely influenced by Christianity. But this, too, like many other things in our culture, is changing. We now like to keep our identity as Irish people separate from our loyalty to any particular denomination. An enlightened awareness of our belief system will demand an interdisciplinary approach that includes history, religious studies, art, literature, politics, economics and moral education.

Artistic expression has always been an integral part of human living and every society has an aesthetic system. As Lawton observes: 'nowhere is there a society, however near to subsistence level, where pots are made without decoration or where there is no attempt to decorate the person or the environment' (1984: 284). Art was once inseparable from the ordinary life of the people but, as it became more secularised, it became more remote from everyday living. What is now considered as art tends to be part of the culture of the upper and middle classes. 'Art correspondents,' says Lawton, 'rarely discuss the aesthetic qualities of cars or furniture; high culture and popular culture are falsely separated' (1996: 45). Yet art remains one of the fundamental forms of knowledge and modes of experience, and is an essential dimension in any comprehensive map of our culture.

Finally, anthropologists tell us that the human species is characterised by a prolonged period of maturation and dependency – we take a long time to grow up. This has resulted in the various practices of child rearing that are the basis of our developed educational systems. Modern educational systems tend to take in more and more aspects of the maturation process, such as health, personal and social relationships, parenting skills and preparation for leisure. The span of education has been lengthened as well as widened; we now talk of educating people from the cradle to the grave, and growing old is as much part of the curriculum as growing up. In earlier cultures, growing up meant a successful transition from youth to adulthood, a process that was never taken lightly. It included much more than imparting knowledge and skills; it was also an initiation into the responsibilities of adulthood. Successful initiation into adulthood was achieved through role modelling and ritual, something that our modern culture has tended to neglect. Can we afford to take for granted that all young people today will automatically negotiate their passage into adulthood? Should we not be exploring how the curriculum can help to make the transition process a more positive and creative experience, especially for the considerable numbers of young men who seem to be losing not only their way in life but also their reason for living?

Lawton refers to his nine systems as cultural invariants or human universals. How do we build a curriculum on his ideas or, to rephrase the question in his own terms, how do we make a selection from the overall culture? To help us, Lawton proposes the following five questions:

- What kind of society or cultural system do we live in?
- In what way is it developing?

- How do its members want it to develop?
- What kinds of values and principles will be involved in deciding this development?
- What kind of education will be necessary to achieve it? (1996: 26)

The overall thrust of Lawton's argument is very compelling; it provides not only a tool for building a curriculum but also a way of analysing and critiquing it. It would be a useful exercise to apply his model to Irish society, but it would also be very difficult, given the centralised nature of our educational system. Still we must not despair. The City of Dublin Humanities Curriculum, which was launched over three decades ago and which we shall examine in Chapter 8, took as its starting point a cultural analysis similar to what Lawton advocates. We conclude this chapter with an example of curriculum integration through the arts.

INTEGRATION THROUGH THE ARTS

Ten years ago, in her survey of drama in Irish post-primary schools, Deirdre Scully had this to say:

> Ireland is renowned for its rich literary heritage, a heritage which includes a remarkable wealth of dramatic literature of international repute. Nevertheless, drama as a practical art form has never been firmly established in the Irish educational system. For the majority of post-primary students, the experience of drama has remained non-practical and mainly confined to the textual analysis of the written word through the study of play-texts within English. (1998: 7)

Today, the position of drama in our schools and indeed of arts education in general has not greatly improved. Despite several official pronouncements on the importance of the arts, we tend to regard them as somewhat peripheral to the serious issues of education and living. The reason, as Professor Colm Ó hEocha pointed out some years ago, is as follows:

> Lack of understanding of the true nature of artistic intelligence has led to a conception of the arts as trivial or merely recreational, with a certain unspecified contribution to make in the area of affective learning. The dominant academic tradition in Irish schools sought to purge itself of such unreliable matter and this process has been accelerated by the new tradition which orients itself by word and number in the new languages and technologies of our age. (Scully 1998: 5)

Artistic expression is vital to our intellectual, emotional, physical and spiritual development as well as being an essential ingredient in all kinds of economic and vocational activities. Without artistic expression, we are culturally bankrupt and socially and economically dysfunctional. Yet we persist in neglecting it in our educational system. I remember once hearing Jerome Bruner remark that he found it puzzling that drama was given such little recognition in the Irish curriculum, despite the fact that our actors and dramatists are famous throughout the world. Surely, he argued, Irish people must have a native genius for drama but why was it not encouraged more in our schools? In the following paragraphs, we describe the efforts of a school in Dublin's inner city to make drama and the arts in general an integrating force throughout the entire curriculum.

Larkin College is situated in one of the most disadvantaged areas in Dublin, with young people traditionally leaving school early. Factors that have contributed to the declining student population are poverty, unemployment and availability of drugs. Despite or perhaps because of these negative conditions, the college principal Noel O'Brien with one of his teachers, Máire O'Higgins, decided to embark on an imaginative programme of curriculum innovation. At the beginning of the school year 2003–04, after a period of prior experimentation, the Learning through Arts Programme was launched. To some extent it was modelled on an existing Learning through Soccer Programme, developed under the leadership of the vice-principal Seán Spillane; both were based on a scholarship scheme and included disadvantaged pupils from outside the school's immediate catchment area. The arts programme, however, is more ambitious in that it aims to integrate a major part of the junior cycle curriculum through the medium of the arts – music, art, dance, drama and key humanities subjects.

The Learning through Arts Programme has four strands. The first, Making Waves, involves the students going on weekly visits to museums, galleries, concert halls and theatres. So far examples have included a tour of the Hugh Lane Gallery, where the visit involved an interview with an art technician engaged in cleaning the bust of Michael Collins; a visit to the Abbey Theatre to see Brian Friel's play *Aristocrats* and afterwards to meet the cast and crew; a visit to *Finders Keepers* at the Peacock Theatre, including a post-show discussion with the director and playwright; an art sketching tour of the Botanic Gardens; and attending the launch of a book, where two of the students performed for the event. The visits help the students to practise new ways of behaving in a cultural space and, although codes of behaviour can often seem trivial, familiarity with art galleries, theatres or concert halls opens the door to a world where the young people of Larkin College now fit in and which they enjoy.

The second strand, On the Shore, encourages artists to come to the school to perform and talk about their work. The students learn how to be a critical and appreciative audience and to understand something about the life of artists. Examples have included a post-show dance class with a member of the Irish Modern Dance Theatre, a pre-show workshop with an actor, a puppet workshop for staff and students, and a mosaic art project with an artist, in conjunction with the Dublin City Council Parks Division.

The third strand, Meandering Stream, brings the artists into the classroom itself. They meet the teachers to find out what topics they are teaching and together they discover the common threads that link the different subjects together, using the arts as a tool. For example in history, the students looked at ancient peoples such as the Romans and Celts, in geography they studied rocks and volcanoes while in Irish they learnt traditional greetings. The artist helped to integrate these three activities by relating the story of the destruction of Pompeii, showing samples of volcanic rock and scripting an imaginary conversation in Irish and Latin between the Romans and Celts for the students to act out. Afterwards they went to the art studio and painted their impressions of volcanoes.

'Still Waters', the fourth strand and the cornerstone of the programme, enables the students to develop the skills of four specific arts disciplines: music, art, drama and dance. Music and art are subjects on the Junior Certificate, which gives the students a concrete goal to aim at. Neither drama or dance, however, has the same status, but Larkin College is in no doubt about their importance, especially drama.

> Drama offers children a voice with which to articulate fears, hopes and dreams. Drama takes the written word from the page to the stage. Engagement in drama gives our children confidence. Poor self-esteem often shatters their dreams. Drama instils self-esteem. Our students also learn to work as a team, trust each other and learn to rely on each other. Drama enhances the English curriculum and builds students' confidence in exams, wherein lies so much success in terms of access to a better future in college and in work. The child that acts out Shakespeare has a stronger sense of ownership of a script than one who simply reads the text. Poetry comes alive through performance. Drama gives our students the tools with which to express themselves through literature, comedy, tragedy and public speaking. (Larkin Community College 2005)

The arts programme is barely four years old and has a fairly restricted intake. It has ambitious targets, however, and aims not only to improve the all-round academic and artistic performances of its participants but to convince other schools of the importance of the arts as an integrating force in the entire curriculum. In this context, an external evaluation of the programme's first year reached the encouraging conclusion that the programme had achieved the majority of its aims, and with the support of the local community and the school's cultural partners it was eventually likely to achieve them all. The most convincing evidence of success, however, can be seen in the story of an individual student:

> One of our best dancers on the Learning through Arts Programme is a boy. He is 13 years old and a very good dancer. Since he came to secondary school he hasn't stopped dancing, despite the risk of being made fun of by his friends. He has found the strength to go on because of the skills he is developing. The dance programme in Larkin Community College catches young people at an age when they are still innocent enough to enjoy dancing. The programme instils in students a discipline of dance that carries them through the challenging teenage years. (Larkin Community College 2005)

In this chapter we looked at the fragmented manner in which knowledge is often presented in our schools and colleges, and suggested some integrating strategies such as the project method and the core curriculum. We also noted the potential of the arts as a force for integration. The chapter concludes our examination of the second element in our overall curriculum rationale. In the following two chapters we introduce the third element – curriculum as process and interaction. Chapter 7 discusses the importance of the teacher's role and how this was reflected in the curriculum development movement in America and England. Chapter 8 describes the curriculum movement in Ireland in the context of the CDU's first projects and school networks.

CHAPTER 7

Curriculum as Process: The Teacher's Role

THE PRACTICE OF TEACHING

The process approach to curriculum emphasises the importance of the relationship between teachers and students in the learning activity. Learning is perceived not so much as the acquiring of a product but as the development of understanding, which is best promoted through interaction and dialogue. A learning dialogue can take place in different ways, sometimes directly between teachers and students, at other times indirectly when we learn from books, audio-visual materials or by participating in various activities.

Learning cannot always be planned or predicted in detail. We are aware nonetheless from our experience as teachers and from research studies on the learning process that there are certain general principles that underlie successful learning. Examples of these principles are as follows:

- Students usually learn better when they are encouraged to participate actively in their own learning.
- Students also learn better when they are encouraged to ask questions and to give reasons for their own answers.
- Learning is consolidated when students are given opportunities to apply it in different situations.
- Learning is enhanced when students are taught how to listen to others as well as to express their own views.

- Learning should be more concerned with promoting broad understanding than accumulating facts.

There are other principles like the above: the essential thing is how and when to apply them – which brings us to the importance of the teacher's role in the curriculum. Jerome Bruner once said that a curriculum is more for teachers than for pupils: 'If it cannot change, move, perturb and inform teachers, it will have no effect on those they teach' (1977: xv). The teacher's role in the curriculum is some-times summed up in the term 'pedagogy', the art and science of teaching. Three models in particular have dominated pedagogical practice: the apprenticeship, didactic, and interactive models. In the apprenticeship model, the student learns primarily by imitating the teacher who consciously demonstrates a particular activity, often turning it into a performance, to show more vividly what is involved in 'doing it right'. The emphasis is on skills and know-how rather than on theory and understanding, and the assumption is that, through constant practice, the required knowledge and skill will grow like a habit. The apprenticeship model suits a traditional soci-ety where the pace of change is slow and the time available to learn is long. Our present-day technological and fast-changing society demands more accelerated forms of learning but, even so, appren-ticeship still has its place and we can never dispense with its practi-cal, hands-on approach. In the long-run, the best results are achieved through a combination of theory and practice.

The didactic model is based on the premise that learners should be presented with the principles and facts that they are ignorant of and that exist in the teacher's mind or in books, maps, databases or other sources of knowledge. This kind of knowledge, as we saw in Chapter 5, is sometimes referred to as propositional and is the tra-ditional academic knowledge that we associate with schools and colleges. It contrasts with the procedural knowledge that is at a pre-mium in apprenticeship. In the didactic approach, the assumption is that know-how will follow from a prior knowledge of principles and facts. The approach is widely used in schools and colleges and often assumes that learners are passive receptacles of knowledge – their minds are considered to be a *tabula rasa*, a blank slate waiting to be written on. The principal danger with the didactic approach is to confuse memory recall with genuine understanding.

The interactive model regards the learner's mind, not as a blank slate, but as something that is already well-stocked with ideas and hypotheses about whatever is being taught. The starting point for the teacher is to interact with learners in order to uncover their construct of the world, why they hold a particular view and think in a partic-ular way. The important issue is not the rightness or wrongness of the learner's view, but its appropriateness as a meaningful way of explaining the world. The teacher's task is to help the learner appre-ciate the difference between knowledge and opinion; an opinion only deserves the title of knowledge when a reasoned justification for holding it can be given. As Bruner puts it: 'Knowledge is what is shared within discourse, within a textual community. Truths are the product of evidence, argument and construction rather than of authority, textual or pedagogic' (1996: 57).

It would be wrong to think that the teacher's role can be neatly summed up in any of the above pedagogies, or even in a combina-tion of all three. Teachers are essentially practitioners; their practice is shaped not only by educational theory but by their own knowl-edge, skill and experience. They are guided by principles that are at once ethical and pragmatic, traditional and modern. They thrive when they are given the opportunity to reflect on their practice and share their insights with their colleagues.

We often refer to the practice of teaching but what do we mean by the term? According to Alasdair MacIntyre, a practice is a coherent and complex set of human activities that a group of people have developed over time, with certain standards of excellence to guide them (1981: 175). These standards are subject to development and redefinition and demand responsible behaviour from all those who are, or are trying to become practitioners themselves. MacIntyre gives two examples: farming and soccer. Both are coherent and com-plex forms of human activity and have many different components, such as planting crops or caring for animals in the case of the first, and dribbling, heading and scoring goals in the case of the second. Farming and soccer have evolved over time and are still evolving. They have rules and standards of excellence and inevitably involve other people.

Many other examples could be given because the nature of human activity is to organise itself into practices. For instance, farming can be compared to a range of occupations like architecture, carpentry, medicine, engineering, painting, plumbing and music making. Soccer reminds us of other games and pastimes that are also practices, such as chess, golf, sailing and mountaineering.

Why do people engage in a practice and submit themselves to the discipline of learning the skills involved and keeping the rules? What satisfaction do the practitioners themselves gain from their practice? Ask any enthusiastic golfer, historian, musician or nurse and you will hear a variety of answers. But they will have one thing in common – the feeling of fulfilment that comes from participating in a worthwhile and demanding activity and acquitting oneself well in relation to one's peers. The satisfaction of taking part in a practice is the joy of playing the game as it should be played or doing the job as it deserves to be done. When we participate in a practice for the sake of its intrinsic worth, it brings its own reward, as Joseph Dunne points out:

> A thing worth noticing about what might be called the economy of a practice – when we stay on the inside of it – is that it is not an economy of scarcity. In other words, if one person really comes to excel, this need not be at the cost of other people's chances to develop their talents. Every achievement of excellence enriches all who participate in or care about a practice; it can be an occasion for admiration or even celebration as well as sometimes, of course, for attempts at emulation. (1995: 73)

There are other reasons for taking part in a practice such as earning money or enhancing our reputation. These are technically known as external goods and as the name suggests are outside the immediate scope of the practice itself and can in fact be achieved by other means. Since a practice involves both internal and external goods, a conflict can easily arise between the two, especially if the latter begin to dominate. When this happens, the practice itself is put at risk. If I am a farmer and all I care about is profit then the temptation to engage in activities that are foreign to the nature of farming will be strong. If I am a footballer and my sole concern is to become famous, then the chances are I will become a ruthless egotist. If I am a teacher and my chief occupation is to produce good examination grades, then my teaching will be narrow and mechanical. The pursuit of external goods may be legitimate but it becomes dangerous when it makes us forget the real purpose of the practice we are engaged in.

This brings us to a fundamental aspect of every practice – it cannot take place in isolation but must always involve other practitioners. I cannot play football, engage in farming or teach a class in complete isolation. I am constantly relating to other people in the practice. There are two aspects to this: first, it is mostly from other practitioners that I learn the skills and competencies that are necessary to the practice and that enable me to attain the standards of excellence that are possible for me. Secondly, the proper exercise of these skills and competencies demands certain moral qualities on my part. I must be honest and patient with myself or I will never learn my trade. I must have courage and persistence when the going gets tough. I must be generous in helping others in the practice, and I must always try to be fair to them and give them what is their due.

We have examined in some detail McIntyre's concept of a practice because it is one of the best ways of understanding the teacher's role in the curriculum. I cannot really teach what I do not practise myself. If I wish to become a good teacher of mathematics or history or engineering, I must first of all be a practitioner in these areas and feel part of the general community of mathematicians, historians or engineers. I must love my practice and try to be better at it and want other people to become interested in it and come to love it too, in other words to become mathematicians, historians and engineers themselves. That is what the practice of teaching means. In Chapter 5 we saw how

Paul Hirst adopted this view towards the end of his career, when he proposed building the curriculum on what he called the practices of living rather than on the disciplines of knowledge. The art of teaching, as Dunne argues, is the ability to engage the students in a reflective conversation on what it means to practise the craft they are learning, whether it is science or music or home economics:

> It is through participation in conversations that arise in the context of focused tasks that people truly develop their repertoires of thinking, feeling, speaking and acting as well as reading and writing. Creating contexts that elicit and sustain such conversations is the great challenge to schools. And the great art for teachers is to be responsible not only to the opportunities and demands of the specific practice but also to the needs, aptitudes, and difficulties of particular pupils. It is the latter requirement that makes them teachers, that is to say people competent not only in the specific practices that give substance to education, but also in the peculiar practice that is teaching itself. (1995: 79)

Most practices have to contend with a bureaucracy that tries to control them. Bureaucracies are part of life and can have a useful function, but they tend to stifle the practices they are meant to support. This is particularly the case with teaching, which is in grave danger of being routinised and trivialised by excessive bureaucratic control. From time to time, however, rebellions break out and attempts are made to assert what the practice of teaching should be about. The entire history of education could be written around the story of these rebellions from one generation to the next. The modern curriculum development movement, which lasted from the late 1950s to the end of the 1980s, is a case in point.

CURRICULUM DEVELOPMENT MOVEMENT

The movement began in the United States in the late 1950s, the Sputnik era, when the American public was shocked at how far they had been left behind in the space race by Russian science and technology. In a climate of near panic, resources were poured into the educational system to update the curriculum, beginning with mathematics and the physical sciences. The foremost scholars in their fields were persuaded to join the venture and help produce curriculum materials based on the most up-to-date knowledge available in the relevant disciplines. Jerome Bruner, a cognitive psychologist from Harvard, was one of these scholars and summed up the thinking behind the new movement in his book, *The Process of Education*.

Bruner begins with the challenging statement that any subject can be taught effectively in some intellectually honest form to any child at any stage of his or her development. But for this to happen, there are necessary preconditions. Teachers must have a fundamental grasp of the essential principles that underlie the subject they are teaching. These principles give structure to the subject, but they should not be regarded as difficult or complicated. The basic ideas that lie at the heart of science and mathematics and the great themes that give form to life and literature are as simple as they are powerful. To be in command of these ideas and themes and to use them effectively requires a continual deepening of our understanding of them. This comes from learning to use them in progressively more complex forms – in what Bruner called the 'spiral curriculum' (1977).

What a scientist does in the laboratory, what a literary critic does with a poem and what a student does in the classroom should all be of the same nature. The difference is in degree, not in kind, because intellectual activity anywhere should basically be of the same nature, whether at the frontiers of knowledge or in the classroom. The pupil learning physics should be a physicist and it is easier for him or her to learn physics behaving like a physicist than doing something else. This 'something else' is the artificial task of mastering a 'middle language' usually through textbooks that talk about other people's conclusions in some field of intellectual inquiry. Teachers should concentrate instead on introducing their students to the inquiry process itself. School physics often looks very little like real physics, social studies are often removed from the issues of life and society, and school mathematics is in danger of losing contact with what is at the heart of the subject – the idea of order.

Mastery of the fundamental ideas of a subject involves not only the grasping of general principles, but also the development of a particular attitude towards learning and inquiry. Students should be encouraged to make educated guesses and hunches and consider the possibility of solving problems on their own. Just as a physicist has a certain attitude about the orderliness of nature and a conviction that this order can be discovered, in the same manner young physics students need a working version of the same kind of attitude in order to organise their learning and make it usable and meaningful. To instil such attitudes into students requires something more than the presentation of ideas; the students also need to catch something of the scholar's excitement about the discovery of regularities in previously unrecognised relationships, with the resulting sense of self-confidence in their own abilities.

Bruner was more than a curriculum theorist, he was also the guiding light behind one of the most celebrated of the early American curriculum projects, Man: A Course of Study (MACOS). The three questions that are the basis of MACOS give an idea of its ambitious scope:

- What is human about human beings?
- How did they get that way?
- How can they be made more so?

Bruner tried to answer the questions by structuring the project around five humanising themes in the evolution of human beings – tool making, language, social organisation, the management of our prolonged childhood and the urge to explain the world. In passing, we can note the similarity between Bruner's themes and Lawton's human universals, which were described in Chapter 6.

MACOS was originally intended for the upper grades of the American elementary school, but this did not mean that it lacked substance or intellectual rigour. 'The more elementary a course and the younger its students,' Bruner argued, 'the more serious must be its pedagogical aim of forming the intellectual powers of those whom it serves' (1966: 73). A good course of studies for any age is justified not only on its content value but also by the intellectual discipline and honesty it promotes and the moral and imaginative powers it stimulates.

For Bruner, the heart of MACOS was its pedagogy, the 'how' rather than the 'what' in the teaching of the course. He advocated four pedagogical strategies, the first being contrast – how to rescue the phenomena of social life from familiarity without making them look primitive or bizarre. The content of MACOS was largely based on a series of purpose-made films on the life of the Netsilik Eskimos at Pelly Bay in northern Canada. By following the activites of a particular Netsilik family throughout four seasons in the Arctic, the pupils got a sense of the Netsilik culture and how it related to their own. As Bruner put it, it was through contrast that they were able to grasp the underlying continuity in all cultures:

> It is characteristic of Netsilik Eskimos, for example, that they make a few beautifully specialized tools and weapons, such as their fishing lester or spear. But it is also apparent that each man can make do with the stones he finds around him, that the Eskimo is a superbly gifted *bricoleur*. Whenever he needs to do something, improvised tools come from nowhere. A flat stone, a little fish oil, a touch of arctic cotton, and he has a lamp. So while the Eskimo footage provides a sharp contrast to modern technological man, it serves perhaps even better to present the inherent, internal logic of a society, any society. Each has its own approach to technology, to the use of intelligence. It is the recognition of this unique integrity in human society, wherever it is found, that children are led from what first seemed like contrast to what is finally seen as continuity. (1966: 94)

Bruner's second strategy was the use of informed guessing and the making of hypotheses and conjectures; the underlying principle here was that any information that the pupils did not ask for should never be given.

> We have a film of Zachary, the father of the Netsilik Eskimo family we have filmed, hunting seal alone by waiting for the seal to come to the surface of a breathing hole in the ice. A seal has about a dozen breathing holes. Which one to stalk? And if the hunting party were six in number, how to distribute them? In fact, we have film of a group hunting seal by watching the breathing holes. But before we show it, we like to get the children figuring out the problem on their own. (1966: 94)

The third strategy was to increase the participation of the pupils through the use of games and simulations that acted as artificial but powerful representations of an underlying social reality. Here, Bruner was anticipating the computer games of our own time and using them as allies of the educational process:

> Games go a long way toward getting children involved in understanding language, social organization, and the rest; they introduce, as we have already noted, the idea of a theory of these phenomena. We do not know to what extent these games will be successful, but we shall give them a careful try. They provide a superb means of getting children to participate actively in the process of learning – as players rather than spectators. (1966: 95)

The final strategy was to make the pupils more aware of their own learning processes, how they went about finding information and how they used it, the kind of guesses and hypotheses they made and how these could be verified, how to discover things on their own and above all how to discover connections in what they had learnt.

> The cultivation of such a sense of connectedness is surely the heart of the matter. For if we do nothing else, we should somehow give to children a respect for their own powers of thinking, for their

power to generate good questions, to come up with interesting informed guesses. So much of social studies until now has been a congeries of facts. We should like to make the study more rational, more amenable to the use of mind in the large rather than mere memorizing. (1966: 96)

MACOS was disseminated widely – marketed would be a better description – in the US and other countries. It was often controversial because of its content and assumptions about human and animal evolution. Its portrayal of what was sometimes considered to be primitive and brutal behaviour, both human and animal, caused angry reactions, such as the following from an anti-MACOS group in Arizona:

A steady diet of blood-letting and promiscuity is presented through games, records, nightmarish films, booklets and pictures ... the children are also taught that we humans are related to the chimpanzee. The immature, impressionable child is therefore induced to believe that man is only an advanced animal. (Jenkins 1980: 221)

Bruner himself was well aware of the potential of MACOS to stir up emotions, and referred to the course as 'dangerous stuff'. But he also passionately believed in its integrity and its power to bring out the best in pupils and teachers:

The paramount virtue of the course, as one teacher put it to me, was that it posed problems in such a way that teacher and student both knew that they were together at the frontier of their thinking, brooding about the nature of man. If I did not know at the start, I certainly know now that you cannot address that question in school without plunging into the central political issue of education. (1984: 198)

I remember the first time I came into contact with MACOS. It was in the early 1970s shortly before I left Ballyfermot, when I was invited to attend an OECD conference on curriculum in Dublin. The conference examined how the early curriculum projects in the US, Canada, Britain, France and Sweden could be adapted by other countries that were interested but had not the resources to develop large-scale projects on their own. The conclusion I came away with was one of which I think Bruner would have approved. We should not be dazzled by glossy materials or overawed by hugely resourced projects. What mattered was the quality of the thinking behind the projects and the kind of pedagogy they implied.

MACOS was introduced into Britain in the mid-1970s by Lawrence Stenhouse and one of his colleagues, Jean Ruddock, through the medium of training courses for teachers. The CDU was represented at one of these courses by Tony Crooks and myself and this ultimately led to the introduction of MACOS into Ireland. The course was expensive as it involved the use of films, student booklets, teacher manuals and a variety of posters, slides, worksheets and games. It was purchased by the Dublin City library service and given on permanent loan to Ballyfermot Vocational School where it was introduced to a number of second-year classes in 1972–73. The Ballyfermot experience of MACOS was evaluated by Tony Crooks who found that the majority of the students rated it among the subjects they liked best. It was particularly beneficial for non-academic students. Most of the teachers regarded the course as worthwhile but some felt it neglected the spiritual element in human beings and reinforced prejudices regarding sex roles (Crooks 1978: 286–305). The course was also used as a pilot study in the CDU's early work. Bruner would have been pleased with this because it fitted closely with his own ideas about the purpose of MACOS:

> The course was ultimately designed with change in mind. I always had the feeling that the main thing that was worthy about the course was that it could be used as well for teacher training and, used in that way, it would produce quite unpredictable results in what teachers would do with the course afterwards. I gather

from everything I have been told that this indeed is the case. (1980: 225)

A CURRICULUM PIONEER

When I started teaching, it was generally accepted that, although a teaching qualification was necessary to enter the profession, the best way to learn your job was by doing it. Later, after teaching in a variety of schools in England and Malta, I returned to Ireland to take a professional qualification. At the first lecture I remember the professor saying that his course would only benefit people who had at least five years teaching experience. He was right. The course was largely theoretical but I think I benefited because it enabled me to reflect on my previous teaching in the light of the theories and principles I was now learning.

I began my teaching career in Ireland in the early 1960s. These were exciting years because the country had begun to open up to new ideas from outside. The world of Irish education was waking up as news of exciting curriculum projects in England, America and Sweden was beginning to filter through. The Schools Council for England and Wales was a fruitful source of ideas at the time. The Council had been set up in 1964 as a joint venture between central government, the local education authorities and the teacher unions. The Council initiated a great variety of projects, which were staffed by small teams who worked with a network of pilot schools along the lines of the then widely accepted research and development model – research, develop, evaluate and disseminate.

Lawrence Stenhouse was the director of one of these curriculum projects from 1967 to 1972. His project arose from one of the School Council's major preoccupations at the time, that the forthcoming raising of the school leaving age to sixteen years would result in large numbers of average and below average students remaining longer at school and consequently putting the traditional curriculum under stress. Stenhouse based his project on what he called a vernacular version of the classical humanities curriculum.

His understanding of what this implied was taken from one of the Council's publications:

> The problem is to give everybody some access to a complex cultural inheritance, some hold on their personal life and on their relationships with the various communities to which they belong, some extension of their understanding of, and sensitivity towards other human beings. The aim is to forward understanding, discrimination and judgement in the human field – it will involve reliable factual knowledge, where this is appropriate, direct experience, imaginative experience, some appreciation of the dilemmas of the human condition, of the rough hewn nature of many of our institutions, and some rational thought about them. (Schools Council 1965: 60)

Stenhouse was a gifted, charismatic person who delighted in challenging the accepted orthodoxies of his day. It is said that when he was appointed director of the Humanities Curriculum Project (HCP) he told his sponsors that he expected to be given the right to fail, thereby turning on its head the accepted maxim at the time that all curriculum projects were doomed to succeed. His sponsors, though somewhat taken aback at his request, gave him permission to experiment, which he did with style and audacity. His definition of curriculum was challenging – a proposal or a hypothesis that should be tested in the practical reality of schools and classrooms. His starting point was the very ground forbidden by Tyler – the activities of the teacher. These should be planned by asking the following two questions: what kind of knowledge should the student learn and how should the teacher facilitate this learning?

Stenhouse set about translating the answers to these questions into a curriculum suitable for average and below average teenagers by having them study a number of controversial issues. A controversial issue was defined as one that involved a problem, about which different individuals and groups urged conflicting courses of action, and for which society had not found a solution that could be universally accepted. It should be an issue of sufficient significance that each of the proposed ways of dealing with it was objectionable to some section of the community and so bound to arouse protest. The protest could result from a feeling that a cherished belief, an economic interest or a basic principle was being threatened. When a course of action was formulated that virtually all sectors of society accepted, the issue was no longer controversial.

A controversial issue then is one that divides pupils, parents and teachers, and often it is the specific case not the general rule that causes the controversy. For instance, it is widely accepted that war is undesirable, but whether a particular war in Iraq or Northern Ireland is justifiable can be highly controversial. Similarly, the assertion that sexual self-control is desirable is scarcely controversial, but whether this necessarily excludes active sexual relationships between unmarried people can be controversial. Stenhouse and his team chose nine controversial topics for HCP – war and peace, education, the family, relations between the sexes, people and work, poverty, living in cities, law and order and race relations.

The methodology of the project was what made it well known and indeed controversial – a discussion-based approach with the teacher acting as a neutral chairperson. This methodology was underpinned by a number of principles. The teachers had to renounce their authority as experts capable of solving value issues, since this authority could not be justified either epistemologically or politically. Instead, they aspired to being neutral chairpersons and tried to avoid the use of their traditional authority position to impose their own views on the pupils. They were expected, however, to maintain a procedural authority in the classroom. This meant that the fundamental educational values of rationality, imagination, sensitivity and readiness to listen to the views of others were built into the classroom procedures. These procedures helped the pupils to understand divergence of views and to work together through discussion and shared activities where differences were respected and minority opinions protected from ridicule and social pressure.

In sensitive issues, the teachers were careful to protect the privacy of pupils who were any way at risk, for instance pupils from broken homes were borne in mind when discussing the family or relationships between the sexes. Above all, the aim of the classroom activities was to promote understanding. The teachers were urged never to force pupils towards opinions or premature commitments that could harden into prejudice, nor to see a particular virtue in the pupils coming to a change of view. Instead, the pupils were led to understand the nature and implications of their own point of view, and helped to grow into adult responsibility by assuming accountability for their own opinions. Whether or not the pupils changed their point of view was not always significant for the attainment of understanding.

The growth of understanding was crucial for Stenhouse and he made two points in particular about it. Firstly, he believed that teachers as well as pupils should grow in understanding; in other words the teacher was cast in the role of a learner. The second point Stenhouse typically expressed as a paradox: understanding was chosen as an aim because it could never be fully achieved. It could be deepened but there must always be a dispute about what constituted valid understanding. Teachers and pupils had to accept that it was their task to explore together the meaning of understanding.

Stenhouse himself felt that the most important thing about HCP was the concept of the neutral chairperson. There were many misunderstandings about this, chief of which was the notion that teachers were forced by the project to abdicate their authority. This was far from being true. Teachers, Stenhouse argued, should always maintain their position in authority but they should moderate their claim to being an authority by ensuring their pupils did not rely on them as arbiters of truth. Nonetheless, the kind of authority he advocated was in reality revolutionary and had the potential to cause tension in schools, especially when HCP pupils made unfavourable comparisons between their own classrooms and the more traditional teaching in other classrooms.

HCP was principally taught through discussion with groups of about sixteen students usually seated in a semi-circle. The informal seating arrangement was considered important as it emphasised the non-authoritarian role of the teacher. The discussion the project was aiming at was not the type popularised by media chat shows – a performance meant to entertain and judged by the criteria of fluency, animation and balance of contributions. HCP was different and, in proposing the aim of understanding, it called into question the values that are cherished in popular discussion. For example, it is not necessary that everybody should strive to say something: learning to listen is quite as important as learning to speak and we should not be satisfied with a pace of discussion that gives no time for reflection. There are all sorts of discussion that need to be looked at afresh in the light of promoting genuine understanding. For instance, is it a good thing that in a discussion group only two people speak in a twenty-minute sequence? If understanding is our aim, the question can only be answered by discovering whether the understanding of the group as a whole is being enhanced. In this context, silence may be just as important as fluency.

A good HCP discussion was a disciplined affair, fed by evidence from many different sources – songs, poems, extracts from novels, plays and biography, letters, memoirs and historical works, readings in social science, journalism, advertisements, questionnaires, statistical tables, graphs, maps and plans, cartoons, photographs, paintings, drawings, films and audio-tapes. Anything or anybody that contributed towards a meaningful exploration of the issue under discussion could be classified as evidence. For instance, a HCP group in Ireland, which explored the theme 'war and peace', invited two speakers to address them, one a well-known pacifist and the other a strong supporter of the IRA.

We have taken HCP as a case study of what became known as the process model in the modern curriculum development movement. Stenhouse himself once said that the major weakness of the model was that it rested on the quality of the teacher, but the same factor, he added, was also the model's greatest strength. The importance of HCP was its potential to improve the learning process by enabling teachers to improve their professional expertise through a more enlightened awareness of what they were doing and how they could do it better.

Stenhouse's insistence on the centrality of the teacher's role led him to formulate the idea of the teacher as a researcher. It is not enough, he declared, that the work of teachers should be studied by others, they need to study it themselves. Teachers should continually reflect on their work in a structured way and this process of reflection can be the basis of a genuine research programme. Stenhouse defined research as systematic enquiry made public. This is a simple, sensible and inclusive understanding of the meaning and scope of research and is a healthy antidote to much of the high-blown rhetoric that often surrounds the subject.

In the early 1970s when the CDU was getting off the ground, Stenhouse, who was greatly interested in its progress, came to Dublin to participate in a seminar for some of the teachers involved. On that occasion, I asked him whether his own project was something that only exceptional teachers could operate. I was surprised at his reply: 'HCP often works best for those teachers on whom the profession has gone sour.' After Stenhouse's death in 1982, some of the teachers who had worked with him chose a quotation from his writings as an inscription on his memorial in the grounds of the University of East Anglia: 'It is teachers who, in the end, will change the world of school by understanding it.'

In this chapter we looked at the vital role of the teacher in the curriculum and how this was reflected in the modern curriculum development movement, especially in the work of two pioneers, Jerome Bruner and Lawrence Stenhouse. In the following chapter, we shall examine how the movement influenced the work of the CDU, particularly in the establishment of its first projects and in the way it created networks of innovative teachers and schools.

CHAPTER 8

The Early Work of the Curriculum Development Unit

PILOT PROJECTS

The early 1970s witnessed an awakening of interest in curriculum innovation in Ireland, both inside and outside the formal educational system. In 1970, new curriculum guidelines for primary schools were published. The following year saw the founding of the Irish Association for Curriculum Development (IACD), spearheaded by John Harris, Kathleen Quigley, Bryan Powell and Tony Crooks. The IACD stimulated debate on curriculum matters among teachers, parents and the general public through its journal *Compass* and the organisation of lectures and conferences. In 1972, the first prison education service in Ireland was established with the introduction of pilot courses for young offenders in St. Patrick's Institution, Dublin, under the leadership of Edmund Burke and a team of teachers from Cabra Vocational School. In the early 1970s too, as we have seen earlier, the Shannon and Dublin curriculum centres came into being. Both were influenced by the curriculum development movement in America and Britain that we discussed in the last chapter. The director of the Shannon centre Diarmaid Ó Donnabháin relates how he came to launch his first pilot project after attending a three-week course on curriculum development at the University of East Anglia, sponsored by the OECD and the Volkswagen Foundation:

The course was in three parts. In the first week, we visited some typical examples of schools in the England of 1971. In the second week, we carried out a daylong critical study of each of five major national curriculum development projects. In the third week, the participants were invited to design, with the assistance of the facilitators, a proposal for a curriculum development project to be implemented in their own country. I prepared a proposal for an integrated studies project on Social and Environmental Studies which I presented to the Department of Education some months later, and so I found myself on a February afternoon in 1972 with Anton Trant and the late Bryan Powell facing the Assistant Secretary of the Department of Education, the late Seán O'Connor, and being given the approval to go ahead with our proposals. Anton embarked on the ISCIP and Humanities projects while we introduced the Social and Environmental Studies Project (SESP) to schools in the mid-west and subsequently to the Cork region. (1998: 40)

Like Shannon, the CDU also planned to launch a project in social and environmental studies, a newly established area in the primary curriculum. It was intended that the project would have two dimensions: science- environmental studies and humanities-social studies. This was a very ambitious plan, too ambitious as things turned out, with eight different subjects integrated into a single project. The plan was probably unworkable in its original form, and it comes as no surprise to find that in September 1972, when the CDU began to function, it had been considerably modified. The single all-embracing project had in practice become two separate projects, one in science the other in humanities. A third was to follow a year later, in outdoor education.

The science project was called the Integrated Science Curriculum Innovation Project (ISCIP) and was designed by Bryan Powell. It was an adapted version of the Tyler approach to curriculum, described in Chapter 4. Objectives were first specified and content and methods devised to implement them. Materials in the form of student work sheets were produced by a small group of practising science teachers, known as the writing team. The materials were given to teachers in a number of pilot schools to try out and were then modified and reissued. The overall direction of the project was in the hands of an inner cabinet comprising Bryan Powell, the director; Melvyn Freestone, the assistant director; Elizabeth Oldham, the evaluator; and the writing team, comprising Kris Bridges, John O'Riordan and Jim McCarthy.

Although the ethos of ISCIP was brisk and business-like, its general philosophy was not lacking in idealism. Its aim was to teach science as science should be taught, that is with an emphasis on 'enquiry and experimentation, understanding and constructive thinking rather than the mere accumulation of facts which could be regurgitated to satisfy examination requirements' (CDU Annual Report 1972–3: 1). The project sought to make the students aware of those aspects of science that played an important part in their everyday world, while also giving them a genuine experience of the scientific method: 'They will be introduced to and use some of the apparatus that scientists use, they will experiment and have the opportunity to communicate their observations and conclusions' (CDU Annual Report 1972–3: 1).

ISCIP represented an integrated approach to the learning of physics, chemistry and biology, similar to other science curriculum projects of the period, like Scottish Integrated Science and the West Indies Science Integrated Project. It comprised separate units on themes like matter, electricity and ecology. The integrated approach was relatively new at the time and excited strong feelings both for and against, as Rose Malone, a later director of ISCIP, observes:

> Integrated science was the prevailing mode in curriculum development in school science for over a decade and thus became identified with change and innovation. Consequently, it bore the brunt of expectations from those who favoured change and the brunt of criticism from those who favoured the retention of the status quo. (1987: 63)

ISCIP was a tonic for a CDU still feeling its way through its infancy years. The project had a clear rationale and a simple and well-defined structure. Powell had considerable status among science teachers and, very soon after the project's inception, several secondary schools showed an interest in joining. Curriculum development had arrived on the Irish scene with a flourish.

Humanities, the second of the CDU's early projects, lasted from 1972 to 1993, a remarkable record for a curriculum project anywhere. It was the brainchild of Tony Crooks and was essentially a three-year junior cycle programme integrating English, history and geography. Although Crooks designed Humanities within the broad scope of the national syllabi in English, history and geography, he set out to give the project a completely new content. He approached the task by asking a group of teachers from four CDVEC schools to undertake a feasibility study with the general aim of giving students the opportunity to understand both themselves and their own environment. The teachers also undertook to study and adapt ideas from three contemporary curriculum projects in humanities/social studies, two in Britain and one in the United States. At the end of the feasibility year, they came together and agreed on the outline of a new three-year programme.

Two basic assumptions underlay Humanities. The first related to the methodology which endeavoured to complement that of the primary curriculum, with an emphasis on enquiry, discussion, project work and use of the local environment as a laboratory for learning. The second related to content: Irish culture was the basis of the programme, with culture interpreted as the total way of life of a people. The project aimed to give the students an appreciation of the diversity of their cultural heritage by helping them realise that there were different kinds of Irishness, urban and rural, nationalist and loyalist, English speaking and Irish speaking, Catholic and Protestant.

The project began with a local and regional study in the first year, and then introduced contrasting studies in terms of place and time in the second year. An imaginative contrasting study on the Aran Islands was designed by one of the Humanities teachers, Paul O'Sullivan. The islands have several appealing features for a project like Humanities: they have a distinctive culture, life-style, and environment, there is a wealth of literature in Irish and English about them, every major phase in Irish history is represented on their landscape and very importantly they are accessible for field trips. In the final year, Humanities broadened out to embrace contemporary issues like population, environment and the world of work.

Humanities was fortunate in the teachers who taught and developed the programme. It was also fortunate in its publishers, Michael O'Brien and Séamus Cashman, who decided to make the project's materials available to the general public in the form of attractive books, written by some of the teachers. Some of the books proved highly popular with a broad readership, notably *The Celtic Way of Life* by Agnes McMahon, *Viking Settlement to Medieval Dublin* by Dermot Stokes, *A World of Stone* by Paul O'Sullivan and *Dublin 1913: A Divided City* by Gary Granville.

The most remarkable thing about Humanities was its methodology, which was based on the process approach to curriculum. It was designed in large measure by Crooks who believed that its most essential element comprised the teachers themselves:

> The success of the programme depends not on the publication of materials or on alternative examinations (though both of these are very necessary). It depends on the quality of teachers who teach the programme. In this way, the materials and the assessment procedures are only the means to improve the quality of teaching and therefore of learning. The most important means to improve this quality has been the meeting of teachers on a weekly basis in the schools to plan and assess their work, and the meeting of school representatives in the CDU. It is this which is integral to the successful implementation of the project and to the lasting changes that have taken place in schools. (1978: 445)

The importance of the methodology was noted in an evaluation of the project carried out by the Department of Education. The evaluators saw the methodology as essentially based on pupil activity, where the normal role of the teacher was that of adviser to small groups or individual students involved in their own research. The underlying principle was that discovery is generally its own reward and that students enjoy the challenge of doing things for themselves.

> Their individuality is respected, and they very soon realise that they, not the subject matter, are of primary importance. The teacher is no longer seen as someone who is chiefly concerned with skills and information but with subtly stimulating and directing the pupils' own investigations. (Ó Máirtín and Ó Ceallaigh 1981: 58–9)

The methodology was a demanding one for the teacher and in this regard the evaluators pointed out the need for vigilance and tact to avoid possible disaster. Whereas the traditional curriculum was more concerned with imparting a predetermined amount of information, Humanities aimed at the personal growth of the individual student through the pursuit of knowledge and skills. The overall aim was to make the students better human beings with greater control over their own lives and greater mastery over their environment. As the evaluators noted, the Humanities classroom took on an exciting meaning:

> It's where the work is planned, facts are compiled and presentation is worked out. It's a base. Pupils leave the classroom to do surveys on cars, shops, factories, farms and so on. Local history can be examined at first hand in its monuments and buildings and other extant markings, and the classroom can serve as a focal point where the results can be discussed and compared and presented for the benefit of all. (Ó Máirtín and Ó Ceallaigh 1981: 59)

Humanities came to an end in 1993 and was well served by co-ordinators like Nora Godwin and Dymphna McCartney. It continues to a limited extent as a new subject, Environmental and Social Studies (ESS), which is an amalgamation of Humanities and SESP, the Shannon project. ESS was consolidated nationally under the successful direction of Ancilla O'Reilly and Patricia Loughman. It remains, however, a somewhat emasculated version of Humanities: the two-subject equivalency of history/geography and English has been reduced to single subject status, and the emphasis on teacher-based assessment has been substantially reduced. But the spirit of Humanities lives on, not so much in the materials or examination structures that it left behind, but in the teachers, students, parents, inspectors, administrators, curriculum developers and researchers who have been influenced by it.

Outdoor Education (OE), the third of the CDU's early projects, was very different from ISCIP and Humanities. It was not strictly a curriculum development project at all but an attempt to consolidate and disseminate an innovation that had already been successfully developed. It was an example of what R.G. Havelock calls the social interaction model: the innovation is taken for granted, the problem is how to disseminate it (Havelock 1970). OE had its origins in the enthusiasm that surrounded the launching of Ballyfermot Vocational School in the mid-1960s. The school's comprehensive programme had scarcely begun when we started an adventure education programme; we called it 'outward bound', considering this a more resonant name. We profited from a small donation from a local mineral water company, Taylor Keith, to buy a set of anoraks, boots and rucksacks, and away we went into the great outdoors under the leadership of a keen young teacher named Peter Heery. We did not realise it at the time but we were making history. We thought we were simply doing a natural thing in taking students into the out-of-doors as part of their usual timetable, but we are now credited with being one of the first schools in the country to introduce adventure education as part of the normal curriculum.

The outdoor education movement owes much to the inspiration of Kurt Hahn, the founder of Gordonstown School in Scotland. He was a charismatic, larger-than-life figure, who as a young man spent a year in a darkened room recovering from sunstroke. There he formulated his life-long maxim, 'your disability is your opportunity.'

He believed that young people have great potential for altruism and service to others if they are given the right kind of challenge. In his own words, young people should be 'impelled into experiences' by confronting the rugged outdoors through camping, canoeing, mountaineering and sailing (Hogan 1968: 9–29).

In the early 1970s, we developed a thriving outdoor education programme in Ballyfermot, helped considerably by Joss Lynam and Paddy O'Leary from the Association for Adventure Sports in Ireland (AFAS), and Adrian Ebrill, Liam Lambert and John Burke from An Óige, the Irish Youth Hostel Association. All the first year students took an introductory one-day course in the mountains, while second and third years went on a three-day residential course at the national adventure training centre at Tiglin, Co. Wicklow. Senior students undertook week-long venture hikes combined with voyages on the national sail training vessel *Asgard*, skippered by Captain Eric Healy. Such a programme was no mean undertaking when it is remembered that the school population at the time was close to 800. In my own mind the main reason for the programme was a social one:

As well as providing a dimension of experience, which many young people seem to want, the outdoor education movement also represents an effort, however small, to make the school itself a more human institution. Teachers today will testify to the amount of tension that is growing in the school. Problems in inter-personal relationships are becoming the major preoccupation in many schools. Some of these problems undoubtedly reflect conditions in the family and society at large but they are exacerbated by the closed institutional setting of the school. Bringing students and teachers into a completely different surrounding where they can relate to each other more like human beings and less like prisoners and jailers, would seem to many hard-pressed head teachers a consummation devoutly to be wished for. Outdoor education affords such an opportunity: it comprises a kind of deschooling programme that makes it possible for relationships to grow and real learning to take place. (Trant 1974)

By 1973, the CDVEC had extended the OE programme to five other vocational schools and Peter Heery was appointed co-ordinator. He was later helped by a number of assistant co-ordinators, notably Nick Corish and Calvin Torrans. In July 1974, I proposed to the CDU steering committee that OE should become our third project. The proposal was accepted and, under Heery's leadership, OE started life with six CDVEC pilot schools and a group of pioneering teachers. Most of the principals were highly supportive, especially Jim Shorthall in Ballyfermot, Séamus Rossiter in Clogher Road, Gerry Lannigan in Denmark Street, Tom Holt in Mount Street and John McKay in Coolock. McKay, who later became acting CEO of the CDVEC, played an important role in the development of all the CDU's early projects and laid the foundations in his own school of what was to become the most successful outdoor education department in the country.

In 1976, OE was evaluated by Bernard O'Flaherty, a CDU staff member. In the research literature of the time, there was little which might have been relevant to his work; two evaluation studies had been published in Britain but they contained contradictory messages. In 1971, Basil Fletcher had claimed that outward bound courses were producing marked benefits on the physical, aesthetic, moral and social development of young people, whereas three years later a team of researchers from the University of Liverpool published a counter claim, referring ironically to the outward bound movement as the 'character training industry' (Roberts *et al.* 1974: 11–32).

The most interesting part of O'Flaherty's report described the efforts of OE to combine adventure sports with field studies. Some people at the time doubted that this was educationally feasible but the OE team took a different view: far from being mutually exclusive, the two activities could enhance each other. The evaluator was of the same mind and recommended that an experimental programme combining adventure activities and field studies be initiated. The programme involving five CDVEC schools was duly carried out in 1976–77 and comprised adventure activities combined with field studies in land use, forestation, folk life and social history. The location was Glencree in County Wicklow and the fieldwork was facilitated by the production of a manual on the valley, written by Fergus McGlynn, one of the participating teachers. The results showed that it was possible to combine adventure activities with field studies provided the teachers and students were motivated and thoroughly prepared.

Another of OE's achievements was the establishment in the 1980s of a one-year diploma course for teachers. The course was jointly organised by the CDU, the CDVEC College of Marketing and Design and the Tighlin national adventure training centre, all which co-operated very effectively. The principal of the college Tom Madden, and John Cray, the head of the design department, ensured that the course was validated by the Dublin Institute of Technology. The director of Tiglin Paddy O'Leary provided the adventure skills training, while Peter Heery and I were responsible for the educational dimension. The external examiner Colin Mortlock, a notable British mountaineer, canoeist and educator, also made valuable contributions to the course.

Over the years outdoor education has grown rapidly throughout the country, especially with the rise of Post-Leaving Certificate courses (PLCs) from the 1980s onwards. The major thrust, however, is now towards the sport and recreation industry, thus reflecting the interests of our rapidly growing affluent society. The original aims of the OE project, promoting personal development and making outdoor education a force for integrating the curriculum, are in danger of being forgotten.

THE IDEA OF NETWORKING

The main reason for establishing the CDU was to develop a curriculum based on the needs of students and related to their local community. In its first annual report we read the following description of the CDU's work:

> In the Curriculum Development Unit, we start with the assumption that our work is geared to the needs of young people who live in the

greater Dublin area. Their needs and problems are linked with the challenge and opportunity of a fast-growing capital city. Hence, the work of the CDU has a definite Dublin orientation. Secondly, we try in the programmes we are developing to help schools to become more conscious of and more sensitive to their immediate environment. This means making the local area a laboratory for learning and progressing from there in ever-widening circles to the greater environments of Dublin, Ireland, Europe, and the world in general. Schools are encouraged to use the resources of the local environment, and of all the resources available the most important are people. Thirdly, a community oriented curriculum will find itself at odds with conformity. If the school curriculum is to relate meaningfully to the needs of its students, there will have to be differences between one school and another. But we are talking about differences of approach not necessarily differences in standards. We are all anxious to uphold standards but not at the cost of a grey uniformity. (CDU Annual Report 1972–3: 23)

To put this thinking into practice, the CDU adopted a particular strategy, the formation of school-based curriculum development networks. The idea of a group of schools working together to implement a curriculum project was not unknown in the educational world at the time but the CDU made it the foundation of its work and in doing so raised a major question: how many schools should form the ideal network? In reality there can never be such a thing as an ideal network – one that follows a preconceived plan with meticulous exactitude. Every network is a unique entity, whose growth is governed by a set of historical circumstances, and in this the CDU was no exception. It started life with three projects, each based on a small group of schools, all for the most part in the greater Dublin area. The primary target group was the CDVEC schools but other schools in the Dublin area, especially those in the public sector, were not refused admission when they applied. In these circumstances the original network was bound to expand, and so we are not surprised to find that at the end of the school year 1973–74 the

ISCIP schools had increased to thirteen, the Humanities schools to ten, while the OE project, which was just getting under way at the time, had recruited six schools.

During the years that followed, as the CDU's sphere of influence steadily widened, the number of schools increased. By the school year 1974–5, the CDU had established an 'outer ring' of 28 schools from various parts of the country that were interested in keeping in contact with its work. A year later the outer ring had almost doubled while the original network of inner ring schools, which had enlisted in one or more of the CDU's three projects, now numbered 24. Evidently, the CDU's interpretation of networking implied expansion – a policy that sooner or later was bound to lead to conflict with the Department of Education.

The CDU never squarely addressed the thorny question of the optimum size of a network, preferring instead to let events take their natural course. There were two reasons for this attitude. Firstly, the CDU did not have the self-confidence or the official standing to embark on a policy of open recruitment, and secondly, even if it had, the best advice at the time about networking indicated that keeping a low profile paid the highest dividend.

In January 1975, with the publication of the ICE Report, the CDU appeared to have been given important support for its networking policy. The report advocated a radical overhaul of the Irish examination structure in the junior cycle and recommended the establishment of an ongoing service of school-based assessment, supported by external moderation and nationally normed objective tests. Central to this scheme of things was a proposal to set up a system of school consortia, with each consortium comprising seven schools and catering for roughly three thousand pupils in all. The consortia in turn would be further grouped into regional units of seven, each region under the care of a specially appointed field officer with central administrative back-up. In short, the ICE Report was recommending a networking arrangement. The recommendation, however, proved too radical for the Irish educational establishment and was never implemented. The CDU's stance on networking, therefore, remained at odds with the orthodox centralised approach in Irish education and, as such, was destined to remain highly vulnerable.

Besides the question of size, another equally serious problem confronted the CDU's idea of networking – the question of time. When does a network come to an end? A dedicated networker would answer that a network finishes when there is no longer any need for it, but this reply would hardly satisfy the demands of the CDU's sponsors. The Department of Education was concerned over the use of resources and the creation of expectations within the system at large. Trinity was interested in maintaining standards of orthodox research procedures, while the CDVEC was anxious that the CDU's activities should relate to its own schools. Of the three sponsors, the CDVEC was the first to perceive that the essential value of the CDU lay in its ongoing contribution towards teacher development through a networking approach. The other two sponsors took the view that every curriculum venture, including the CDU, should have a well-defined beginning and end.

The argument that a network needs an extended and even indefinite time-span is even in the best of times difficult to make, but in the climate of Irish education in the 1970s and 1980s it was next to impossible to sustain. The CDU was constrained to make continual pleas for short extensions to its original four-year time-span so that it could continue what it had begun. But the pleas were never treated favourably by the Department of Education, whose officials were not likely to be impressed by requests to support an ongoing process of development with no immediate end in sight. Yet, the Department continued to allow the CDU to exist, albeit on an ad hoc and hand-to-mouth basis. The reason may well have been that, despite its misgivings, the Department realised that something worthwhile was going on. This perception was probably reinforced by reports from inspectors who were in close touch with the CDU staff and the pilot schools and had therefore a good idea of what the networking idea meant in practice.

What was the essence of the CDU's understanding of networking? There were two principles that summed up its approach – the primacy of the teacher in the curriculum process and the grouping of a number of schools into a voluntary association to support one another in the task of curriculum change. The two can be seen clearly in the CDU's relationship with its pilot schools where respect for each school's autonomy and freedom of choice was always the starting point. The decision to join one or other of the projects was a voluntary one and the CDU never tried to influence which teachers or classes should participate. But once the decision to join was taken, each school was expected to commit itself to the idea of innovation and be prepared to work with other schools in bringing it about. In such a network there had to be give and take and each school had to accept the discipline of a consensual approach.

The network model of curriculum development was to become the cornerstone of the CDU's philosophy. It was not based on any ingenious theorising but on a pragmatic common sense approach that fitted the tough realities the schools had to live with. It was essentially a support service for teachers, an attempt to link their own aspirations for change with the power points of the educational system. It also provided the context in which the professionalism of teachers could flourish. It sought to replace rigid control from the centre with a process of negotiation, partnership and consensus. It acknowledged the reality that innovation in the system does not come easily or swiftly but nonetheless can be achieved through a responsible and structured process of collective endeavour. The network approach went far beyond what any individual school, no matter how innovative or creative, could achieve on its own.

In this chapter, we looked at the establishment of the CDU's first curriculum projects and the school networks through which they operated. Their great achievement was the innovative climate they introduced into the educational system: other teachers and schools were encouraged to follow suit in a variety of projects and programmes over the following years. The chapter brings to a close our examination of curriculum as process and interaction. The process approach is particularly helpful in dealing with the dynamics of educational change. I remember in the early 1970s a senior inspector from the Department of Education said to me, 'When will you finish this business of developing the curriculum so that we can all settle down again?' I know now that the curriculum will never settle down because it is always changing. Heraclitus was right when he said that everything is in a state of flux; a person cannot step twice into the same river. John Henry Newman expressed the same thing: 'To live is to change and to be perfect is to have changed often.'

The following two chapters describe the fourth element in our overall rationale – curriculum as appraisal of outputs. We shall look at two aspects of appraisal: the evaluation of curriculum programmes and projects in Chapter 9, and student assessment in Chapter 10.

CHAPTER 9

Curriculum as Appraisal: The Politics of Evaluation

SCHOOLS OF EVALUATION

Evaluation has always been an integral part of the curriculum; text books, courses, teaching methods, schools and colleges are continually evaluated by students, parents, teachers, inspectors, journalists and the public at large. It is only in fairly recent times that evaluation has become formalised and the professional evaluators have come into being. We can distinguish two kinds of evaluation: formative, in which, as the name suggests, information is fed back to the participants during the course of the evaluation; and summative, in which judgement is reserved until the evaluation is finished. In practice both types merge into each other.

Although evaluation is a comparatively new discourse, there are many approaches to it. At the risk of simplification, we can identify two types of evaluation: the product or objectives model and the process or naturalistic model. The product model emphasises the specification of objectives and outcomes in the activity that is being evaluated and the evaluator's task is to find out whether in fact these have been fulfilled. The classical way of doing this is to design a series of tests which can be given to the participants before, during and after the experimental period to measure the gains and losses. The model takes on an added refinement if the evaluation succeeds in comparing the experimental with a control group – a group as similar in composition as human conditions will allow but which is not affected by the experiment.

The product model is associated with Ralph Tyler who is sometimes regarded as the father of educational evaluation. In the 1930s Tyler was invited to evaluate progressive education then under attack in America. His study, which lasted eight years, comprised 30 pilot sites and became a major influence in the subsequent development of evaluation techniques. Although several aspects of Tyler's work have since been questioned, his approach became the standard pattern advocated in texts on curriculum and evaluation for many years. The advantages of the model were summed up by Wynne Harlen, a British evaluator, who admired but did not always agree with Tyler:

> It provided a neat picture of curriculum development in which evaluation had a well-defined function. It indicated how students' achievements could be used in modifying and developing materials. It provided for setting up criteria – the objectives – against which the value of curriculum materials could be assessed. It became, in fact, the 'classical' evaluation strategy. (1976: 43–4)

I remember meeting Tyler in 1972 and was impressed by his account of his eight-year study of progressive education. He was very much on the side of the teachers and schools, as was clear from his three basic principles of evaluation – the evaluation should be related to each school's purposes, the teachers should participate in the construction of the evaluation instruments and each school's evaluation programme should be comprehensive.

Tyler defined evaluation as the process of determining to what extent objectives were being realised by a curriculum programme. In his eight-year study, he succeeded in developing a simple and effective model with the following ten steps:

- Express the objectives of the programme in terms of behaviour and content.

- Identify the best situations for trying out the objectives.
- Decide the kind of instruments that will be used to gather the evidence, such as paper and pencil tests, direct observation, interviews, questionnaires and examples of the students' work.
- Check the instruments for validity and reliability.
- Decide on sampling procedures (you don't have to see everything that the students have done).
- Decide on the best way to record the results.
- Obtain results from a number of different activities to get an overall profile rather than a single score.
- Analyse the results and then make hypotheses as to what worked well and what did not.
- Redesign the original programme in the light of the hypotheses.
- Evaluate the programme again to see if the hypotheses are working out. (1969: 104–25)

It has been said that all evaluators who came after Tyler either copied him or reacted against him. Several of his critics had hard words to say about him, but their criticisms were often provoked by the rigid way in which his model came to be used by others. Tyler's own approach was primarily school-based and teacher-oriented and did not excite strong feelings when it was published in the late 1940s; nobody indeed was greatly interested in evaluation at the time. But the 1960s saw the rise of huge social and educational programmes in America, backed by millions of federal dollars. An immediate cry arose for accountability and evaluation as an industry was born, almost overnight. Since so few evaluation models were then in existence, it was understandable that Tyler's model, with its logical and scientific format, was pressed into service.

The reaction against Tyler began in the late 1960s and early 1970s and was associated with evaluators like Lee Cronbach, Michael Scriven, Robert Stake, Ernest House and Elliott Eisner in America, and David Hamilton, Malcolm Parlett, Barry MacDonald and Helen Simons in Britain. The reaction was initiated by Cronbach who, though himself a psychologist of considerable standing, nonetheless questioned the adequacy of psychometric tests to meet the complexity of real-life situations. Helped by a group of colleagues at the University of Stanford, Cronbach developed an interdisciplinary approach, which viewed evaluation as primarily social and political, and should therefore be based on the same processes by which other socio-political judgements were made. Cronbach and his colleagues set out their arguments in a challenging manner and, following the example of Martin Luther's celebrated ninety-five theses that had heralded the Protestant Reformation in the sixteenth century, they drew up their own ninety-five principles, calling for a transformation of evaluation. Their starting point was a declaration of what to expect and not to expect from evaluation:

> Its priests and its patrons, as well as those who desire its benefits, have sought from evaluation what it cannot, probably should not give. The proper mission of evaluation is not to eliminate the fallibility of authority or to bolster its credibility. Rather its mission is to facilitate a democratic, pluralistic process by enlightening all the participants. (Cronbach 1980: 1)

Every evaluator, in Cronbach's view, should be an educator; success is to be judged by what other people learn from the evaluation. The task of teaching people through evaluation, however, is not easy; in a busy world, evaluation reports receive only limited attention and many factors besides the evaluator's conclusions influence the final decisions. Evaluators then should not overestimate their own importance and their reports often fall short of the degree of influence they themselves would like to wield. In order to make a greater impact on their audience, Cronbach offers the following advice:

> With some hesitation, we advise the evaluator to release findings piecemeal and informally to the audience that needs them. The impotence that comes with delay may be a greater risk than the possibility that early returns will be misread. (1980: 6)

Two British evaluators, Parlett and Hamilton, argued for what they called the illuminative approach: evaluation should be 'a paradigm for people, not for plants', and should focus on humanist and cultural issues rather than on technocratic and managerial aspects (Parlett and Hamilton 1976). Other evaluators like House and MacDonald developed Cronbach's thesis that evaluation is essentially political and always entails a particular view of society. People hold different views about evaluation because they differ about what society actually is and what it ought to be. Much of the debate about evaluation is in fact ideology disguised as technology.

Evaluation has also been called the science of the particular: it deals with a concrete, volatile and sometimes dramatic piece of human existence, and, despite our lofty theories about why certain things happen, the basic issues underlying any human situation often tend to elude our grasp. We can only observe the situation as best we can and record what we see.

In this sense evaluators are historians: they tell the story of what is being evaluated and at the same time try to do justice to the individual roles of the various participants. There is always more than one story to tell and the story of what might have been may be the most significant of all. The role of the evaluator as story-teller is particularly emphasised in the case study approach. Robert Stake describes a case study as follows:

> A case study is expected to catch the complexity of a single case. A single leaf, even a single toothpick, has unique complexities, but rarely will we care enough to submit it to case study. We study a case when it itself is of very special interest. We look for the detail of interaction with its contexts. Case study is the study of the particularity and complexity of a single case, coming to understand its activity within important circumstances. (1995: xi)

In some case studies, the evaluator is also an actor in the story – a participant observer, to borrow the terminology used in anthropology. This approach allows the evaluator to identify more fully with the people in the situation being studied and so obtain a more complete picture of their views and concerns. There are also other possibilities in the approach: just as the observer can be a participant, the participants themselves can become observers. This is an exciting scenario for teachers: they can be active participants and co-partners in any research project that is introduced into their classrooms. Laurence Stenhouse once said that every teacher should be a researcher; Tony Crooks in the CDU Humanities project argued that teachers should also be evaluators and reflect on their own stories as classroom practitioners.

EVALUATION AND SURVIVAL

Evaluation, as we have seen, is essentially a political process. It is for this reason that it is regarded warily by the people who are subjected to it and who often view it as a threat to their survival. The CDU is a prime example. During the first years of its life, it had one major preoccupation – to stay alive. Despite the fact that it was sponsored by three powerful bodies – the CDVEC, Trinity College and the Department of Education – the CDU was the child of none of them and its intentions were liable to be misunderstood by all three. It was not a permanent institution, established by statute and protected by precedent and tradition; it was an ad hoc body with nothing to guide it except its own vision and inherent will to weather the various storms that continually threatened it.

It is not surprising then that survival issues coloured the CDU's outlook on curriculum. Faced with the grim choice of growth or death, its philosophy of curriculum development translated itself into a pragmatic and client-oriented approach. Its primary clients were the pilot schools and, if it proved irrelevant to them, it would be ignored and would eventually die. On the other hand, if it satisfied their needs, the schools themselves would press for its continuation. The CDU regarded the schools as the chief evaluators of its work and their judgements were expressed in a simple but very telling manner – they either remained with the CDU network or they left.

This approach to evaluation was fairly primitive, yet it contained much common sense. It was a highly political approach – which was not surprising in an organisation that continually had to sharpen its political skills in its effort to survive. The CDU was discovering for itself what several prominent evaluators were proclaiming at the time, that evaluation is a political process and its varying styles and methods all express different attitudes to the distribution of power.

The question of formal evaluation arose early in the CDU's life and not surprisingly it was the Department of Education that insisted on raising it. In December 1973 I was summoned to a meeting chaired by Seán O'Connor, who had earlier given his sanction for the CDU's establishment. The atmosphere was far from friendly and it soon became clear that O'Connor was displeased. The reason was that he had discovered the CDU was increasing its range of activities and the number of its pilot schools. During the meeting I was bluntly told that he had decided to initiate a thorough evaluation of the CDU's activities and was going to ask an expert of international standing to assess our work – Malcolm Skilbeck, director of the Education Centre of the new University of Ulster at Coleraine.

The news that the Department was contemplating an external evaluation was not a shock; I knew Skilbeck personally and was glad at the chance of having the CDU evaluated by an educationalist of his stature. There was also another reason for welcoming the proposal: it offered an opportunity for enhancing North-South co-operation in education. The previous summer I had participated in an OECD conference on school-based curriculum development organised by Skilbeck in Coleraine, when he had used the occasion to bring educationalists from both sides of the Border more closely together. During the conference he called an informal meeting of all the participants from Ireland, North and South, which resulted in the creation of a small working party, of which I was a member.

Fearing that the Department of Education officials would either change their minds or else lack the resolution to carry out their proposal, I made an informal approach to Coleraine to see if Skilbeck was interested in the evaluation. He was indeed very interested, and so I arranged a meeting in February 1974 between him and two of the Department's officers, Torlach O'Connor and William Hyland, to discuss a draft evaluation proposal which Skilbeck had drawn up. The outcome of the meeting was highly satisfactory from the CDU's point of view; the proposal was favourably received by the Department's officers and thus the first obstacle in the way of launching the evaluation was cleared.

The final version of the evaluation proposal was a carefully prepared document. Skilbeck's original version had been modified as a result of a preliminary visit to Dublin by Don Batts and Harry McMahon, two members of his evaluation team. During their visit they interviewed four members of the CDU staff and one of the Department's officers, and following their return to Coleraine a revised version of the proposal was prepared and sent to the CDU in June 1974 – in time for a meeting of the CDU steering committee four days later. It was intended that a team of four people from Coleraine led by Skilbeck would carry out the evaluation, with a fifth member from the Paris office of OECD acting as adviser. The methodology was to be 'one of consultancy which is informed by the theoretical framework of illuminative evaluation'. The scope of the evaluation was ambitious; it included the CDU's policy objectives, decision-making process and general organisation, its individual projects and their evaluation, its relationship with other initiatives in curriculum development and examination reform in the country, its role in in-service education and its potential as a focus for interinstitutional co-operation (Skilbeck 1974).

Such a wide scope was typical of Skilbeck's general outlook on curriculum development and evaluation, which he saw as an integral part of the larger process of cultural formation. What he was proposing amounted to an evaluation of a substantial part of the Irish educational system and would inevitably include the role played by the CDU's three sponsors. One of the most significant things about the proposal was the emphasis it placed on the CDU itself as distinct from its projects. The CDU was now two years old but many people in the sponsoring organisations regarded it, not as an entity in its own right, but as the locus of three separate projects: Humanities, ISCIP and Outdoor Education. Skilbeck, however, focused attention firmly on the CDU as an institution. Of the eight objectives of the evaluation, five were expressly devoted to the policy, decision-making process, organisation, external relations and arrangements for inter-institutional co-operation within the CDU itself. Only two related to the CDU's individual projects, while one related to teacher inservice, which encompassed both the CDU and its projects.

Skilbeck drew up a detailed evaluation programme, comprising 25 stages. The basic strategy was to ensure a constant flow of information from the CDU to the evaluation team, with periodic feedback to the CDU staff. All of the CDU's files were to be made available and it was proposed to make extensive use of written questionnaires backed up by informal discussion and interviews. People from outside with a close interest in the CDU were to be interviewed and it was also planned to visit some of the pilot schools.

The high point of the evaluation would occur about three-quarters of the way through the process when a two-day series of meetings would take place between the evaluation team, the CDU staff, the steering committee and senior officers of the Department of Education. This strategy was based on a model developed by OECD, with which Skilbeck was familiar. In OECD parlance, the culminating meeting of all the parties involved was called a 'confrontation', a French term that describes very well the dramatic nature of what was intended – a coming together of all the actors in the story in a face-to-face encounter. The confrontation would be the climax of a series of events, meetings, interviews and questionnaires and would contribute towards a heightening of interest in the subject of the evaluation – the CDU itself. As a result of this process the CDU was to assume a higher profile than ever before in its history.

On 24 June 1974 the steering committee formally approved the evaluation proposal and the only condition it stipulated was that a preliminary as well as a final report should be presented by the evaluation team. From then on events moved smoothly and according to plan. The confrontation meeting took place in January 1975, the preliminary report was presented in April, and the final report the following September, one month ahead of schedule.

There can be little doubt about the overall verdict that Skilbeck and his team reached on the CDU's work. The CDU, the report stated, had elected to pursue a policy of support and stimulation for school-based curriculum development and in this it was found to be successful. 'Its approach is defensible in the light of the brief given by the sponsoring bodies, especially the VEC, is appropriate to widely accepted needs of schools, and is in line with international thinking and foreign practice. In fact, the CDU's proclaimed policy is in the vanguard of curriculum thinking' (Skilbeck 1975: 3). This was praise indeed and greatly contributed towards raising the self-esteem of the CDU staff. An external evaluation, after a searching enquiry, had concluded that the CDU's work was valuable and worthy to be put on a par with the best in the international field.

The report did not stop at praising the CDU's achievements, it also looked to the future and in its concluding section recommended that the CDU become a permanent organisation. It should continue to be situated in the university and 'see itself and be seen as a regional curriculum development and innovation centre, with some clearly defined national and local responsibilities' (Skilbeck 1975: 14). Not only should the CDU become a permanent body, it should also expand; since the existing staff was too small to sustain the present and envisaged scale of operation, either the scale should be reduced or the staff enlarged. The evaluation team opted for the latter on the grounds that 'the CDU has raised expectations in the system and disclosed real needs which it has the capacity to fulfil and satisfy provided it can be better supported' (Skilbeck 1975: 14).

One of the major recommendations of the evaluation was the convening of a national conference of interested parties to examine the work of the CDU and consider plans for its future in the context of the report's recommendations. The conference should include foreign experts, possibly recruited through OECD. To achieve the best results, it should take place within a year and the steering committee

and staff should prepare a major policy document on the future structure and programme of the CDU as an input paper.

The idea of a post-evaluation conference was in line with
Skilbeck's own convictions about the basic meaning of the evaluation.
He saw it as a process which should not end with the presentation of
the final report but remain an on-going opportunity for continuing
contacts between Coleraine and Dublin. He made his point clear in a
letter which accompanied the final report: 'An evaluation of the evaluation would indicate the long-term significance of these contacts
and the desirability of continuing and indeed intensifying them.' The
conference would also help the CDU in its efforts to institutionalise
itself. 'It could be a very powerful lever', Skilbeck observed, 'and this
I suspect you are going to need' (Skilbeck 1975*b*).

The conference never took place. Shortly after the presentation of
the final report, Skilbeck left Coleraine to take up a post as director
of the Curriculum Development Centre in Canberra, Australia. His
departure was a great loss to the CDU, which was now emerging as
a curriculum force on the Irish scene and was counting on his continuing support. Certainly, he had shown every sign of a deep interest in the CDU's progress and, before deciding to go to Australia, he
had mooted the idea of presenting the CDU as a case study for the
Open University's course on curriculum studies. The idea, together
with the proposed conference, had to be abandoned with Skilbeck's
departure from Ireland.

Skilbeck's sympathy for the CDU was probably due in large part
to his own espousal of school-based curriculum development, an
area in which he considered the CDU to be very successful. He was
convinced of the importance of the school as a curriculum agent and
was later to express himself on this point in a manner that clearly
indicated his sympathies:

The school is a social institution comprising people in active relationships with one another: it is a living organism which needs to
organize and manage its affairs in such a way that its primary purpose, the education of children and youth, can be achieved in the

best possible way ... We cannot expect a school to be a vital centre of education if it is denied a role of self-determination and self-
direction: the curriculum is the central structural component of
schooling, upon whose reasonable control the educational vigour
of the school and the success of its educational mission depend.
(Skilbeck 1984*b*: 13–4)

How should we classify Skilbeck as an evaluator? Barry
MacDonald once divided evaluators into three categories: bureaucratic, autocratic, and democratic (1976: 126). Although Skilbeck
defies categorisation in many respects, he more easily fits into the
second. 'Autocratic', however, is not the best term to describe
Skilbeck's approach, and if we replace it with the term 'authoritative'
we are better able to catch the distinctive flavour of his evaluative
style. He had considerable authority in the Irish educational scene
and was prepared to use it in focusing attention on what he considered to be important aspects of the CDU's work. He was well versed
in the political niceties of the situation he was evaluating, but he was
also conscious of the danger of becoming too preoccupied with the
politics of evaluation. He preferred instead to see evaluation as only
one ingredient in a complex whole, where the important thing was to
be aware of qualitative issues such as values, aims and criteria. 'It is
helpful to keep in mind', he was later to point out, 'the dependence
of evaluation on other aspects of the educational process, including
everyday institutional practice in schools, colleges and education
offices. Curriculum evaluation would make a good servant but a bad
master' (Skilbeck 1984*a*: 5).

The significance of the Coleraine evaluation was more in the
process it initiated than in the report it produced, and in this regard
we are reminded of Lee Cronbach's words:

The cumulative and indirect contributions of an evaluation can be
as important as the effects on the program studied ... A program
evaluation that gets attention, whether or not it affects the immediate fate of the program it studies, is likely to modify the prevailing

view of social purposes, of attainable goals and of appropriate means of action. (1980: 156)

Skilbeck certainly succeeded in drawing attention to the CDU but his optimistic aspirations for its future did not materialise. The tenuous nature of the CDU's existence remained unchanged and survival continued to be its major preoccupation. Why then, it could be asked, was the CDU not warned by the evaluators of the difficulties in store? This would probably have been to expect too much from the evaluation team; they were not prophets and could not be held responsible for the complex interplay of relationships that were to affect the CDU's destiny. In hindsight, however, it could be said that the Skilbeck evaluation had a blind spot: in stressing the CDU's potential as a permanent centre within the university, with national as well as regional functions, it raised hopes and expectations that could not be fulfilled. The alluring prospect that the report put forward was never feasible in the context of the political realities with which the CDU had to contend. Skilbeck had strongly advocated that the CDU should anchor itself in the university school of education and take on a national role with the support of the Department of Education. In theory he was right: there was much to be said in favour of a centrally supported CDU working closely with a university school of education. But in practice the arrangement was unworkable, as later events were to show. As it turned out, there was no place for the CDU within the university and the Department of Education remained fundamentally suspicious of and at times openly hostile to the CDU's continued existence.

The irony of the Coleraine report was that it underplayed the significance of the most committed and supportive of the CDU's three sponsors – the CDVEC. There were probably two reasons for this. Firstly, throughout the entire evaluation period, Sheehan, the CEO of the CDVEC, was on leave of absence with the Commission of the European Communities in Brussels. Secondly, the vocational educational committee itself had been suspended since 1969, when Dublin City Council and its attendant committees had been disbanded by the Government and replaced by a special commissioner. This state of affairs was to last until 1974 when a newly elected coalition Government reinstated the City Council and a new vocational education committee was appointed. At the time when Skilbeck and his colleagues were carrying out the evaluation, the CDVEC was preoccupied with adjusting to a new regime and was not greatly concerned with what was happening in the CDU.

Nonetheless, the importance of the Coleraine evaluation should never be lost sight of. It had a pronounced effect on the morale of the CDU, more than any other evaluation in its history. Skilbeck himself, although removed from the Irish scene after 1975, remained in contact and for many years continued to exercise an influence on the CDU's destiny. He had intended the evaluation to be the beginning of a fruitful and exciting link between the CDU and the Education Centre at Coleraine and although this hope had faded with his departure from Ireland, the CDU always kept alive the interest he had fostered in the educational scene north of the Border.

GUIDELINES FOR EVALUATORS

Elliott Eisner (1985) has put forward the view that the evaluator should be a connoisseur, and he went on to define connoisseurship as the art of appreciating something and communicating this appreciation to others in an appropriate way. This is an important observation about the nature of evaluation: it is as much an art as a science and, with this maxim in mind, I now put forward some suggestions about how would-be evaluators should behave. The suggestions are offered from two stand-points: firstly, the experience of being subjected to several evaluations in my own work in the CDU and, secondly, the experience of acting as an evaluator myself for seventeen years on the Wider Horizons Programme of the International Fund for Ireland, like a poacher turned gamekeeper (see Chapter 13).

- Don't leave the situation you are evaluating in a worse shape than you found it. Evaluation is a political activity and usually adds a further complication to an already complex political

186

scene. Remember that evaluation is about the use of power, and thus the evaluator should try to ensure that all the players are on a level playing field. An evaluation is a political exercise and of its nature will move the political scene backwards or forwards as the case may be. No evaluator can be neutral, nor can he or she afford to be but, in the political power game, the evaluator should at least try to be on the side of the angels.

- It is particularly important to include the sponsors among the actors being evaluated. Their actions and attitudes have an important bearing on the entire project – the way they give out money to the participants, the conditions they impose and their real but often unstated expectations. The sponsors will probably object to being evaluated and may even be outraged. But persist: an evaluator should be brave.
- Be flexible in the use of evaluation instruments, whether quantitative or qualitative; pick whatever suits and be aware of their limitations. Evaluation is a very imperfect science and at the end of the day, the evaluator has to make an enlightened guess.
- Be humble: many evaluations in the past have failed and many more have gone unheeded.
- Don't attach too much importance to the statements of objectives that people make; these are usually more hopeful than realistic, the kind of rhetoric that is used to please the sponsors and help the money flow.
- Remember Cronbach's advice about an evaluator being an educator: success is to be judged by what others learn. Also, it may be wiser to release findings piecemeal and informally as they are needed. Final reports often come too late, when the action has already moved on. Good evaluators are good communicators, so avoid being ponderous, pseudo-scientific and over-addicted to detail. The first test of an evaluation report, like any other piece of writing, is not to bore the reader.
- Try to start a debate on the situation being evaluated. This is often more important than issuing a report; if the evaluation is any good, the debate will continue after the report is forgotten.

- If possible work as a team; the more points of view in an evaluation the better.
- An evaluator needs many virtues. We have already suggested humility and courage; we could add patience, tact, humour, common sense, a concern for fair play and of course the willingness to say what people may not want to hear.
- An evaluation usually generates interest, energy and resources, but it should never be seen as an end in itself. Its fundamental purpose in any educational setting is to bring about an improvement in the quality of people's learning. Keep in mind that your evaluation has to fit into the busy and complex round of activities that make up the lives of the people being evaluated. Good evaluators always know their place, do not over over-rate their own importance and never take themselves too seriously.
- An evaluator is a storyteller and every story is a mix of comedy and tragedy. We should remember that telling a story is an art in itself – it may sound simple but it is not. The ability to tell a good story is essential if the participants are to understand what is happening to them and how they can learn from the evaluation. To tell a person's story is to validate their lives and affirm their efforts. It is a sacred trust and not all evaluators are aware of it. Every voice deserves to be heard and sometimes it is only the evaluator who hears it.

In this chapter, we looked at the arrival of evaluation on the educational scene and the various schools of thought and practice it has given rise to. We saw how evaluation is essentially a political activity, and we examined how this is illustrated in the way the CDU was evaluated. We concluded with some suggestions to would-be evaluators. The following chapter is devoted to student assessment, which is another aspect of curriculum as appraisal. Assessment should be an integral part of the entire curriculum. In practice, it has become separated from it, mostly with unfortunate results – particularly with reference to external examinations.

CHAPTER 10

Student Assessment

A Good Servant but a Bad Master

It was Socrates who said that the unexamined life is not worth living but one wonders what he would have thought of the Irish examination system. From second level onwards, our curriculum is driven by examinations. We teach to the test and by doing so put the cart before the horse. We disregard warnings to the contrary – that assessment should never be separated from the curriculum but always be an integral part of teaching and learning. We forget the vital distinction between assessment as the servant of learning and assessment for managerial purposes such as selection, certification and monitoring standards. We ignore the undesirable results that follow managerial assessment – the distortion of the curriculum, devaluing the work of teachers and students and lowering the very standards assessment purports to raise.

The dominance of managerial assessment is not new. We are told that in seventh century China young men were recruited to the civil service through a three-tier examination system, where as many as 20,000 candidates were guarded by soldiers as they answered written questions for two days from dawn to dusk (Hyland 1998: viii). In nineteenth-century India, the civil service examinations concentrated on literacy, penmanship and conformity, which were considered important qualities for civil servants at the time. In Ireland, in the second half of the nineteenth century, a payment-by-results assessment scheme was operated at elementary and secondary levels. Elementary school pupils were orally examined by inspectors while secondary pupils took external written examinations at the end of the school year. The scheme also operated in England, the United States and Australia and was severely criticised by prominent educationalists at the time. Matthew Arnold described it as a 'game of mechanical contrivance' through which pupils could be coached to pass examinations without really knowing how to read, write or count properly (Hyland 1998: ix).

Arnold was complaining of the evils of teaching to the test in his own day, but the practice has persisted into modern times. I remember in my own schooldays learning English, geography and history by writing out and learning by heart model answers to examination questions dictated by the teacher. Later on as a young teacher in London, I had to coach nine- and ten-year-old children to pass a selection examination for grammar schools by giving them endless practice in intelligence tests.

Over two decades ago, Donal Mulcahy remarked that passing the public examinations and amassing points for admission to third-level institutions was the overriding objective of Irish schools. The results of such an examination-led curriculum are predictable: what tends to be taught is what is examinable and what is most examinable is often of least importance. Other forms of teaching and learning, such as debating, questioning and investigating, come to be regarded as wasteful of time.

> Originality, which has been known to be associated with error, may be seen as a loser's strategy in the race for marks ... There is little time for the non-book or non-vicarious but time-consuming learning experiences. Most of all, there is little time for learning what real learning is, what it means, and how to go about it. (Mulcahy 1981: 161)

Is the Irish practice of assessment any better today? There have been some improvements, a few concessions towards alternative modes of assessing but in general the traditional written examination remains the norm. We can take some comfort that we are not alone; recent research on assessment in several other countries reveals the following depressing picture:

- More attention is given to marking, grading and processing the results, rather than giving feedback to improve learning.
- There is a tendency to assess quantity and presentation rather than the quality of learning.
- The usual practice is to compare students with each other rather than assess individual learning needs, with the result that low attainers become discouraged.
- Tests tend to measure rote and superficial learning.
- There is little discussion or sharing among teachers about various methods of assessment, and little attention paid to the records of previous assessments carried out by other teachers.
- Most assessment practices are not primarily concerned with the learning needs of students.

(Black and Wiliam 1998; Assessment Reform Group 1999; Black *et al.* 2003)

The last point is the most worrying of all. If assessment does not serve the needs of students, then it is failing in its most important task. Clearly, the educational world has lost sight of something fundamental: divorcing assessment from learning is like turning a valuable instrument into a dangerous weapon.

ASSESSMENT FOR LEARNING

If we are to make any progress in designing assessment modes that do not adversely affect the way students learn, we must first of all discover what is going on in the classrooms. We are aware that learning takes place there but we are not always sure why or how. To find some answers, UK academics Paul Black and Dylan Wiliam undertook a research project that produced important results. The researchers were chiefly interested in the way learning could be enhanced by the use of formative assessment, which they defined as an activity undertaken by teachers and students to provide feedback and so modify the teaching and learning in which they were engaged. With this end in view, Black and Wiliam surveyed 580 research studies in assessment as reported in articles and books. The studies were taken from several countries, covered a wide age range, from five-year olds to university undergraduates, and included different subjects. The researchers reached the following conclusion:

> The main plank of our argument is that standards are raised only by changes that are put into direct effect by teachers and pupils in classrooms. There is a body of firm evidence that formative assessment is an essential feature of classroom work and that development of it can raise standards. We know of no other way of raising standards for which such a strong *prima facie* case can be made on the basis of evidence of such large learning gains. (Black and Wiliam 1992: 2)

Two years later, the authors were joined by colleagues from King's College London in a four-year project that explored ways of making formative assessment a practical reality in the classroom. Thirty-two teachers of maths, science and English from six secondary schools under the local education authorities of Medway and Oxfordshire participated in the project. The project team devised four assessment strategies – oral questioning, written comments, peer and self-assessment and the creative use of written examinations.

Although there is nothing new about any of the strategies, they had the merit of making the teachers and students conscious of the assessment practices they were used to but usually took for granted. The teachers found that if they wished to make assessment an integral part of learning they had to make fundamental changes in their own pedagogy. The students discovered that, as their own participation in assessment increased, they had to take more responsibility for their learning. The project as a whole demonstrated that a commitment to assessment as a tool of learning meant a radical change in the culture of the classroom – what amounted to a new contract between teachers and students. Let us look briefly at each of the four strategies.

Asking questions during the course of a lesson is probably one of the oldest forms of assessment, but we scarcely ever think about the way we do it and what effect it has on our students. The project teachers began their work by trying to 'widen the gap', that is, to increase the waiting time between the questions they asked and their students' replies. This they found quite difficult to do, as one teacher reported:

> Increasing waiting time after asking questions proved difficult to start with, due to my habitual desire to add something almost immediately after asking the original question. The pause after asking the question was sometimes painful. It felt unnatural to have such a seemingly 'dead' period but I persevered. Given more thinking time, students seemed to realize that a more thoughtful answer was required. Now, after many months of changing my style of questioning, I have noticed that most students will give an answer and an explanation where necessary without additional prompting. (Black *et al.* 2003: 33)

Other teachers had similar experiences. When the waiting time was increased, more students answered, their responses were longer and more confident, and they challenged or improved the answers of fellow students and offered alternative explanations. The teachers found themselves putting more thought into the questions they asked and paying more attention to the replies they received:

> Not until you analyse your own questioning do you realize how poor it can be. I found myself using questions to fill time and asking questions which required little thought from the students. When talking to students, particularly those who are experiencing difficulties, it is important to ask questions which get them thinking about the topic and will allow them to make the next step in

the learning process. Simply directing them to the 'correct answer' is not useful. (Black *et al.* 2003: 34)

What strikes me in particular about the above comments is that for a teacher there should be no such thing as a wrong answer, only one that is more or less appropriate. Every answer can give a clue about how the student thinks – even an 'I don't know' answer can be a serious reply that merits further exploration. This of course is not a modern discovery as we know from Plato's description of Socrates' method of asking questions.

The second strategy was about the written feedback teachers give their students. This usually takes the form of a grade, a written comment or a combination of both. The project teachers were surprised to discover that students made learning gains when they were given written comments only, whereas they made no gains at all when given grades or a mixture of grades and comments. It was contrary to what the teachers expected but they were willing nonetheless to try out the comment-only approach. They soon found that it made its own demands:

> The important feature of this technique of course is the quality of the comment. A blank, non-helpful comment, such as 'Good work Jaspaul, this is much neater and seems to show that you have tried hard', will not show any significant change in attainment because it says nothing about the individual's learning. There is no target and the students, although aware that the teacher is happy with them, could not be blamed for thinking that neatness is everything and that by keeping all of their work neat from now on, they will attain high grades. Students are not good at knowing how much they are learning, often because we as teachers do not tell them in an appropriate way. (Black *et al.* 2003: 44–5)

When the project teachers gave grades as well as comments, the students were only interested in the grade and in how it compared with that of others. Their focus was on winners and losers rather than on the work itself and how it could be improved. But when the teachers changed to comments only, a surprising thing happened.

> At no time during the first fifteen months of comment-only marking did any of the students ask me why they no longer received grades. It was as if they were not bothered by the omission. I found this amazing, particularly considering just how much emphasis students place on the grades and how little heed is taken of the comments generally. Only once, when the class was being observed by a member of the King's College team, did a student actually comment on the lack of grades. When asked by our visitor how she knew how well she was doing in science, the student clearly stated that the comments in her exercise book and those given verbally provided her with the information she needed. She was not prompted to say this. (Black *et al.* 2003: 45–6)

The change to comment-only marking was also accepted by the school authorities, inspectors and parents, who saw it as a way of creating a culture of success where students could progress by building on their previous performance rather than being compared with others.

The third strategy was self- and peer assessment. In practice, each complemented the other. Self-assessment was the ultimate proof that the students were taking responsibility for themselves as learners, while peer assessment acted as a very powerful motivator:

> The students know that homework will be checked by themselves or another girl in the class at the start of the next lesson. This has led to a well-established routine and only on extremely rare occasions have students failed to complete the work set. They take pride in clear and well-presented work which one of their peers may be asked to mark. Any disagreement about the answer is thoroughly and openly discussed until agreement is reached. (Black *et al.* 2003: 50)

Personally, I can vouch for the motivating power of peer assessment. I once taught English to a class of seventeen-year-old boys in Ringsend Technical Institute. They were bright and self-confident, but more interested in their technical studies than the delights of English literature. Essay writing in particular they regarded as a pain, something artificial and irrelevant. Their first attempts showed this only too clearly – long-winded, dull and boring. I selected one essay at random, asked the author to read it aloud and told the rest of the class that they would be the critics. The young man visibly paled as a sleepy, uninterested class suddenly came to life, commenting on the essay in language I would scarcely dare to use. But as it dawned on them that they too would have to face the music, their comments became more restrained and thoughtful. They were learning the first rule of writing – never bore the reader. In subsequent classes, I limited the length of the essays to a single page so that everybody could have their turn at reading aloud. The quality of the writing improved dramatically.

Peer assessment naturally complements peer teaching, in which some students excel. When practised in small groups, it provides an excellent opportunity for student co-operation. It also helps to make the assessment criteria, which should really be the same as the learning criteria, more transparent, thus enabling the students to acquire the objectivity they will need for self-assessment.

The fourth strategy, the creative use of written examinations, meant that the students came to regard the examinations not as hurdles to be jumped but opportunities to reflect on their understanding of what was being tested. This is easier said than done as most examinations, especially if they are external, can be threatening for students and teachers alike. Many of us have memories of a bad examination experience at one time or another in our lives, which may have had lasting effects. I do not count myself as an exception but fortunately I also have memories of a very different kind. I am not talking about the intoxicating experience of examination success – that too has its drawbacks and is often of little educational value – but of being shown how little examinations count in the long run. During my undergraduate studies, I took philosophy as a subsidiary degree subject. A pass was all that was required but this was by no means guaranteed. We all knew we would have to submit to the rigours of sitting a three-hour paper, accompanied by the usual feverish pre-examination cramming. Our professor, an enlightened young Franciscan, had other ideas for us. At the beginning of the year he made a proposal: if we consented to forget about the examination and concentrate instead on doing philosophy, he would let us know the main items on the paper a week before. We readily agreed: we all passed the examination and at the same time succeeded in learning some philosophy.

The King's College team also wanted their teachers to forget about examinations because of their negative influence on the new assessment techniques they were putting into practice. But the teachers refused: the examinations were a reality they could not ignore. A compromise was reached that the assessment strategies would be used as far as possible in preparing for the examinations and in reviewing the results. The students were asked to prepare their own examination questions and afterwards to compare and discuss them among themselves. The exercise turned out to be a stimulating and productive way of revising their work and also proved more effective than the traditional methods. One of the teachers explained:

> Answering other people's questions and discussing solutions with the whole class is a very effective way of concentrating on topics that need to be revised rather than spending time on what is already known. Students have had to think about what makes a good question for a test and in doing so need to have a clear understanding of the subject material. As a development of this, the best questions have been used for class tests. In this way the students can see that their work is valued and I can make an assessment of the progress made in these areas. When going over the test, good use can be made of group work and discussions between students concentrating on specific areas of concern. (Black *et al.* 2003: 54–5)

The aftermath of the examinations was a similar opportunity for creative reflection, as another teacher pointed out:

> Now, the papers are returned and students work in small groups to agree on answers – in effect coming up with their own mark scheme. This works best in practice, I have found, if only a few questions are tackled at a time, then the class share information, and make sure that they are in agreement with the official mark scheme, then on to the next few questions. Initially, this tended towards 'I must be wrong because I'm the only one who has that answer', and that is still a problem with lower ability students who lack confidence. Quickly, however, the middle ability and more able pupils realize that the best answer is not necessarily the majority one, but the one that can be best justified. (Black *et al.* 2003: 55)

An Irish project on assessment for learning under the auspices of the NCCA got under way during the school year 2003–4, with two school networks in Cork and Sligo. By the second year of the project, 96 teachers from a wide variety of subject areas and a range of second-level schools were participating. The project, which is co-ordinated by Hal O'Neill, NCCA education officer, has built on the evidence and experience of its English counterpart in testing the applicability of assessment for learning in an Irish context.

A report on the project at the end of its second year reached the following conclusion:

> Assessment for learning promotes innovation in classroom organisation and management. It favours approaches to assessment that are characterised by collaboration between teacher and learner. It encourages teachers to adjust their teaching in the light of their observation of the work of their students, to introduce greater degrees of differentiated teaching and to develop strategies that promote self-assessment in students. (NCCA 2005: 20)

The project has important implications for the quality and format of the information that teachers give to parents on the progress of their students. The current phase is concentrating on gathering examples of students' work with accompanying comments from teachers for publication on an NCCA website. This will be a key way of encouraging other teachers to trust their own professional judgements in assessment matters.

The overall message of both English and Irish projects is that assessment can be a positive part of the learning process and can help students to be beneficiaries rather than victims. It seems to me, however, that this is true only when the teachers themselves are in control of the tests. External examinations are a different matter, both in the UK and in Ireland. In this country, we have a particular difficulty in allowing teachers to assess their own students as part of the public examinations. We tend to put our faith entirely in external assessment, as if there were no other alternative. But this is not necessarily the case; there are other alternatives, as we shall see in the following section.

ALTERNATIVE MODES OF ASSESSMENT

It is sometimes said that teachers are afraid of examining their own students because of the possibility of pressure from parents and the public in general. This concern has to be taken seriously. It is not a happy situation for any teacher to feel that he or she can be left in a vulnerable position because of a mark awarded in an examination. The situation, however, need not be regarded in black-and-white terms. We can enjoy the advantages of both forms of assessment, internal as well as external, provided we ensure the teachers play an active part in the examination system in a way that respects and at the same time protects their professional integrity. We can bring this about if the assessment process is situated in a framework of cross-moderation, that is, where the overall responsibility for the marks awarded rests with a group of teachers rather than an individual. The cross-moderation process can be effectively operated by a number of schools co-operating together and monitored by the inspectorate. A similar system was proposed over thirty years ago in the ICE report but was rejected, possibly because too much was being attempted with inadequate resources at the time. The same idea, however, was successfully implemented by the CDU over a period of fifteen years for the students following its two first projects, ISCIP and Humanities. It is worth noting that no teacher in these pilot schemes ever reported being pressurised by students or parents.

The examination modes operated in ISCIP and Humanities were in the context of the Intermediate and Group Certificate. The Intermediate was established in June 1924 when the Intermediate Education (Amendment) Act put an end to the previous system of financing of schools, partly on the basis of their public examination results. In 1947, a second public examination was instituted, the Group Certificate, to cater for the needs of vocational schools. This dual system remained in force until the 1960s, when an effort was made to liberalise the post-primary curriculum by introducing new and broader subject syllabuses. The examination format, however, remained largely unchanged – written terminal examinations, devised centrally and applied nationally. It was this system that the CDU was challenging when it sought a new method of examining its two projects.

The first indication that the Department of Education might be prepared to let go some of its control over the examinations came from one of its senior officials, Seán O'Connor. In February 1973, shortly after he had been appointed secretary, O'Connor met Tony Crooks and myself, and we told him we were anxious to discuss the possibility of alternative examination modes. The meeting was informal and O'Connor was in a generous mood. He was not unsympathetic to our request, he said, and advised us to contact the Chief Inspector Richard Foley. I met Foley the following March and, although he was against tampering with the established examination structures, he agreed that the CDU could make its case to individual members of the inspectorate.

Throughout the next three months, we tried to win the interest of some of the inspectors. Our efforts were well received and the following May a one-day seminar was organised in Hawkins House, the headquarters of the secondary schools inspectorate. As an input paper, we prepared a document that argued the case for a change:

> In Ireland, changing the curriculum must necessarily entail changing the public examination system. Exams are the most powerful determinants of the post-primary curriculum and it would be wise never to ignore this. But there is no reason why the exams themselves cannot be used as creative agents for change. To do this we must be prepared to experiment and to support schools and teachers who are willing to try out new ideas. The important point is that whenever a new curriculum experiment is launched in a responsible way, there must be equal commitment from the officials in charge to experiment with new modes of examining to fit the new projects. If this does not happen the projects will not be taken seriously by teachers, students and parents. (Trant 1992: 16)

Immediately after the seminar, a working party comprising five inspectors and five CDU representatives was established to devise a framework for the experimental examination modes. Within two weeks it had completed its task and reached the following conclusions. The inspectors agreed to moderate the experiment, and five inspectors were appointed from three examination subjects, one each from science, English and Irish, and two from history/geography. They arranged to meet the CDU staff one day per month to plan and review the experiment and also have the opportunity of meeting teachers from the pilot schools. The conclusions show a remarkable commitment from the inspectors to the task of bringing the new modes into existence, and events over the ensuing months were to witness, if anything, an increase in this commitment. By early June, when I again met the chief inspector, Foley told me he had changed his mind about tampering with the established examination system and was now in favour of the new modes. The working party had by this time divided into two subcommittees, one for ISCIP and the other for Humanities, with the purpose of formulating detailed proposals on the operation of the modes. Both worked quickly and succeeded in completing their task before the end of the year.

The story now took a new turn. Not all the inspectors had been involved in the discussions; an important section, the vocational schools branch, had been left out. In retrospect it was a strange omission but something over which the CDU had no control. In theory, there was a unified inspectorate for the entire system but, in practice, there were three separate branches – primary, secondary and vocational – and up to this point the vocational branch had played no part in the negotiations. In January 1974, Micheál Ó Súilleabháin, one of the vocational inspectors, complained to me about leaving the vocational branch out in the cold. I tried to reassure him and a month later I was invited to meet the assembled body of vocational inspectors at their headquarters in Apollo House to explain what was being proposed. The senior inspector Tomás Grennan was absent but two months later he declared himself on our side.

The scene was finally set and all the relevant inspectors, secondary and vocational, had been won over. Crooks and I thought it would now be opportune to make a second approach to O'Connor, if only to remind him of the progress that had been made since our original meeting in February 1973. The meeting took place on 11 June 1974 and on this occasion Hugh Healy, the acting CEO of the CDVEC, was also present. O'Connor was again sympathetic and promised he would make an immediate decision. He was as good as his word; ten days later we were notified that the Department had approved the new examination modes.

It might seem an exaggeration to describe the new modes as revolutionary but, in the context of a highly centralised and rigorously controlled system, the description is not unjustified. The modes themselves were simply constructed. The ISCIP mode comprised continuous assessment, accounting for a quarter of the total marks, and a paper set from a question bank supplied by the teachers, accounting for an additional third. The rest of the marks were for one of the existing written papers from the national examination, thus linking ISCIP securely to the traditional system. Humanities, on the other hand, was more radical. Like ISCIP, it contained a measure of teacher assessment, accounting for 30 per cent of the total marks. But, unlike ISCIP, it made few concessions to the national system, with 70 per cent of the total marks being divided between student portfolios and three Humanities papers, devised and marked by examiners drawn from the teachers themselves.

With the permission to operate the new modes, the CDU was given what amounted to a stake in the national system – a small one it is true, but which nevertheless implied a partnership with the inspectorate. The partnership pointed towards the future, for although the permission was for one year only, it would be difficult if not impossible to limit the application of the modes to such a short period. The pilot schools had already committed their first and second year classes to the new projects with a view to the classes sitting the examinations at the end of their third year, and the schools would have protested vigorously if the modes were suddenly terminated.

ROLE OF THE TEACHER UNIONS

The CDU next began the task of persuading the teacher unions to support the new modes. There were two unions involved, the Association for Secondary Teachers, Ireland (ASTI) and the Teachers' Union of Ireland (TUI). Both were opposed to teachers participating in any form of assessment for the public examinations without receiving remuneration. Their position had given rise to a longstanding dispute with the Department of Education and was an obstacle in the way of any new initiative involving teachers in the continuous assessment of their students.

In the CDU, we were well aware of these sensitivities and so in December 1975 and again January 1976, I wrote to the presidents of the two unions asking for their co-operation. The National Executive of the TUI reacted favourably and promised their co-operation for 1976 – the year the modes were due to operate. The ASTI, however, would not allow its members to participate unless they were paid. This presented the CDU with a problem but it was confined to ISCIP only and involved only five teachers and three schools. We sought to resolve the problem by persuading the schools to make a reduction of one class period per week in recognition of the assessment duties the teachers were undertaking. I wrote again to the ASTI president asking that the modes be allowed to continue because they were experimental and were being implemented in controlled conditions for a limited period of time. But he rejected the offer because 'the Department of Education, with whom our dispute regarding payment for assessment really lies, would be in no way involved with this arrangement' (Trant 1992: 170).

We now found ourselves in a dilemma, caught in a dispute between two powerful institutions, the Department of Education and the ASTI, and the prospect of successfully operating the new assessment modes, at least on the ISCIP side, looked bleak. The following March, however, a solution emerged which saved the day. The ISCIP co-ordinator Bride Rosney devised a formula acceptable to all parties – she herself would act as an independent assessor in the schools involved in the dispute. The arrangement operated smoothly for the rest of the school year, so much so that the ASTI agreed to operate it again the following year.

Having successfully pacified one union, the CDU then had to reckon with the other. The trouble with the TUI began with one of the local branches, the Dublin City branch, to which a large number of the ISCIP and Humanities teachers belonged. In September 1976, the branch secretary issued a directive instructing all members not to teach ISCIP or Humanities. The reason given was a ruling from the TUI annual congress the previous June that, except in the case of official pilot projects, continuous assessment should not be undertaken without appropriate payment. Neither ISCIP or Humanities, it was stated, were entitled to be recognised as pilot projects after 1976 and so the branch proceeded to place a ban on its members attending any meetings in the premises of the CDU.

The ban had an immediate effect and the majority of the pilot teachers stopped attending meetings. The outlook was now alarming. For a body like the CDU, which was pledged to work with teachers to further their professional development, a ban of this sort was the equivalent of a death sentence. We decided to appeal to the TUI national executive. When the two sides met we put forward the argument that the CDU was now operating a bridging year – an extra year granted by the Department of Education in which it planned to undertake a comprehensive review of what had been achieved during the previous four years. The bridging year, we said, offered an opportunity to put forward proposals to the Department regarding the terms under which teachers should be engaged in curriculum development and assessment procedures. As the year had been officially permitted by the Department, ISCIP and Humanities should be accorded the status of pilot projects undertaken for a limited duration, which was one of the conditions that the TUI had originally stipulated for participating in continuous assessment.

The TUI president was unmoved. He was bound, he said, by the terms of the TUI congress resolution of June 1976, and there could be no continuous assessment without appropriate remuneration. Payment for assessment and a better teacher ratio were the main requirements if the TUI was to entertain any thoughts of settlement. It was clear that the union was determined to take a tough line despite our plea that the CDU had no bargaining power in the matter of payment. On 19 October the Dublin City branch renewed its ban and this decision was later endorsed by the National Executive. The ban had now become fully official and the situation looked ominous.

It was against this background that the two sides came together again on 17 December. This time the CDU representation included the CEO of the CDVEC Jerry Sheehan and some members of the CDU steering committee. The meeting ended in stalemate with no solution in sight. Sheehan, however, was shrewd enough to detect some signs of willingness to settle. He privately contacted the TUI executive and made an offer which they accepted.

The solution was a compromise: the teachers would each be paid £15 for attending an inservice seminar on assessment. For both sides this was a face-saving exercise. The CDU could argue that the teachers were not being paid directly for taking part in assessment procedures; to have yielded on this point would have incurred the wrath of the Department of Education, which was determined that no precedent would be established on the issue. The TUI executive on the other hand could claim credit with its members for ensuring that money would be paid, albeit indirectly, in recognition of the teachers' involvement. The executive was also probably glad to be rid of a dispute that had been thrust on it by one of its local branches. The settlement was welcomed by the ASTI, which, although not in dispute with the CDU, was glad to accept payment for its members and consequently no longer insisted on a separate independent assessment.

During the ensuing six months the CDU worked out a formula with both unions that allowed the teachers to continue with the assessment procedures. In return, they were given a goodwill payment of £25 per annum and a time allowance of one teaching period per week for planning sessions. A further allowance of one teaching period per month was given to a representative from each pilot school to attend meetings in the CDU. In the years that followed, the formula operated successfully and was the basis for a long period of harmony between the CDU and the unions.

The core of the arrangement was a cross-moderation procedure that enabled the teachers to come together in small groups to agree on assessment criteria and monitor their own marking and grading schemes. The system was afterwards developed by the CDU and was greatly appreciated by the teachers who participated in it. It was essentially a form of assessment in-service training, which covered many of the issues described above in the section on assessment for learning. A typical cross-moderation meeting was like a court of examiners. It ensured that all major decisions about marking and grading had the approval of the entire group, which comprised not only teachers but also inspectors from the Department of Education.

No individual teacher, therefore, could be blamed for a decision to pass or fail a particular student.

PARLIAMENTARY QUESTIONS

Although the support of the teacher unions was essential for the successful operation of the experimental modes, ultimately it was the Department of Education that had the last word. We have seen how the inspectorate had enthusiastically participated in the design and initial implementation of the modes, but this was not sufficient to ensure their survival. The senior administrators had also to be won over and this proved a very difficult task. In February 1978, after the modes had been in existence for two years, we were informed that ISCIP and Humanities were to be evaluated and phased out by June of the following year. Obviously not everyone in the Department of Education was convinced that the projects were a good thing.

The CDU had a final card – to bring the issue into the public domain. At the end of May we called a meeting of the principals of the pilot schools and put before them the problem we were facing. They felt the issue was as much their responsibility as ours and resolved to take action on their own initiative. There was no mistaking their determination to make a stand and to put whatever pressure they could on the Minister for Education John Wilson. Their strategy was two-fold. Word of the Department's intention to abolish the modes was given to the news media and in particular to the educational correspondent of the *Irish Times*, who kept the story alive during a vital seven day period in early June. The lead given by the *Irish Times* was followed by some of the other dailies and the story was also taken up by RTÉ.

The second strategy was more telling. A number of principals approached their local TDs with the result that on 1 June 1978 the issue surfaced in Dáil Éireann during a debate on the education estimates. When the Minister had finished his opening address, he was immediately followed by Deputy E. Collins, the Fine Gael education spokesperson. Collins attacked the intention to abolish the modes in trenchant terms:

> I firmly believe that the case is in fact one where the civil servants in Marlborough Street do not like to see the slightest bit of power passing out of their hands. The pilot scheme was something I welcomed. It was making excellent progress and the attitude of the Department now really makes me sick. I believe this is a backward step of monstrous proportions when one looks at the need to develop the curriculum. It is a shocking decision on the part of the Minister. I condemn it out of hand, and if and when we get back into Government, hopefully at the next election, I can assure the House that if I am ever Minister for Education I shall reverse that decision and ensure that the scheme and other schemes like it will get full support. (Collins 1978)

Collins was followed by the Labour Party spokesman on education Deputy J. Horgan, who was also incensed. Horgan deplored the decision to end ISCIP and Humanities because it undermined a development that was 'authentic, school based, real and important to children'. He agreed with Collins in laying the blame on the excessive centralism of the Department of Education. The innovation, he asserted, 'is being knocked by the Department because it is not under their direct control. That is the beginning, the middle and the end of it' (Horgan 1978).

The attack was resumed three weeks later when Deputies M. Keating and E. Collins raised parliamentary questions about the CDU's future and the fate of ISCIP and Humanities. Notice of a parliamentary question has to be given some time in advance, so that the minister concerned has time to receive a full briefing. When John Wilson rose to answer his questioners, it was obvious that he had a prepared statement on the CDU's work. He repeated the terms of the Department's letter of 20 February about the two projects being evaluated, but significantly made no mention of terminating them. On being pressed by Keating on this point, he was prepared to concede some ground: 'I am very flexible with regard to years. I want to look at the work which has been done with a view to putting it on a larger stage' (Wilson 1978*a*).

Clearly the Minister had softened the line taken earlier by the Department. This became apparent a week later when two further parliamentary questions were asked on the future of the projects, this time by Deputies R. Ryan and F. O'Brien. Ryan, who represented a large Dublin constituency, probably put his finger on the point that caused the Minister greatest worry – 'the considerable concern of parents, children and teachers in the Dublin area' (Ryan 1978). Pressure from the public was mounting and Wilson knew this. He decided to make a concession: he told the Dáil he was prepared to extend the modes until 1980, one year longer than had been decided by the Department (Wilson 1978*b*).

The CDU had won a significant victory. The Minister for Education had publicly reversed the decision of his own Department to phase out ISCIP and Humanities within a year. But there was a downside to the victory. Wilson had made no definite promises; all that the CDU had won was a stay of execution and the Department had time on its side. An important battle had been won but not necessarily the war. The crucial test would come when the CDU came to renew its request to operate the modes after 1980.

Wilson's decision was greeted with delight by the teachers of ISCIP and Humanities but the uncertainty about the future of the projects was by no means ended. Over the succeeding years, the CDU had to request permission on an annual basis to continue with the modes, until eventually in the early 1990s the Humanities mode, the last to survive, was phased out.

One of the most significant achievements of ISCIP and Humanities was to demonstrate that teachers could be entrusted with the running of public examinations and that the examination system itself could contain flexible forms of assessment without endangering standards of excellence.

This was in no small part the result of the ongoing interest and support of a number of inspectors who had been designated by the

Department of Education to monitor the operation of the projects in the schools and liaise with the CDU staff in the implementation of the new assessment modes. In the case of Humanities, a special committee was established, which met on a regular basis and comprised six inspectors and two CDU representatives. The group was humorously referred to in Irish as 'Coiste na hÉigse', the poetry committee, but there was no question about the seriousness of its intent and the importance of its role. The operation of the examination system was now being decentralised – admittedly in a very small way, but nonetheless symbolic of what could be achieved in the future.

ISCIP and Humanities began thirty-five years ago, but the official attitude to the assessment modes they pioneered has changed very little in the meantime. Surely the time has come to grasp the nettle and launch a new initiative in assessment that will involve all the main partners in the education system. The time is ripe for such a venture, especially within the framework of the current junior cycle. The Junior Certificate Programme could lend itself very readily to carefully structured pilot projects that integrate assessment into the curriculum. We now have experience of a range of different assessment modes that we can call on. We can introduce them with built-in safeguards about the duration of the experiments, the nature of the teacher involvement, the status of the validation process and the adequacy of support, monitoring and feedback mechanisms. All these factors were successfully taken into account in the case of ISCIP and Humanities, and the major stakeholders at the time, the Department of Education and the teacher unions, were happy to participate. A determined and imaginative response is once again needed and no reasonable person will object to a venture that stimulates a more open, fruitful and positive debate about the issue of assessment in the Irish education system.

The chief concern in this chapter has been to show that, despite strong external pressures, assessment should always be considered an integral part of the curriculum. To show that this is possible, the development of alternative examination modes in ISCIP and

Humanities were given as examples. The chapter concludes with a plea for a national initiative in assessment in the context of the Junior Certificate Programme, which involves all the partners in education.

We have now finished the analysis of our four-fold rationale: curriculum as instrumental, content, process and appraisal. We next turn to three case studies of curriculum in action. Chapter 11 is devoted to the CDU's early work in the area of educational disadvantage and the following two chapters deal with a wider stage – saving the environment (Chapter 12) and peace and reconciliation on the island of Ireland (Chapter 13).

PART III

Case Studies of Curriculum in Action

CHAPTER 11

Curriculum on the Margins

EDUCATIONAL DISADVANTAGE

Catering for the educational needs of the less fortunate in our society has always inspired the efforts of educators down through the ages. It seems to me that often the most imaginative and exciting curriculum projects are found on the margins of the system, in situations where status is not a barrier to learning, and the spirit of experiment and adventure is not stifled by the dead hand of bureaucracy. It is on the margins that we discover the power of education to liberate the human spirit from ignorance, oppression and meaninglessness. In my Ballyfermot years, I remember how we were thrilled at the new approach to remedial education and that no pupil should ever be dismissed as backward and uneducable. I think it was then I realised that applying the term 'remedial' to a particular group of students was wrong and that all education should be remedial. We are all disadvantaged in one way or another and we all need the encouragement of good teachers. But some students are more disadvantaged than others because the help they need to reach personal fulfilment has been for one reason or another denied them. We rightly call such people deprived.

The *Concise Oxford Dictionary* defines deprivation as the condition of being dispossessed; in this sense deprivation is a recurring theme in the history of the Irish people, so much so that it must surely be part of our collective consciousness. Between the seventeenth and nineteenth centuries, the majority of the people were dispossessed of their lands, laws, language and almost their religion. The most terrible deprivation of all and the most enduring in its effects was the all-pervasive poverty to which great numbers were subjected. Visitors to the country in those years were aghast at what they saw. One eighteenth century traveller, the indefatigable Arthur Young, was clearly shocked by what he witnessed: 'Speaking a language that is despised, professing a religion that is abhorred and being disarmed, the poor find themselves in many cases slaves' (Thomson 1976: 74).

The chronicle of deprivation and poverty in Ireland reached its culmination in the catastrophe we know as the Great Famine (1846–48). This event, which left 800,000 dead and millions lost through emigration during the famine and in the years after, has etched itself deeply into the race memory. Less well known is the fact that, throughout the preceding three decades, one in every three years saw a famine with an accompanying fever in one part or other of the country. By the time the Great Famine arrived, poverty, hunger and disease had almost become a way of life. So too had unemployment. In 1836 the Report of the Commissioners on the Poor estimated that over half a million labourers were unemployed for over thirty weeks of each year and as a consequence their dependants, who numbered nearly two million, were in distress (Ó Tuathaigh 1972).

The aftermath of the Great Famine brought an economic recovery of sorts but poverty and unemployment remained familiar features for the next century and a half and were a direct cause of the continuous emigration that almost bled the nation to death. Irish people did not just leave their country, they fled from it. Deprivation then is not a new phenomenon and if we meet it again in present day Irish society, it should be with a recognition and compassion born of long endurance.

EARLY SCHOOL LEAVERS

The CDU has always been concerned with educational disadvantage and its foundation documents were at pains to justify curriculum reform in this context. It was not until the late 1970s, however, that the CDU was able to launch a major project in the area of disadvantage. The opportunity arose with the inauguration of the European Action Programme on the Transition from School to Work and Adult Life. The programme had originated in a proposal by the European Commission in 1976 concerning the increasing number of young people who were failing to find work after leaving school.

The CDU's involvement in the European Transition Programme was through the Early School Leavers Project (ESLP). The coming of ESLP was a special event because its sponsors included the European Commission as well as the Department of Education. Together with two other Irish projects, one in Shannon and the other in north Mayo, ESLP was part of a network of projects established by the Commission throughout the member states. It had a higher profile than any of the CDU's earlier projects, and a voice in the control of its destiny was essential to the Department of Education.

The project defined early leavers as students who derived little or no benefit from their schooling, left at the earliest opportunity, were unsuited to the world of work and consequently drifted from one job to another or remained more or less permanently unemployed. The problem was recognised as complex, involving three sets of factors:

- personal, relating to health, ability and interests;
- home and environment, relating to deprivation, unemployment and delinquency;
- school, relating to curriculum, organisation and interpersonal relationships.

The last of these was the chief concern of the project staff and in this context they considered the public examinations to be a particular difficulty. In their view, success in school was determined by the values of the examination system; some students thrived on examinations but others lost out. The latter did not measure up to the demands of the examinations; for one reason or another they did badly and what was worse they themselves and often their teachers

217

expected they would do badly. Their defence was to drop out of school, which was hardly surprising since nobody likes a threat that they cannot cope with. We all need status, security and a sense of achievement and, if we are in a place where these are denied, we will either rebel or drop out. Garry Granville, the first co-ordinator of ESLP, painted the following picture of the typical early leaver:

> With few exceptions, the young people who leave school at or before the age of fifteen, without having received a Group or Intermediate Certificate, can be said to have derived little or no benefit from their schooling. The logic of school programmes culminating in examination achievements has escaped them, and their ten or eleven years of schooling has left them no tangible reward nor in many cases anything more than a minimal level of competency in the basic life skills. Because schools have been inadequately equipped and structured to meet the needs of this group of students, there has been a tacit tolerance of their disappearance from school. (1982: 21)

ESLP lasted from September 1979 until June 1982. It had three dimensions: a school programme for early leavers, an out-of-school work exploration centre and a work release programme for young women. The school programme developed an alternative curriculum for early leavers with assessment based on student profiles. The programme culminated with the award of a school-based certificate, developed in conjunction with five of the participating schools, Coláiste Dhúlaigh, Coolock, Coláiste Eoin, Finglas, Marino Vocational School, Blakestown Community School and Caritas College, Ballyfermot.

The work exploration centre was based in the campus of Crumlin College of Business and Technical Studies, courtesy of the principal Phil Galvin. Under the leadership of Colm Rock, eighteen projects were carried out, each lasting a week and producing items like bedside lockers, dolls' cots, metal candle-holders and playground slides. The centre created a workplace atmosphere, with production targets, time-keeping and tea breaks. Points were earned in lieu of wages and, on completion of their tasks, the students received a diploma. The emphasis throughout was on personal achievement, which was of particular importance to young people with a record of failure in the traditional curriculum. Experience of success and the recognition of their work made an agreeable change from their previous schooling.

The work release programme for young women originated in the Liberties area of Dublin where the principal of the local vocational school, Terry Doyle, had noted that many girls left school early to take up work in the clothing trade. Their motives were due more to family and social pressures than any antipathy towards school and, although they were fortunate in obtaining jobs during a period of recession, their long-term prospects were poor. With the co-operation of their employers, a ten-week course was devised by ESLP team member Hanna O'Brien, involving the attendance of eight girls at the vocational school for one afternoon a week. Initial research indicated that the girls needed specific work-related skills combined with social and life skills. The teacher responsible for the course, John Hammond, took an informal approach, with group discussions, project work and visiting speakers. Work-related topics included industrial organisation, trade unions, relationships between workers, pay-slips, income tax and insurance, while life skills included the use of leisure time, communication, citizen rights and the use of community resources.

The significance of ESLP lay more in its overall impact than in its individual parts. This point was noted by Malcolm Skilbeck at a dissemination seminar organised by the project in summer 1982. According to Skilbeck, the project had raised a fundamental paradox – the need to focus on a particular group but at the same time to see the group as part of society as a whole, not as a sharply separated category. It was in this context that the traditional perception of the early school leaver as a failure had to be questioned:

If we use the language of failure we are bound to ask ourselves the question: who has failed – we the educators or they the drop-outs?

Or is it perhaps the social and economic orders that are at fault? One of the points that has come through strongly in this seminar is that educators now openly recognise that the system, whatever that may mean, has failed or has been unable to provide adequate resources for all whom it purports to serve. (1982: 72)

Skilbeck had put his finger on the core issue ESLP was trying to address: the causes of early leaving went beyond the students and the schools and were to be found in the nature of society itself. But how could teachers, schools and well-intentioned curriculum projects change deep-seated social attitudes and practices? The danger, as Skilbeck pointed out, was that the solution offered by a project like ESLP could result in a kind of educational apartheid, a curriculum that was alright for the low achiever but not good enough for the top tier.

Is that really what we want? Do we want to see the alienated and the dispossessed on the bottom tier of such a structure? If we do not want it, can we nevertheless avoid it? Does consideration of the particular needs of a specific group, however large and politically ominous, necessarily commit us to a kind of educational and social stratification which many of us have been trying for years to scale down if not eliminate? Will our strategies at the stage of generalisation of these pilot studies take account of the consequences for school and society of this underlying trend? Surely these are questions to be addressed in the further work of the pilot projects. (Skilbeck 1982: 72)

The CDU was well aware of the issues raised by Skilbeck and regarded them as relevant to all its project work. The CDU response was implicit in its own philosophy and style of curriculum development. Worthwhile curriculum change involved the creation of new traditions in the teaching profession and new attitudes in society in general. This process was bound to be slow and could not be achieved within the limited scope and timeframe of the usual curriculum project. The dynamic of curriculum innovation had to be kept alive over several years and built into as many projects as possible. The CDU viewed its projects as opportunities to enlist pioneer teachers in the overall enterprise of creating a new educational tradition to underpin worthwhile curriculum change.

The ESLP external evaluators, James Callan and Elizabeth Hilliard, were perceptive enough to recognise the context in which the CDU was trying to address the issue of early leavers, and that any solution to the problem would have to be a broadly-based one, focusing not on a particular product but on the development of a new climate for the unmotivated, non-examination student.

> It is recognised that the work of the CDU over the past ten years has been a major catalyst in promoting curriculum developments in difficult areas under very difficult circumstances. The CDU has been a pioneer in this area in the absence of a clear policy from the central authority, the Department of Education; it has been a pioneer in stimulating teacher development in the absence of adequate teacher training and in-service training programmes in our universities. It has been a pioneer in its attempt to tackle complex issues of certification for the non-academic and very often the economically poor students in our system. (1984: 303)

The evaluators were less complimentary on how far the ESLP staff had embarked on a process of systematic and reflective analysis of the underlying issues of early leaving. This was unfair, especially as the evaluators themselves admitted that 'the potential benefits of a curriculum project that has been in existence for three or four years, only begin to become apparent as the project is being terminated.' The CDU, for its part, was in no doubt about the importance of what ESLP had achieved and was determined that its work should continue. An opportunity to do so arose fairly quickly after the project ended. The overall results of the Transition Programme were sufficiently satisfactory for the European Commission to embark on a second round of pilot projects. Invitations to apply were again issued to all the member states and the CDU, sensing the opportunity to continue its work in disadvantage, submitted another proposal to Brussels, this time targeting the educational needs of Dublin's inner city.

DUBLIN INNER CITY EDUCATION PROJECT

Dublin is usually considered a Viking foundation, dating from the nineth century, but its origins probably go back further. It was not until the mid seventeenth century that the city began to expand in earnest, when it grew from a population of only 9,000 in 1659 to about 80,000 in 1700. Dublin continued its rapid growth throughout the eighteenth century, when it acquired the elegance and splendour that made it the second city of the English speaking world after London. In 1801 came the Act of Union and with it the dissolution of the Irish parliament, an event that had a blighting effect on Dublin's growth. The city's glorious reign was over. The population, nonetheless, continued to grow and by 1911 had reached 398,000. In 1921, Dublin became the capital of the new Irish state and still it continued to expand; by 1926 the population of the city and the suburbs totalled 419,000 (National Economic and Social Council 1981: 42–6).

The growth of Dublin, especially up to independence, was an uneven affair and resulted in the emergence of two cities, one for the rich and the other for the poor. The contrast was noted by Frederick Engels when he visited the city in the mid-nineteenth century. He was impressed by Dublin's aristocratic quarter, which he described as 'laid out in a more tasteful manner than that of any other British town', but the poorer districts he found to be ugly and revolting: 'The filth, the dilapidation of the houses and the utterly neglected conditions of the suburbs beggar description and are beyond belief' (NESC 1981: 63). By the beginning of the twentieth century, the contrast between rich and poor was still evident and the destitution of the inner city slums had become notorious throughout the western world. Patrick Geddes, in his evidence to a 1913 Parliamentary inquiry, declared that the city had 'a more numerous submerged class than anywhere else I know' (NESC 1981: 65). This submerged class was memorably depicted in Sean O Casey's plays and later in James Plunkett's novel, *Strumpet City*.

From the 1930s onwards, with the provision of local authority housing in the suburbs, the worst of Dublin's slums began to disappear. The clearances, however, were accompanied by a declining population and general decay in the inner city environment, which has lasted almost to the present time. It is not surprising to find the conditions of deprivation reflected in the attainment of the children. Researchers have noted the stark contrast between the educational achievement of inner city children compared with that of the more affluent suburbs. Despite such difficulties, or perhaps because of them, Dublin's inner city has been the location of some imaginative initiatives. In 1969, the Department of Education, in co-operation with the Dutch Van Leer Foundation, established a five-year experiment in pre-school education in Rutland Street in the North inner city. The project, one of the first of its kind in Europe, was followed by a number of similar initiatives in other disadvantaged parts of the city, which tried to disseminate the original methodology (Holland 1979).

Ten years later the CDVEC established a subcommittee on education and training in the inner city, where there were five vocational schools at the time. The ensuing report called attention to the high numbers of remedial pupils and recognised the damage that this could cause to the public image of the schools unless all the educational interests involved came together to formulate a comprehensive policy for remedial education. One of the report's major recommendations was that 'a special educational intervention be made ... in which curricula appropriate to the area might be used and in which the school day could be varied to suit the circumstances of the area' (CDVEC 1979: 1). What the CDVEC was in fact recommending was a meaningful community education policy for the inner city.

The recommendation might well have gone unheeded were it not for a dramatic development in the political arena that brought the issue into the full glare of national publicity. In January 1982 Garret FitzGerald's Coalition Government fell and the consequent general election failed to give any of the contending parties an overall majority. When the 23rd Dáil met the following March, it found itself in the dilemma of a hung parliament. Charles Haughey, the leader of the Fianna Fáil, eventually found he could form a minority government but only with the support of left-wing independent deputy Tony Gregory, who represented Dublin's north inner city. Gregory, who now found himself a virtual king-maker, was able to bargain for a substantial package of social and economic measures for the inner city in return for his vote. As part of the package, it was agreed to declare the north inner city an educational priority area and build a new community school there.

The 'Gregory deal', as it was popularly known, received wide media coverage and was debated at length in the Dáil. Some people regarded it as a cynical exercise to secure political power but others pointed out that, whatever the motivation behind the deal, it was in a good cause and should be accepted at its face value. The CDVEC was particularly interested in the educational dimension of the deal, as it already had plans of its own to build a school in the north inner city. On 15 April 1982, the CEO Liam Arundel met Gregory and persuaded him to merge his plan with that of the CDVEC. It was agreed that the school proposed for the area would be a community college under the auspices of the CDVEC (CDVEC 1982).

The community college was an exciting concept and went well beyond the remit of a typical VEC school. Some of the most imaginative elements in the plan came from one of Gregory's advisers, Fr Michael Casey, the pastor of Our Lady of Lourdes in the north inner city and a graduate of the Ontario Institute of Studies in Education in Canada. Casey submitted a five-page document, which formed the basis of the agreement reached by Gregory and the CDVEC. He proposed that the new college should mark a radical departure from the traditional pattern of education, which in his view was no longer adequate:

> In the past, schools have failed the children and people in the north inner city. Being middle-class institutions with middle-class

teachers who had to impart middle-class knowledge in order to achieve middle-class goals through a middle-class medium, language and methodology, the schools were alien objects, as if from outer space. Massive illiteracy, a huge drop-out rate and consequent feelings of failure by both pupil and teacher have led to great wastage of human potential, energy and money. With contrary, ill-defined and often conflicting agendas the two (school and community) never matched and the larger entity, the environment, always inevitably won. (1982: 1)

Casey wanted the college first of all to have a clearly defined community philosophy. It should cater for both children and adults, be person and community-oriented, foster formal and informal learning and prepare people for employment and unemployment alike. It is interesting to note the influence of the Brazilian social reformer Paolo Freire on Casey's thinking, especially regarding his ideas of education as liberation:

The education engaged in by the community college will therefore be more than 4 x 2 schooling (what's learned between the four walls of school and the two covers of a book). It will draw strongly on people's innate interests, potential and skills, and will value life experience (experiential learning). It will foster academic, manual and social skills in the context of the educative community, where all staff, pupils, and adults are co-teachers and co-learners for the good of all. The education will be for the liberation and development of the human person and the building of structures conducive to this. In keeping with the theory of education enunciated above, the community college will develop in the pupils the ability to discriminate and analyse their life situation, and endeavour to develop their skills and human potential so as to enable them to take control over their own lives or 'name their world'. (Casey 1982: 1)

The Gregory deal was short-lived. Eight months later, the political wheel of fortune turned once more. Haughey's government fell and Garret FitzGerald returned to power. The planned community college was put on hold and had to wait fifteen years before it was eventually built as the present Larkin College. The interest in inner city education, however, was kept alive by a growing community movement in both the north and south inner city. It was in this context that the CDU decided to look for an inner city location for its new proposal to Brussels. In summer 1983 this aspiration became a reality when Fr Philip Kelly, the pastor of St Catherine's in the south inner city, offered a home for the project in his parish primary school in School Street, which was only partly occupied at the time. The following September, the Dublin Inner City Education Project (DICE) came into being.

The aim of DICE was the social and vocational preparation of young people with poor prospects of employment in order to enable them to acquire a degree of independence in a changing society. Three target groups were envisaged: students completing their schooling and with poor employment prospects, young people who had left school and were still unemployed, and young women with poor employment prospects. The same three groups had been part of the ESLP remit, so it was obvious that DICE was meant to continue where ESLP had left off.

DICE lasted for four years and two of its activities, a school programme for early leavers and a work exploration centre, were direct continuations of ESLP. DICE, however, was more radical in its community involvement: it developed two community-based programmes, one in School Street for unemployed young people, and the other in a nearby apartment block for young women, many of whom were mothers of small children. The School Street centre became one of the most visited locations of all the European Transition projects. Most of the young people in the centre had dropped out of school at fourteen years or even earlier and some had never transferred from primary school at all. Many had experienced the poverty, ill health and emotional troubles associated with a severely disadvantaged background and not a few had had brushes with crime, vandalism and substance abuse. The centre's efforts to counter these adverse influences was by any reckoning an ambitious undertaking.

The starting point of the programme was to take the young people seriously in trying to identify their needs and involve them in seeking solutions to their own problems. Under the leadership of Siobhán Lynam, the staff created a friendly atmosphere, warm and positive, informal and informative, open and responsive. The centre became a space where the young people could become self-aware and self-confident. They were encouraged to be themselves and grow as individuals (Stokes 1988). The activities comprised social and personal education, craftwork, film-making, job searching, counselling and a variety of cultural and recreational pursuits. The high-point was the mid-day meal, which was planned, prepared and served by the young people themselves. The mealtimes were moments of community interaction and many distinguished visitors felt privileged to be invited as guests.

The great achievement of School Street was to demonstrate the possibility of providing a successful educational milieu for young people who had become alienated from the mainline system. Afterwards, the School Street model was to have an influence on the establishment of Youthreach, a national programme offering integrated vocational preparation and work experience to disadvantaged early school leavers.

The other activities of DICE were understandably a little overshadowed by the fame of School Street but they represented solid and worthwhile achievements in their own right. The school programme under Gary Granville and later Geraldine O'Connor succeeded in consolidating the work of ESLP for low achieving pupils in 30 postprimary schools in the greater Dublin area. The programme for young women was located in an apartment in Fatima Mansions, one of the largest and most deprived of the flat complexes in the south inner city. This programme, led by Mary Owens, comprised home budgeting, child care, family planning, home-crafts, literacy and numeracy, personal development, outdoor recreation, aerobics and body care. It helped the young women to solve some of the problems which confronted them by discovering that they themselves had the resources to challenge and change their situation. The work exploration centre, also a direct inheritance from ESLP, expanded its activities under Colm Rock's direction and found a new home in a splendid Georgian building in North Great George's Street.

By the time DICE came to an end it had come to be recognised as one of the leading European initiatives in educational disadvantage. This was underlined in April 1987, when the CDU was commissioned by the Department of Education and the Youth Employment Agency to organise a conference on the theme, 'Disadvantage, Learning and Young People', which was attended by delegates from many parts of Europe. The conference presented the experience of the three Irish projects that had participated in the second Transition Programme as well as several vocational and community education projects at home and abroad. The speakers included Damian Hannan from the ESRI, Tony Crooks, the deputy director of the CDU, and Nano Brennan from the Conference of Major Religious Superiors.

In his paper, Hannan took a broad view of early leavers which included not only young people who dropped out but also those who had finished their compulsory schooling with poor examination results. He estimated the annual number of early leavers at 4,000 and felt that, for many of these, the traditional curriculum was 'too abstract, too formal and too dependent on post-school extrinsic rewards'. These young people needed a radically different curriculum along the lines of the pilot projects presented at the conference, which were pupil centred rather than subject based, experiential and integrated into daily life. The curriculum should be based on learning from doing, and use projects and practical work rather than books and formal instruction. Also, the relationship between teacher and students should be more egalitarian and interpersonal. All the answers were there, Hannan concluded, but if we ignore them, have we not in effect chosen early leaving as one of our unspoken objectives? (Hannan 1987: 43–51).

Tony Crooks, who had replaced Gary Granville as co-ordinator of DICE when the latter departed to the Curriculum and Examinations

Board, identified the typical characteristics of a successful programme for disadvantaged young people. First of all, the purpose of
the programme, unlike the traditional school course, was determined not by examination outcomes but by personal needs – 'the
real life situation of each individual will define the starting point for
learning.' Although the content of the various programmes varied, in
all cases the importance of the local area and community was understood. The programmes also emphasised literacy and numeracy and
the personal, social and vocational skills necessary for living and
working in today's world (Crooks 1987).

Many of the programmes were modular and focused on short-
term goals which could be achieved within a few weeks, unlike the
targets in traditional schooling which are usually two to three years
away. The short-term goals were often combined with user-friendly
assessment based on participation and affirmation. The milieu in
which the programmes took place was carefully planned, friendly,
comfortable, suitably equipped and tastefully decorated. The calibre
of the staff was crucial, and equally crucial was a good support
structure – encouragement from management, regular staff meetings and opportunities for inservice training. Finally, the programmes were usually presented to the young people as a contract
they could negotiate before entering into it (Crooks 1987).

Nano Brennan posed a fundamental question: what is the nature
of educational knowledge? The traditional answer is that it is a
rational and academic form of knowledge, abstracted from particular persons and situations, and representing an understanding of
general principles. This kind of knowledge is mediated through
rational, abstract categories, usually in the form of disciplines or
subjects. The model is Greek and Christian in origin but it does
not reflect the oldest strands in the Greco-Christian experience of
knowing.

An older form of knowing can be found in Greek epic and drama
and in biblical narrative. It is 'a more basic form of knowing, one
that is rooted in existence and expresses itself in symbol, narrative
and action'. It is a participative and holistic form of knowing, which

has two dimensions: praxis and integration. The first means reflecting on our experience of reality in order to transform it. The second is a holistic way of perceiving things which arise out of everyday experience.

Brennan considered that the second form of knowing best described what the various programmes presented at the conference were trying to achieve; it complemented the first form but should never be seen as something inferior to it:

> This is our most basic form of knowing. It is represented more by the least rewarded in our society, for example, women and socially disadvantaged minorities. Because of its association with these groups, it is considered as invalid or inferior educational knowledge. In fact it is the foundation for rational academic knowledge. Educational knowledge, therefore, should be perceived as an interaction between the different forms of knowledge, that is, integrating praxis with the rational. (1987: 144–5)

When DICE came to a close, the CDU had high hopes of continuing with its major activities, both in the schools and the community. This was not to be. On 4 June 1987, the Department of Education announced without warning that the staff of the CDU would have to be reduced to two people and its entire work programme would have to be significantly scaled down and restructured. Henceforth the CDU's plans would have to conform to the Department's wishes and carried out according to the Department's guidelines. The Department had in fact just stopped short of closing the CDU down.

Throughout the summer of 1987, the CDU fought for its life. The immediate effect of the Department's edict was the scattering of the CDU's staff: twenty project and five administrative staff left during the summer months. Some had their contracts terminated, while others, who had been long-term staff members, were allocated to schools throughout the CDVEC. The latter, although fortunate in the sense that they had jobs to go to, felt deeply humiliated because they were thrust without ceremony into schools that neither expected nor wanted them. The only staff who remained in the CDU were the director, deputy director and a token administrative staff – a skeleton crew on a stricken ship.

The CDU did not die. Its survival was due to the efforts of several key people, including the CEO of the CDVEC Liam Arundel. The cost of recovery was considerable: all the long-term plans had to be abandoned including the follow-up activities for DICE. However, one exception was made and that was the network of schools following the programme for early leavers. This the CDU continued to support for a period of ten years with marginal funding and with the help of dedicated co-ordinators like Patricia McCarthy and Liz McSkeane. The number of participating schools grew over the years and by 1996 it had reached forty. At that stage, the Department of Education and the NCCA had come on board. The programme was given official status and increased resources and, as we have seen in Chapter 4, it began its national implementation stage as the Junior Certificate School Programme (JCSP).

OPTION FOR THE POOR

We have been discussing curriculum at the margins or what could be more broadly called 'the option for the poor'. Cynics may say that the poor will always be with us but in today's world they are assuming an added significance. They are a dispossessed and growing group at the margins of a fast changing society and may exercise a radical influence on the direction of that change. The poor of today are not as biddable as the poor of by-gone years, nor even of the recent past. Writing in the 1980s, sociologist Liam Ryan warned that failure to find economic solutions for poverty could have major repercussions in politics, religion, education and cultural life generally: 'In the process, the wheel of values and attitudes may turn significantly, the marginal may well become the central, and terrible beauties may again be born' (1984: 104). Ryan was referring to poverty in Ireland a generation ago, but in today's global society the effects of poverty affect everybody.

Who are the new poor? The first challenge we face with regard to poverty is to renounce whatever preconceptions we may have about it. Poverty, we are reminded by theologian Denis Carroll, must be viewed in its totality, in its forms, causes and effects. It is any kind of underdevelopment or deprivation of the necessary means to live decently. It can be hunger, homelessness, bad health or a lack of access to the goods and services that are the right of everybody. It can be voicelessness in the decisions that affect one's life, or lack of participation in the social process. 'Poverty puts a question mark over easy talk about the common purpose of the goods of the earth. It rises up to mock the Genesis command about the stewardship of creation. What kind of stewarding can be exercised by those who are deprived even of the means to live?' (Carroll 1987: 186).

Poverty is an evil that oppresses the human spirit, yet one of the great surprises of the modern world is the revival of religious thinking and practice in the face of poverty and oppression, as we see in the liberation theology movement of some Third World countries. God is perceived as being meaningfully present among his poor and those who serve them, and this perception is lighting up the Gospel today for many people. As Carroll points out, the option for the poor commits the Christian Church to understanding and denouncing the mechanisms that generate widespread deprivation. 'It means challenging the prevalent structures in Western countries and the dominant international economic order. It is nothing less than a conversion from old alignments and narrow institutional concerns to a much less comfortable solidarity with the victims of injustice' (1987: 190).

The option for the poor also presents a challenge to educators. We must be prepared to question existing orthodoxies about the nature of educational knowledge and the justice of existing forms of selection and assessment. We should remember that all hegemonies, whether in politics, economics, religion or education, defend their position with arguments that in the last analysis are based on power and privilege. Is it too much to hope that something similar to the liberation theology movement can happen in the world of education, that in serving the disadvantaged, teachers can rediscover the dignity, purpose and satisfaction of being true professionals? Could it be that the school, for all its difficulties and doubts, is still one of the few credible human institutions, if only it is given freedom to serve disadvantaged communities in a meaningful community context? These are questions that arise from what we have said about the CDU's work with the disadvantaged and although the answers are neither certain or clear, we should at least feel that in raising the questions in the first instance the CDU deserves credit.

In the years that followed, initiatives relating to disadvantage and social justice were to remain at the heart of the CDU's work, as exemplified in various projects such as: the rehabilitation of long-term psychiatric patients, led by Colin Pollard; poverty issues in the curriculum, led by Rose Malone and Sandra Gowran; Irish for students with learning difficulties, led by Angela O'Connor; human rights, development, equality and intercultural education, led by Aidan Clifford, Karen O'Shea, Barbara Gill and Mary Gannon; the Youthreach programme for early school leavers, led by Liz O'Sullivan and Bernie Reilly at CDVEC level, and Dermot Stokes at national level; consumer education led by Cláir Ní Aonghusa, Miriam O'Donoghue and Mella Cusack; community literacy led by Michael Greene; and education and vocational preparation for unemployed adults, led at national level by Helen Keogh.

This chapter was devoted to a case study of the early efforts of the CDU in educational disadvantage. When we apply our four-fold rationale to the study, we find that the specification and implementation of aims and objectives is seldom emphasised. The curriculum content is usually experimental and practical rather than academic or abstract. Process and interaction are at a premium; the emphasis is on a holistic way of perceiving reality, based on everyday experience. Finally, curriculum as appraisal in the traditional mode is of little interest to people searching for more participative and less threatening forms of assessment.

In the following chapter we look at our second case study – education for a better environment.

CHAPTER 12

Saving the Environment

ENVIRONMENTAL CRISIS

In 1970 the International Union for the Conservation of Nature and Natural Resources (IUCN) called a conference on environmental education in Nevada, USA. At the time the term 'environmental education' was new and the conference's aim was to try to define it. It proved a difficult task and what emerged was not so much a definition as a broad description, which afterwards received worldwide acceptance. Environmental education is not a new discipline but rather a process, in which values are clarified and concepts, skills and attitudes developed in order to understand the complex pattern of relationships between a people's culture and their biophysical surroundings (IUCN 1970).

Environmental problems of one kind or another have been with us for a long time, but by the 1960s and early 1970s they had assumed an international dimension; there was now a growing awareness that the entire environment was at risk and something should be done to save it. Several factors contributed to this awareness. Firstly, there was the influence of the written word, as certain books and reports caught the public imagination. In 1962, Rachel Carson's *Silent Spring* graphically illustrated the effects of the misuse of synthetic pesticides and insecticides (Carson 1965). Other environmental prophets quickly followed like Paul Ehrlich, Ralph Nader and Barry Commoner (McCormick 1985). In 1972 two influential reports appeared within months of each other: *Blueprint for Survival*, published by the *Ecologist* magazine and *Limits to Growth*, prepared by the prestigious Club of Rome (Goldsmith *et al.* 1972; Meadows *et al.* 1972).

A second and more important factor was a succession of well-publicised environmental disasters. In 1966 a slag heap, poised above the Welsh mining village of Aberfan, collapsed and killed 144 people, 116 of them children in the local school. In 1967 the oil tanker *Torrey Canyon* spilled 875,000 barrels of oil into the English channel, an event followed two years later by a 77,000 barrel blow-out at Santa Barbara off the California coast. There have been far greater disasters since then, notably at Chernobyl in 1986, but *Torrey Canyon* and Santa Barbara were the first in a long line of such incidents and had a pronounced effect on public consciousness.

A third factor was the rise of popular protest groups. These began in the 1960s, with the hippies spearheading a movement that rejected the obsession of older generations with success and security. Materialism, technology, power, profit and unbridled economic growth were seen as some of the greatest threats to the environment. In 1970, this popular environmental movement received added impetus, when Earth Day on 22 April attracted thousands of people to various meetings and events – more than 11,500 across the United States alone. Earth Day convinced large numbers of the need for change and one of its legacies was the growing support for pressure groups such as the Sierra Club and Friends of the Earth.

A fourth factor was the influence of international organisations like IUCN, United Nations, OECD, Council of Europe and the European Community. For many people in Europe, the first awakening of environmental consciousness dates from European Conservation Year, inaugurated by the Council of Europe in 1970. Two years later the United Nations held a conference in Stockholm, which issued a memorable declaration alerting the whole world to the impending environmental crisis:

We see around us growing evidence of harm caused by human beings in many regions of the earth: dangerous levels of pollution

in water, air, earth and living things; major and undesirable distur-
bances to the ecological balance of the biosphere; destruction
and depletion of irreplaceable resources; and gross deficiencies in
the man-made environment of human settlement. (United Nations
1972)

The United Nations declaration has far-reaching implications: an
environmental crisis of such proportions is a terrifying comment on
the plight of humankind today. Human beings, in common with
other living species, dwell in a narrow band of land, air and water
on the surface of the third planet from the sun. But unlike other
species, we have developed technologies and social and economic
systems that consume vast amounts of resources, cause rapid and
bewildering changes and overload our environment with waste. We
even have the potential to destroy ourselves. The message of the
environmental movement is that the task of our generation is to pull
back from the brink by realising that by our decisions and actions
we not only determine the quality of our lives but we also have in
our hands the fate of future generations.

It was because of the above four factors that the modern environmental movement was born and, like many similar movements, it
sought to enlist the help of educators to further its aims. At first the
educational response was modest and limited to what was called conservation education, an area of the curriculum largely confined to
geography and biology. But from the 1970s onwards, especially with
the involvement of various international organisations, conservation
education was considerably broadened and became the equivalent of
a modern educational crusade. Environmental education had arrived.

EUROPEAN ENVIRONMENTAL NETWORK

In Chapter 8 we examined the idea of networking. It is an idea that
lends itself very readily to the environmental movement, especially
when it challenges governments and multi-national corporations.
A demand for free access to the information on which important

planning decisions are based and the liberty to protest against what are perceived to be environmentally dangerous actions are the hallmarks of modern environmental groups. A good example is Greenpeace, which brought environmental protest to world-wide attention in the early 1970s by sending its members into the American and French nuclear weapon zones 'to interfere with and provoke public protest against these test runs for Armageddon' (Lipnack and Stamps 1986: 51).

The idea of establishing a network for the promotion of environmental education throughout the European Community was first put forward in June 1974 by one of the European Commission officials in Brussels, Patrick Daunt. Daunt, who had been a headmaster in a comprehensive school in England before he joined the Brussels bureaucracy, designed a simple but attractive model. He proposed that the member states would sponsor a network of primary schools already actively engaged in environmental education. The network would have two aims: dynamic and seminal. The dynamic aim meant that the schools would improve the range and quality of the environmental education they provided by co-operating together and learning from each other's experience. The seminal aim intended the schools to become models of good practice that would be imitated by other schools in the European Community.

The pilot schools were to be designated by the national ministries for education in collaboration with their local education authorities and would be representative of different geographical and social situations in the Community. The age range would be upper primary and lower secondary, approximately nine to fourteen years. A full-time co-ordinating agency would be appointed to run the network's activities and a steering committee would be established comprising representatives from the national ministries and the Commission.

Daunt's plan represented a European model to achieve a European objective. It was also simple and concrete, and received a favourable hearing from the national ministries. The financial implications were clear-cut: since the schools chosen would already be actively engaged in environmental education, it was not foreseen that there would be any significant costs for the member states. The educational implications of the idea were attractive: the network aimed to build on creative work already in progress and to establish a base for the development of teaching methods, the creation and testing of learning materials, and the inservice training of teachers.

Having successfully mooted the idea of a network, Daunt decided to test it by commissioning a feasibility study. The study would have two elements: firstly examples of outstanding practice would be selected from all the member states, and secondly the views of key people in environmental education in Europe and elsewhere would be consulted. By December 1974 Daunt had decided who would carry out the study; he contacted the CDU and offered us the contract. In his letter to us, Daunt mentioned that he had heard favourable reports of its school-based approach to curriculum development and, as an ex-headmaster himself, he was probably in sympathy with this approach. Besides, the location of the CDU in a well-known university had not gone unnoticed. 'The TCD siège is good on the side of prestige', Daunt noted in a memorandum to his superior, Hywel Jones (Trant 1992: 339).

The CDU completed the feasibility report by April 1976. Its main purpose was to secure the support of ministry officials in the member states and in all cases this was given. There was a wide variety of views about the nature of the network and the pace of its development. Some ministries were in favour of pressing ahead as quickly as possible and two gave the names of the schools they wished to nominate; others were more cautious and felt that the idea should be implemented slowly. Another year, however, was to elapse before the Commission took the next step, and by this time the initiative had passed from Daunt to one of his colleagues, Richard Geiser. Geiser was convinced that the CDU would be the best institution in Europe to co-ordinate the network, since on the evidence of the feasibility report it had already established the necessary contacts. He decided to hold an inaugural meeting of representatives of the national ministries, a body which would also act as the network's steering committee. The slow machinery of issuing and answering invitations according to Community protocol then began and it was spring of the following year before preparations were finally completed. Eventually on 28 February 1977, the representatives of the national ministries, or national experts as they were officially called, assembled in Brussels and gave their blessing to the venture. The European Community Environmental Education Network (ECEEN) had come into being.

The network lasted for nearly ten years, from March 1977 to December 1986. It had two phases, the first for primary (1977–81) and the second for post-primary schools (1982–86). Each phase contained 30 schools and generated a variety of activities, materials, documents, discussions and not a few controversies. The network had three levels of membership: the pilot schools, the national experts and the Brussels officials. The linking agency was the CDU, which put together a co-ordinating team led by Danielle Durney and myself.* We regarded the teachers as the key people in the network and from the outset we consulted them on all vital decisions. In June 1977, representatives from all the participating schools met for the first time in Dublin and agreed an agenda for the following year. This democratic procedure was followed during the ten years of the network's existence and the annual programme of activities was basically the same as that agreed in Dublin – teacher and pupil exchange visits, project work on agreed themes, teacher seminars, production of materials, publication of a newsletter, *Milieu*, in five European languages, and dissemination of the network's experience.

The second level of membership comprised the national experts. The experts were seasoned bureaucrats who were inherently suspicious of utopian schemes and radical philosophies. They were happier with the traditional pyramid structure of authority than the informal and participatory style of networking. They tended to

---

* The other members of the team during the ten years of its existence included Kathleen Barrington, Patrick Colgan, Tony Crooks, Karen Dubsky, Nora Godwin, Lesley Haye, Joe Hogarty, John Moore, Brian Muldoon, Bernard O'Flaherty, Bride Rosney and Mariella Savoia.

exaggerate the distinctiveness of their individual educational systems, of which they were the jealous guardians. They were very different from the teachers, whom they regarded as occupying a lower place in the decision-making process. It was difficult, therefore, to reconcile the two groups; the experts as the representatives of the national governments were cautious and conservative while the teachers were filled with missionary zeal and often impatient at official constraint. The co-ordinating team tried to occupy the middle ground, endeavouring to reconcile each side with the other and both with the Brussels bureaucracy, which comprised the third level of the network's membership. It was not the happiest model for a creative networking experience.

Four years after its inception, the network came up against its first major crisis. The crucial question was whether it should have a second phase and, if so, what should happen to the schools of the first phase. A secondary question, but one of great importance to the co-ordinating team, was who would secure the contract for the new phase. These questions were debated with great interest by the network members but the key decisions were in the hands of one individual in Brussels, Claus Stuffmann. Like Daunt and Geiser before him, Stuffmann was a committed European who fully agreed with the ideology of the network. He was a warm supporter of the co-ordinating team and well-disposed towards their claim for a renewed contract. But the continuance of the network into a second phase was by no means a foregone conclusion because the budget had now become an increasing strain on the Commission's funds; nor could the co-ordinating team expect that they would be automatically reappointed. By this time the network had become more widely known and other European research institutions were interested in bidding for the role of co-ordinator.

By summer 1981 Stuffmann had made up his mind. At the network's annual seminar in Paris, he announced that there would be a second phase, which would last for four years and be devoted to post-primary schools. At the same time, the first phase schools were to be given a supplementary year to consolidate their work. He also announced, to the great satisfaction of the Dublin team, that the co-ordination of the network would remain with the CDU.

At the end of 1982, the network scene changed yet again; Stuffmann was now no longer in charge and his place had been taken by Arturo Monforte. Monforte had been associated with the network from the beginning but was never very enthusiastic about it. A lawyer by profession, his main role was to draw up the network's contracts and budgets, which, according to the Commission's regulations, had to be done on an annual basis. In these matters Monforte showed himself to be hard-headed but on the whole even-handed. He considered himself a cynical realist and once said that the main reason for the network's existence was an oversight on the part of the Commission.

Despite his cynicism, Monforte was prepared to play his part, once the network was an item on his agenda. He kept a tolerably good working relationship with the co-ordinating team right up to the end of the second phase in December 1986. But after that date things began to change. Speculation was again rife about the possibility of a third phase and who would be the co-ordinating agency. Notwithstanding the fact that the director of the Commission's environment service Anthony Fairclough had declared himself in favour of another phase and of retaining the Dublin team, Monforte refused to commit himself. The cost of the network, he argued, had now reached such a level that, according to the Commission's rules, a public tendering process would have to take place before a new co-ordination contract could be given.

In November 1985 matters came to a head when Fairclough announced a major initiative, called European Year of the Environment (EYE), which was to begin in March 1987. It now became clear that this would absorb all the time, energy and money that Brussels had available and consequently the future of the network was highly problematic. Throughout 1986 and for six months into 1987 the co-ordinating team tried to rally support in Brussels but to no avail. In July 1987 they finally gave up hope and disbanded.

The European network ended, to use T.S. Eliot's immortal line, not with a bang but a whimper. It was in many ways imperfect and did not match the classic model of network theorists. But it had its good moments and some of these happened in unexpected places. Ireland, for instance, a country where the network made little impact during its lifetime, afterwards developed a network of its own, as we shall see in the following section. There were similar examples in other member countries. We leave the final word to one of the national experts, Charles Linsingh from Belgium, who wrote me the following words of encouragement shortly before the network ended:

> I presume that like everyone else you must have moments of doubt about the future of environmental education. I have been reflecting on events and I believe that one should not underestimate the long-term result of the network's activity. Change occurs in ways that are hidden, unofficial and invisible from the outside. Sometimes I find myself being pleasantly surprised. (Trant 1992: 358)

THE NETWORK'S ACHIEVEMENTS

From the beginning, the network was never unduly concerned about defining environment education, being content to accept whatever interpretation each member state put forward. This was wise because it avoided the danger of becoming embroiled in arguments arising from different cultural and national viewpoints. Besides, there was no shortage of international guidelines on environmental education drawn up by bodies like the Council of Europe, IUCN and UNESCO. What was special about the network was the way it tried to translate these guidelines into practical curriculum realities. As one network report put it:

> We must be able to describe the different sets of conditions that make successful teaching about the environment possible. We must set about discovering what works best in the classroom and

why. We must be able to devise pilot projects if we are to get a clear idea of content and methodology. In a word, we need case studies of environmental education in action. (Trant 1992: 347)

Implementing and publishing these case studies was one of the achievements of the network. They comprised accounts of school projects, carried out under different conditions and over different lengths of time, varying from a week to an entire year. All the projects followed the same general methodology, which usually began with a study of the local area. This approach has a long tradition behind it that pre-dates by many years the modern environmental movement. It is the natural extension of the school curriculum and the place where much of the child's learning can be reinforced by direct experience. No matter where it is situated, be it a deprived city centre or a remote village in the mountains, the local area contains the essential elements that make up any society. It is a window into the affairs of humanity.

The central concept in local studies is recognising how different components of the local scene relate to each other to form unified patterns. This demands an integrated approach to learning because the immediate environment raises questions for which the traditional school subjects have no cut-and-dried answers; it stimulates the excitement of embarking on a study without always being able to predict the outcomes. The primary schools in the network usually had no difficulty with local studies, but in the secondary schools, where subject teaching was the norm, the integrated approach was more problematic. Nonetheless, the network contained many examples of interdisciplinary teaching and, although it was difficult to achieve, there can be no doubt about the radical nature of what was being attempted. I said as much at the time and I have not since changed my mind: 'No other feature of environmental education challenges the existing system of education as profoundly as the interdisciplinary approach. If it were to take hold in the curriculum, a radical shift in the education power structure would inevitably follow' (Trant 1986: 20).

The network also encouraged a problem-solving approach. The methodology is not unique to environmental education but the network put its own stamp on it:

> Problem-solving means being active and activity means movement and bustle. One cannot imagine a problem-solving approach being kept within the confines of the school. In many ways the school is an artificial world. Life is waiting outside with its raw edges and its unsolved problems. The world outside invites the school to examine real-life problems and contribute something, no matter how small, to their solution. The nature of the problem will dictate the type of activity, a polluted river to be analysed or the causes of traffic congestion to be studied. The problem itself will impose its own discipline and its own methodology. (Trant 1992: 351)

Even quite young pupils became involved in studying local problems. For instance, when the pupils of a small village school at Pesche in south Belgium learned that it was planned to build a dam on the local river that would result in the flooding of a large part of their valley, they resolved to become involved in the ensuing controversy between the authorities and citizens opposed to the dam. They decided on a project that would help them evaluate the controversy and at the same time make them aware of the complicated tensions between human needs and those of nature. In this way they would learn how to research environmental matters and organise their work independently. They would also come into contact with people with conflicting points of view.

The pupils first noted that people always need water, but how much? They examined the Council of Europe's water charter and other documents about the supply and demand for water. Discussion ranged from the broad implications to the effects on their own kitchens and bathrooms. In small groups, they discussed each other's reactions to the issues and then pinned up wall charts showing that people always seem to need increased supplies of water.

The next step was to consider the solution suggested by the water authorities in their own area – the construction of a dam that would submerge many acres of an undisturbed valley. As it happened, the pupils built a dam long before the authorities built theirs; a school-room model took shape putting a tangible form on the plan that was arousing local controversy. First the pupils unfolded a large-scale map of the area and then went out to observe the hills and hollows, the trees and homesteads, the fowl and fish that lay behind the contour lines. They gathered various posters, newspaper articles, reports and leaflets used to support or reject the building of the dam, and assessed them not only on their arguments and possible impact, but on their general content, type of language, layout, and use of words and colour. The inhabitants of the village were asked for their opinions, giving the pupils an opportunity to note how people per-ceive the same thing in different ways.

To compare their own model with those that really existed, the pupils spoke to people whose areas and lifestyles had already been changed by dam construction. Documents and maps showed the physical changes, while the local inhabitants were questioned on whether or not the water authorities had been faithful to the prom-ises made before the erection of the dams. The pupils drew up an illustrated gain and loss sheet – on one side the authorities' argu-ments for the dam and the benefits it would bestow, on the other the inevitable losses to the community.

The ability of the pupils to read maps and handle model-making materials came into play in the building of their model dam, some of them becoming teachers to their classmates as their own skills increased. One group provided a slide and tape show of wildlife in the threatened valley, writing and recording the text themselves and supplying the incidental music. The entire project ended with a school exhibition, to which the pupils invited their parents. The disputed dam was eventually built but not before the authorities had made concessions to the local community. For the pupils, the whole event was a rich learning experience (CDU 1979: 31–4).

ENVIRONMENTAL NETWORKING IN IRELAND

Ireland's involvement in the European environmental network was never strong. The Irish pilot schools themselves were committed and enthusiastic, but the problem lay at official level where little interest was shown. In the last year of the network's life, the co-ordinating team conducted a survey of all the pilot schools throughout the European Community and the picture that emerged from Ireland was not encouraging. Progress in implementing environmental ideas was slow and many teachers in the Irish pilot schools were conscious of the conservatism of their educational system. 'Time-tables remain unaltered', the survey noted, 'and in one case an environmental education project had to be carried out outside school hours' (Trant 1992: 358).

The Irish experience, however, had some positive aspects: in one instance the network played a significant role in helping to forge a bond between the educational systems in the two parts of the country, North and South. When the network began in 1977, the United Kingdom signified its willingness to participate by nominating two pilot schools, one in Hertfordshire and the other in Aberdeen. The co-ordinating team were keenly interested in having a school from Northern Ireland and they raised the matter with Daunt in January 1979. Daunt was willing to help and conveyed the request to the Department of Education and Science (DES) in London. He was shrewd enough to give the DES an acceptable reason for acceding to the request – the need to widen the UK involvement in the network in order to make it more representative of its major regions. Daunt anticipated that the result would be the inclusion of a Welsh as well as a Northern Irish school. The team were satisfied with the bargain, and so the plan went ahead. In June 1979 the DES duly invited both the Welsh and Northern Irish education authorities to nominate a pilot school each. The new schools were given associate as opposed to full membership but in practice there was little difference between the two. As far as the co-ordinating team was concerned, the important thing was that the road was now open to co-operate with their colleagues across the Border, led by Chief Inspector Tom Shaw.

The North/South dialogue that ensued was a good example of European co-operation. It gave rise to exchange visits between teachers and pupils on both sides of the Border and also led to the presentation of North/South bilateral reports at the network's annual seminars. The protocol of the European Community allowed for such bilateral co-operation, which became the basis of a North/South network in environmental education, known as European Action for the Environment (EAE).

EAE survived the demise of its European parent, and was supported by Co-operation North (later Co-operation Ireland) and by the two departments of education, North and South. It was co-ordinated by the CDU and comprised 28 post-primary schools, operating in seven groups. The activities comprised joint field-work projects conducted over two or three days. A survey carried out by the co-ordinating team in 1992 found that 90 per cent of the students enjoyed the activities. One noted: 'I think doing something for yourself is far better than listening to other people talking about it, so for me it was the most enjoyable thing.' Another commented: 'I enjoyed the trip to Co. Clare immensely. It was exciting meeting people for the first time. The trip was very interesting. I enjoyed the active schedule we had, along with the flora and fauna of the Burren' (CDU 1994: 38).

The co-ordinating team, comprising John Medlycott and myself, produced the bulletin *Environmental News* and organised an annual exhibition that was the highlight of the year's work. The 1992 exhibition was held in the Environmental Information Centre in Dublin and was visited by more than 25,000 people over a period of two weeks. It was opened by President Mary Robinson, with a speech that captured the essence of what we were trying to do:

The European Action for the Environment Project is about schools in both parts of the island of Ireland working together. Close collaboration, such as that which has taken place here, helps to focus young minds in the direction of the things which they share rather than of those which divide them. This places it at the heart of efforts to promote the European dimension in education in two member-jurisdictions of the European Community. The project is also about being European and concerned about the kind of place in which tomorrow's Europeans wish to live together. These students are learning to view their world in terms of its complexity of physical and human processes. They are encouraged to look upon that complexity without fear, recognising past differences and errors in attitudes to the environment, but building upon these in search of something better. (*Environmental News*, April 1992)

EAE was eventually merged with a North/South network on European Studies, thus ending the CDU's involvement. The merger was decided by officials from the two government departments of education on the pretext of administrative convenience. One suspects, however, that there were other reasons for their decision and that the CDU's approach to networking may not have fitted in with bureaucratic notions of control. The idea of environmental networking, however, did not disappear: in 1996 the CDU helped to create another network, again involving North/South co-operation in a European framework. The rationale and strategy were devised by Professor Adrian Philips from Trinity College in conjunction with Aidan Clifford and Barry Walsh from the CDU, and the nine participating Irish schools were located in Down, Dublin, Mayo and Wicklow. The network lasted for two years and produced a resource manual for teachers entitled 'Linking Environmental Education and Community Enterprises Programmes' (CDU 1998). The CDU is currently consolidating its environmental work through the Education for Sustainable Development programme.

TOWARDS A NEW STORY OF THE EARTH

The environmental crisis is still with us, the time-line to disaster is shorter and the stakes are higher. The threat of global warming, which the *New Scientist* (12 February 2005) called 'the most crucial scientific question of the twenty-first century', is more pressing than it was at the beginning of the environmental movement. Sleeping giants, of whom we are only dimly aware, are being awakened. Fifty years ago, the environment was a minority interest, something that only well-meaning nature-lovers were bothered about. Today the environment is the concern of everybody; it relates to every aspect of the world we share and depend on for survival. It influences everything we do, how we live, work and play. It affects our health, safety and the quality of our lives. We are all involved and all responsible for the problems of the environment. Our very survival demands that we co-operate in the search for solutions.

We are also becoming aware of the connection between what we once thought of as separate problems – poverty, famine and environmental degradation. Finding answers to these problems is no longer a question of charitable interest but a matter of justice. We have a duty to use the earth's resources wisely and ensure that they are shared fairly among people less fortunate than ourselves. We need a new environmental ethic to guide us and a new story of the earth to sustain it. We are proud of our modern scientific and technological achievements but we no longer have a foundation story that gives meaning to our presence in the world. In the west, we once had such a story, based on the Book of Genesis and interpreted in a framework of Greek philosophy and Christian theology. From the Middle Ages onwards, however, the story began to break down as Western science and religion parted ways. The story was discarded and never replaced and now we sense the loss. We have evidence in plenty that points towards a worldwide environmental crisis, but we need more than evidence; we need conviction and passion to motivate us. We need a story to believe in and a cause to serve.

In 1967 Lynn White wrote a controversial article in *Science* magazine on the causes of our ecological crisis. These, he argued, were not caused by the destructive power of modern science and technology as was often claimed, but from the exploitive attitude to nature that had been encouraged by Christianity. There were exceptions to this, White admitted, notably Francis of Assisi, 'the greatest radical in Christian history since Christ', who tried to depose human beings from being kings over creation and set up instead a democracy of all God's creatures. Whatever we may think of White's argument, his conclusion is worth pondering:

> Since the roots of our troubles are so largely religious, the remedy must be essentially religious, whether we call it that or not. We must rethink and re-feel our nature and destiny. The profoundly religious but heretical sense of the primitive Franciscans for the spiritual autonomy of all parts of nature may point a direction. I propose Francis as a patron saint for ecologists.

Rethinking and re-feeling our nature and destiny – what a challenge for educationalists. It will mean putting together a new story of creation by revisiting not only the Book of Genesis but also the creation myths of other cultures. It will mean listening to the astonishing stories that scientists are telling us about the formation of the universe, the birth and growth of planet earth, the evolution of life and the exploration of space. It will entail presenting all these stories imaginatively, illustrating and embellishing them with music, art, drama and poetry.

As well as a new story, we need a new environmental ethic, a sense of being the stewards and not the masters of creation, and an awareness of the need to walk lightly on the earth and leave few footprints behind. This ethic must be grounded in a personal value system, for it is not sufficient that we think globally, we must act individually and locally. Like charity, our environmental ethic should begin at home, in our own houses, schools and communities. We should also revisit the values of the Gospel – living simply and unostentatiously, sharing our goods with people in need and understanding that the meaning of our lives is to be found in a context that extends beyond our own interests.

To make all this a curriculum reality, we shall need the co-operation of scholars from different disciplines, a genuine interdisciplinary project. Thirty years ago, when I first became involved in the environmental movement, the notion of interdisciplinarity was only a discussion point, an ideal not a reality. Things are changing. People are realising that grave problems demand radical solutions and the time has come to sink individual preferences and prejudices into a common endeavour. Such thinking will be the basis for a worthwhile curriculum venture when economists, historians, scientists, sociologists, artists, musicians, philosophers, theologians and poets will join the ranks of the environmentalists. The project is already beginning to happen, and Lynn White would surely be pleased to learn that the Christian Churches are also joining in, even if their arrival is, as Seán McDonagh remarks wryly, 'a little breathless and a little late' (2004: 81). In the fractious world of education, the environmental challenge may yet be the catalyst that brings us all together.

This chapter presents a case study of one of the greatest curriculum challenges of our time – implementing a meaningful strategy in environmental education. We described the CDU's efforts in this field and how it applied its own experience of networking on the wider European stage. Looked at in the light of our curriculum rationale, the case study has the following characteristics. The early projects in the 1960s and 1970s had a strong emphasis on scientific content, but during the following years it became clear that the study of the environment should encompass as many disciplines as possible. Thus was born the interdisciplinary approach, based on an interactive and process-orientated methodology. The various international environmental bodies have tended to stress aims and objectives; at first these were stated in terms of content but later on attitudinal objectives made their appearance. Regarding appraisal, many educationalists have sought a place for environmental education in the public examination system, but this goal is more easily achieved within a mono-disciplinary rather than an interdisciplinary framework.

The next chapter contains our final case study and a new arrival on the curriculum scene: peace and reconciliation on the island of Ireland.

CHAPTER 13

Peace and Reconciliation

CONFLICT AND PEACE IN IRELAND

Peace and reconciliation is a comparatively new area that has not yet become established in the school curriculum. It is particularly relevant in Ireland, but it may be helpful to situate it first of all in an international context. In 1996, the UNESCO Commission on Education described the modern scene in sombre terms:

> The contemporary world is too often a world of violence that belies the hope some people place in human progress. There has always been conflict throughout history but new factors are accentuating the risk, in particular the extraordinary capacity for self-destruction humanity has created in the course of the twentieth century. Through the media, the general public is becoming the impotent observer, even the hostage, of those who create or maintain conflicts. Education has up to now not been able to do much to alleviate that state of affairs. Can we devise a form of education that might make it possible to avoid conflicts or resolve them peacefully by developing respect for other people, their cultures and their spiritual values? (1996: 91)

In the Commission's view, the resolution of conflict should be an integral part of the curriculum and should involve two things, getting to know other people and experiencing with them a shared purpose in life. The first implies an awareness of the diversity and similarities among all human beings, the second means finding common ground for co-operative activities:

> When people work together on rewarding projects that take them out of their usual routine, differences and even conflicts between individuals tend to fade into the background and sometimes disappear. People derive a new identity from such projects, so that it is possible to go beyond individual routines and highlight what people have in common rather than the differences between them. (1996: 93)

How do these principles apply to us in Ireland? We live on a small island of about 100,000 square kilometres. Our people for the most part speak the same language and the majority practise one form or other of the Christian faith. We share a common history of several hundred years of colonisation, and have benefited or suffered from the experience, depending on which point of view you take. We also share the same material culture and to an outsider we look alike, wear the same kind of clothes, eat the same kind of food, drive the same kind of cars and look at the same kind of television programmes, more or less.

Yet for all that Ireland is a divided country. A political border winds its tortuous way over 400 kilometres, dividing fields and farms, rivers and lakes, roads and railways. If you walk along this border, in some places you are in danger of losing your way and wandering unawares from one jurisdiction into the other. But the border is a symbol of a deeper division of minds and hearts among people who live together on the same island. Historically, we have had difficulties in living at peace with each other and we cannot agree on the way the island as a whole should be governed.

The reasons for these divisions have been explored at great length by politicians, church leaders, historians, sociologists, economists, psychologists, anthropologists, journalists, novelists, dramatists, poets and film makers. The volume of research and publications on what is sometimes called the Irish Question is enormous. There has been a huge outflow of scholarly work since 1969, the beginning of the current phase of 'The Troubles', so much so that the researcher Professor John Whyte was able to examine no fewer than 540 serious works which had appeared mostly between 1969 and 1990, all purporting to explain the reason for the conflict (Whyte 1990). Whyte published his book over a decade and a half ago and since then the flow of commentary has not abated.

The various explanations for the conflict in Ireland all lead us to conclude that there are three strands to the problem and therefore three related dimensions to its solution. We can approach the situation as a complex amalgam of three sets of relationships:

- firstly, within Northern Ireland, between two antagonistic communities, who live side by side in the same jurisdiction;
- secondly, within Ireland as a whole, between the people North and South, who have to share the same island;
- thirdly, between Ireland and Britain, who have to live together as neighbours and agree on the best way the island of Ireland is governed.

The core of the problem is essentially linked with the issue of identity; there are different ways in which people in Ireland express their identity and these ways can conflict with one another. Hence, the views and perceptions that people hold about each other are often expressed in hostile terms. The perceptions may or may not be grounded in reality; the important thing is that people hold them firmly, often passionately, and sometimes have been prepared to kill for them. This has led to a conflict going back through the centuries and has left a legacy of bitterness so deep that often no solution seemed possible. No matter what remedy was suggested there always seemed to be one group or other that remained intransigent. But despite all the intransigence, peace eventually came. In 1994 a shortlived cease-fire was declared. It was renewed in August 1996 and has lasted to the present. Today, hopes are high that an important corner has been turned, as all the political parties in Northern Ireland begin to co-operate together in a power-sharing executive.

The peace did not come about by accident. People over the years have laboured at laying the foundations. The conflict that endured for so long and engendered such enmity also brought a wide variety of reconciliation initiatives at all levels of society. Individuals and organisations from various parts of the country, North and South, have shown a willingness to come together to search for a basis of mutual understanding and co-operation. On the political level, one of the most notable achievements was the Good Friday Agreement of 1998, which was brokered by the British and Irish Governments with most of the political parties in Northern Ireland and ratified by national plebiscites, North and South. Although the agreement has been tested several times in the years following its signing, it still remains the basis of the peace process and for many people the best hope for what is still an uncertain future.

WIDER HORIZONS

For seventeen years, I was personally involved with one of the organisations that worked to build up the peace process in Ireland, the International Fund for Ireland (IFI). The Fund came into being against a very bleak background. The Troubles were in full swing and were causing economic deprivation as well as political instability. Violence and civil unrest were contributing to high unemployment, low investment and deterioration of the physical infrastructure in Northern Ireland and in many parts of the southern border counties. The closing of Border roads had cut off many towns and villages from their natural trading hinterlands and reduced cross-border contacts to a minimum. But despite the general gloom there were also signs of hope. In 1985, the Anglo-Irish Agreement was signed, emphasising the need for an awareness of reconciliation at all levels: cross-community in the North; cross-border between North and

South; and east-west between Britain and Ireland. Article 10 of the agreement recommended that a special fund be set up to promote the economic and social development of cross-community and cross-border relationships, especially with regard to 'those areas of both parts of Ireland which have suffered most severely from the consequences of the instability of recent years' (Hadden and Boyle 1989: 42). This was the context in which the Fund was born.

The IFI was established in 1986 by the British and Irish Governments with the overall aims of promoting economic and social advance and encouraging contact, dialogue and reconciliation between nationalists and unionists throughout Ireland. The two aims are interdependent: contact and dialogue are made possible through economic and social regeneration, and stability and prosperity are the prerequisites of reconciliation and mutual understanding. In this regard the motive for establishing the Fund was remarkably like that of the founding fathers of the European Economic Community: war between the nations of Europe can be prevented by building bonds of economic co-operation between countries. As the Fund's first chairperson expressed it:

> Nobody is so naive as to suppose that money alone can buy peace, or that money could, or should, be used to subvert deeply-held principles or beliefs. But discord, conflict and violence flourish in conditions of economic instability and disadvantage, and contributions to viable and self-sustaining growth may provide a foundation upon which a more peaceful and prosperous society can be built. (International Fund for Ireland 1987: 3)

The IFI is an organisation formally recognised in international law and attracts considerable international financial support, chiefly from the United States and the European Union but also from Canada, Australia and New Zealand. Although it derives from the Anglo-Irish Agreement, the Fund itself is not political and its independence is guaranteed by the British and Irish Governments. It has a management board of seven members appointed by the two

Governments with observers from the US, Canada, Australia, New Zealand and the EU, and also has its own secretariat based in Belfast and Dublin. The Fund implements a number of programmes in cross-community and cross-border co-operation in areas like urban and rural development, economic and community regeneration, tourism, technology and business enterprise. One of these programmes is called 'Wider Horizons'.

Wider Horizons aims at promoting employability and reconciliation through vocational preparation, training and work experience. Small groups of young people between 18 and 27 years are sent abroad for periods of up to two months to obtain relevant training and work experience, mostly in the US, Canada, Australia, New Zealand and the European Union. Each group usually comprises 21 people and has a cross-community and cross-border representation in the ratio of one third Northern Catholics, one third Northern Protestants and one third from the South.

The programme makes an impact on the lives of its participants by sending them into situations very different from what they are used to, and where they are challenged by others who know very little of the differences that divide them. Ensuring that each group functions as a unit requires preparation well in advance of the overseas experience. In practice, there are three distinct phases in the group's activities – a preparatory phase in Ireland, an overseas phase where the group undertakes its main task in a particular area of training and work experience, and a return phase where the participants reflect on their experience and apply the fruits of their training and work placements in securing a job and furthering their careers.

PROMOTING EMPLOYABILITY

If we are to build peace in Ireland today, we must look for things that unite rather than divide us; we must identify goals that we share and can be achieved through mutual assistance and co-operation. A good example of a shared goal is seeking to enhance the employment opportunities of disadvantaged young people. Here is a goal that everybody can agree on and that allows for flexibility and creativity in its implementation.

For two decades, Wider Horizons has helped 12,000 young people through vocational projects usually involving an overseas location. Estimating the extent to which their employability prospects have been improved is not easy and the programme does not claim in all instances to have found people jobs. What it does offer is the opportunity to live and work in a neutral surrounding, free from the stress and negative influences of the home environment, where the young people can more easily gain work competencies and develop the personal qualities that make them better equipped to find and keep a job when the project is over.

Employability skills can be broadly divided into two kinds, general and specific. General skills comprise ability to communicate, willingness to take initiative, self confidence, mobility, motivation, responsibility, willingness to learn and relate to others, self-discipline and the ability to present oneself well. Specific skills relate to particular work sectors and processes. Judging from the responses from both leaders and participants, there is evidence that Wider Horizons has had a pronounced effect on the general employability skills of its participants, especially on their personal and social competencies. As one project leader put it:

> Where there is structural unemployment, the skills that enable you to get and keep a job are personal skills rather than vocational competencies – the ability to sell yourself, to convince employers that you are the best person for the job. Young people who have been through Wider Horizons are much better at getting and keeping jobs because of their understanding of the world of work and their role in it. (Trant and McSkeane 1994: 21)

The programme has been particularly successful in improving the work motivation of young people from employment black-spots, where a large percentage of the workforce can be unemployed. This point was noted by several project leaders and the following comment from one of them is typical:

> Wider Horizons reinforces the young people's desire to get a job back home. They want to work. Before they go abroad, they just don't think they're going to get jobs. They don't see themselves as employable. What happens when they go out there is they start to see themselves as workers. I think it's because their personal effectiveness is improved. There was Michael, he didn't want to go at all. He wanted to stay at home and be cocooned. When I saw him over in Toronto, he was a different person. He was out working four days a week, you see. That affects a person's self-esteem. (Trant and McSkeane 1994: 74–5)

For many disadvantaged young people, the experience of having a real job overseas alters their self-image and their hope for the future. In addition, the challenge of living away from home accelerates the process of maturing, something that is reported by both leaders and participants. When the leaders were asked to specify the nature of the personal changes they observed in the young people, almost all of them noted an improvement in maturity, independence and communication skills. The next most frequently mentioned change was attitude to work: the young people return from their projects in a more positive and hopeful frame of mind about their future careers. This corroborates the impressions of the participants themselves, as summed up by one young woman:

> I never thought I would be able to get a job but you have to go out and hunt for one. The effect that working in Canada had on me is now I think you can do anything if you just try and if you get the chance. (Trant and McSkeane 1994: 76)

Have we any hard evidence that Wider Horizons is achieving its employability aim? An evaluation conducted through questionnaires and interviews over a period of three years and involving over 700 participants showed encouraging results. The evidence from the questionnaires indicated a trend from part-time to full-time and from unskilled to skilled employment. The trend was evident in all age groups and education levels and seemed attributable to the Wider Horizons experience. The project leaders and administrators also considered that the employability targets were being met. As one of them put it:

> Many who join the projects have had experience of temporary, seasonal and 'under the counter' jobs. These young people are encouraged to take relevant qualifications and aim at higher quality work placements. (Trant *et al.* 2002: 86)

RECONCILIATION

When we turn to the reconciliation aspect of Wider Horizons we find plenty of scope for debate. The targets here are much harder to measure, possibly because there is a greater difficulty in defining them in the first place. In broad terms it can be said that bringing people together from different sides of the divide in a meaningful, purposeful and non-threatening way has been a very beneficial experience. There is plenty of evidence to show that participants genuinely look beyond the stereotypes they formerly held of each other and in many cases they form close friendships.

In the early days of Wider Horizons, any attempt to introduce reconciliation activities into the projects was looked at warily. The topic was considered an explosive one and not many project leaders felt competent to handle it. The best approach, it was felt, was an indirect one where all that was needed was to bring a group of Northern Catholics and Protestants and Southerners together to carry out a challenging project overseas. Reconciliation would then happen of its own accord. It has to be said in retrospect that there was some wisdom in this approach and positive relationships among the participants did indeed result and in many cases flourished. But there was also a hit and miss element about the whole affair and, although the projects usually went well, we never really knew why.

With the passing of time, four things emerged in the programme's approach to reconciliation. Firstly, the process was reckoned to be too important to let it happen as it were by accident. It was decided, therefore, that the project leaders, as part of their preparation, should take a leadership training course that included reconciliation skills. In some ways, this turn of events was forced by the young people themselves who persisted in raising cross-community and cross-border issues during the projects. In these leadership courses, outside expertise is often availed of, but the best trainers are from within the programme itself – experienced project leaders who have learned their skills through practice.

Secondly, it is now generally accepted that reconciliation should be understood in a broad manner, encompassing any issue that tends to divide people; this includes racism, homophobia and gender issues as well as sectarianism, which are all seen as expressions of prejudice. A debatable point is whether the different forms of prejudice are related. Most project leaders feel they are and regard the broad approach as the most acceptable to the young people themselves.

Thirdly, it is becoming clear that reconciliation, like employability, should be based on the development of the whole person. Prejudice is especially difficult to combat when the individuals concerned are themselves vulnerable, fearful and disadvantaged. Hostile attitudes and behaviour towards others derive as much from personal insecurity and low self-esteem as from ignorance and lack of contact. A similar situation exists with regard to employability where studies have found that the young people most likely to be chronically unemployed have usually very little belief in themselves or in their future. Consequently, personal development is probably the most important contribution that the programme is making to the development of both reconciliation and employability.

Fourthly, Wider Horizons is lending itself particularly well to what could be called institutional reconciliation. The programme comprises not only individual participants but also the various organisations to which they belong and identify with, such as training centres and community and youth groups. A typical Wider Horizons project will demand co-operation from a number of organisations, and this co-operation extends in two directions: cross-community and cross-border. Every project is based on organisations that cater for Northern Catholics and Protestants and for people from the South. Several observers of the conflict in Northern Ireland have pointed to the close connection between the reconciliation of individuals affected by the conflict and the reconciliation of the institutions with which they identify. Individual and institutional reconciliation go hand in hand (Farren and Mulvilhill 2000).

The entire programme rests on an ethos of partnership that transcends religious and political divisions. The partnership ethos is reflected in the Wider Horizons executive, which is made up of representatives of the national training agencies, the Department of Employment and Learning in the North and FÁS in the South, along with members of the Fund's secretariat and the programme's evaluators (A. Trant, J. Medlycott, W. Hurst and S. Morrow). Partnership is something that Wider Horizons has inherited from the Fund itself. Under the IFI banner, all kinds of institutions – State and voluntary, North and South – have come together over the past two decades to develop and implement a range of projects. This would not have happened at the time it did if the Fund had not been in place to lead the way for other cross-border bodies to follow.

Is Wider Horizons succeeding in its task of reconciliation? The evaluation, already referred to, attempted to answer this question by using three independent measures: friendship and social contact between the participants; their perceptions of each other's community; and an internationally recognised measure of tolerance and prejudice. All three measures corroborated one another in showing positive gains. In measuring prejudice and tolerance, the evaluation used the Bogardus Social Distance Scale, which required the participants to choose one from seven levels of social distance. They were asked if they were prepared to accept someone

- as part of their family, for example through marriage;
- as a close friend;

- as a next-door neighbour;
- as a work companion;
- as a citizen of their country;
- as a visitor only to their country;
- as someone who should be expelled from their country.

In this way it was possible to discover the perceptions of the participants of each other's religious, social and political differences. The overall results of the survey indicated an increase in tolerance, between Catholics and Protestants in the North and between Northerners and Southerners in general.

Perhaps more revealing than the figures were the comments made by the participants about each other. Typical expressions used were: 'just like us', 'do the same things', 'ordinary', 'normal' and 'no different'. These kinds of comments were made by 38 per cent of the Northern Protestants (increasing to 51 per cent by the end of the projects) and 42 per cent of the Northern Catholics (increasing to 44 per cent). One participant illustrated the change of attitude in the following words:

> My attitude towards Catholics was one of hate. All I wanted was to hurt them but now I don't care. They are just like me and I have some close Catholic friends. (Trant *et al.* 2002: 41)

It should be noted that the evaluation also looked at racial attitudes among the participants and reached some less comforting conclusions. The evidence suggests that racial prejudice was greater than cross-community or cross-border prejudice. A similar result was recorded in a research report by Connolly and Keenan, who found that people in Northern Ireland are about twice as likely to be unwilling to accept and mix with members of minority ethnic communities than they would be with those from the two main religious traditions (Connolly and Keenan 2000). Other studies have shown that racist attitudes in the South are also a problem. It would seem then that the scope of education for peace and reconciliation will have to be widened to meet the growing challenge of racist prejudice both North and South.

The work of reconciliation is laborious and demanding, and requires patience and constant effort. We must not be surprised or unduly upset when we meet with setbacks. For instance, a research project at the University of Ulster showed that, despite the improvement in community relations between Northern Catholics and Northern Protestants over the period 1989–99, there was a downward trend over the following two years in attitudes towards living and working together and towards mixed religious schools (Hughes and Donnelly 2002). We should take heart, however, at the thought that today there are many people and organisations in Ireland, North and South, engaged in the work of reconciliation and peace building, and the sum total of their endeavours can make a difference. Notable among these organisations is the EU sponsored Peace and Reconciliation Programme, which since 1994 has promoted a great number of peace initiatives, including a citizen education project led by Aidan Clifford and Karen O'Shea from the CDU.

We must also be patient and persistent in our reconciliation efforts and be prepared for the long haul. The Franco-German Exchange Programme, which has reconciliation aims not unlike those of Wider Horizons, is now forty years in existence and some commentators report that it has made a substantial contribution towards promoting good relations between the two countries involved. But this was only discerned after a generation of young people had been given the experience of participating. The lesson for us in Ireland is that we should work towards establishing permanent national structures for peace and reconciliation to underpin the achievements of the pilot programmes and ensure continuity when these are eventually terminated.

Finally, can we ever be sure that our efforts towards reconciliation are succeeding? We leave the last word on this difficult question to a Wider Horizons project leader:

How do we know that reconciliation is happening? We know it is happening when people can be themselves and talk about themselves and their own background without fear, when they understand themselves and where they are coming from, face up to what they do not know about others and learn to regard them as human beings like themselves. (Trant *et al.* 2002: 83)

This chapter concludes our third and final case study of curriculum in action. When we examine the study on the basis of our curriculum rationale, we note the following. In the vocational preparation and training aspect of Wider Horizons, aims, objectives, outputs and appraisal are at a premium. There is considerable variety in the content of the various projects, but little emphasis on process or interaction. In the reconciliation aspects, on the other hand, the order is reversed: interactive activities are considered to be vital, content remains varied, but aims, objectives, outputs and appraisal are not a priority.

Our final chapter returns to the question of values and selects three as a basis for an educational vision.

Conclusion

A Vision for Education

REGARD FOR TRUTH

This book opened with a chapter on values in the curriculum and, throughout the following chapters, we looked at values of one kind or another; they are the key issues today not just in education but in society at large. The story we tell through the curriculum is a story about the good life – the things that are worth knowing and striving for. The curriculum is an attempt to make sense of our world, internal and external, and to enable us to make choices about what is worthwhile. There are many worthwhile things and many values that could be emphasised, but if I were asked to pick those that underpin my own vision for education, I would select three – a regard for truth, the ability to live together and a commitment to use our talents in the service of others. These three values sum up what the book is about.

In his Nobel Prize speech in 1970, Alexander Solzhenitsyn quoted one of his native Russian proverbs, 'one word of truth outweighs the whole world.' In Russia, he said, the most popular proverbs are about truth; they express the people's experience, often bitter, with astonishing force. In Gaelic too, we have proverbs about truth, one of which Solzhenitsyn would have liked: bíonn an fhírinne searbh – truth can have a bitter taste. In Ireland today, truth indeed can have a bitter taste. We are bemused by the scandals that have come to light, but more so by the hypocrisy of some of some of our leaders who have tried to hide them. We are now inclined to treat statements from public figures with caution if not cynicism; spin is the in-thing and anyone who tells the unvarnished truth can be regarded as naïve.

A regard for truth, and the conviction that truth exists even though it is often difficult to find, should be a primary value at all levels of education. We never fully arrive at the truth but the quest for it is what matters. The search is perennial and every age has posed its own questions about how to find it. Seven centuries ago a certain student asked one of the great minds of the age, Thomas Aquinas, for advice on the subject. We know little enough about the student, except that his name was John and he was young, eager and perhaps impatient to find some clever technique through which he could gain speedy access to the treasures of knowledge. Aquinas took him seriously and wrote a reply that is still relevant. Most of the letter is not devoted to the specifics of learning at all, but to a much broader issue – how we should live. If Brother John wanted to arrive at the truth, he must not fling himself headlong into the ocean of knowledge but go gently by way of the little streams – *per facilia ad difficilia*, difficult matters should be learned by mastering the easy ones first.

What Aquinas was advocating comes as no surprise to any practising teacher. If we wish to direct our students on the road towards truth, they must practise an ordered and disciplined way of going about things. True learning rarely happens through instantaneous flashes of insight – although these do come from time to time – but through a gradual process of understanding. We are not angels but a mixture of body and spirit, and in order to learn we have to use all our powers. That takes time and effort. Learning can be a joy, but can also cause pain and tears; a disciplined way of life is necessary. The distinctive virtue of the student is what Aquinas calls *studiositas*. This, as the modern commentator on Aquinas, Victor White, reminds us, is not – contrary to what we might suppose – a matter of fortitude but of temperance:

> It is not, that is to say, a bold aggression against difficulties and obstacles, an affair of wet towels, clenched teeth, furrowed brow,

but contrariwise a bridling, a controlling, a directing of desire – of the innate desire of the intellect to know. (1947: 17)

Learning is slow, laborious work that cannot be done in a hurry through cramming or mechanical techniques. That is why Aquinas began his letter to Brother John with advice on how he should live rather than how he should study. It was probably not what the young man wanted to hear, that he should be slow to speak, keep to the solitude of his cell, commune with the Almighty, guard against unnecessary distractions and be on good terms with his fellow students. To our modern ears, all this may sound somewhat strange. We have lost the taste for silence and probably consider the study habits of medieval monks no longer appropriate. But we are in danger of forgetting that a quiet and reflective mind is one of the greatest benefits of education and in order to learn we must first listen and pay attention. 'The development of the faculty of attention', notes Simone Weil, 'forms the real object and almost the sole interest of studies' (Weil 1959: 66). The ability to give our undivided attention to people and things is a rare gift. 'It is almost a miracle, it is a miracle. Nearly all those who think they have this capacity do not possess it' (1959: 75).

Today we are pressurised by masses of information and subtle and persistent propaganda to accept uncritically the myriad of messages directed at us. Never before, perhaps, has there been such a need for the educated mind, which can reflect on the difference between knowledge and opinion. Those who wish to discover the truth, Aquinas once said, must be able to listen to their doubts. The attainment of truth is like unravelling a knot; before untying it, you must first examine it. In the same way, if you do not examine your doubts, you will not know where you are going and probably will never get there.

A regard for truth demands the courage to make mistakes and also the courage to admit we have made them. The way to truth seldom coincides with the right answer that is so much esteemed in the traditional school examinations; the opposite is more likely. Examinations are the accepted criteria for measuring academic success but truth has little to do with such success. Success is too often an illusion, an onlooker's word from the side-lines of life. People who come to grips with life and achieve something worthwhile come to realise that difficulties and failure are often more valuable than success.

The quest for truth is like setting out to climb a difficult mountain. The closer we approach, the more we discover – deep ravines and broad valleys, formidable cliffs and gentle slopes, blinding rain and breathtaking vistas. We are continually surprised at the mountain's many faces. Truth, too, has many faces which can take a lifetime to explore – scientific truths, historical truths, aesthetic truths, to mention only three. But the scientist, the historian and the artist are climbing the same mountain, they are all striving to catch a glimpse of the same truth. It is this vision that should underlie the entire educational process and if our teachers give us a glimpse they will have done us a great service.

LEARNING TO LIVE TOGETHER

The ability to live together is my second overarching educational value. Human beings, Aristotle once said, are creatures who are meant to live in a community context. But genuine communities that enable their members to respect and care for one another are rare. They should be places where people feel secure, where their lives have meaning and where they feel a bond of friendship with each other. Above all, communities should be places where communication takes place; this is the defining mark of any community, particularly a learning community, which is what a school is supposed to be.

One of the problems of our age is the depersonalised nature of many of our institutions, which are often too large and bureaucratic to allow any meaningful human interaction. Schools are no exception. The dominant model of schooling remains custodial with the result that schools in some respects still resemble a nineteenth century factory or prison. This can result in alienation which in turn has a negative effect on learning. Real learning only takes place when teachers and students regard each other as human beings, not as people trapped in their roles. Education should be a meeting of minds and a process of personal encounter.

Community is an overused term today and its application to education has probably not been helped by designating some schools in particular as community schools. Every school should be a community school but the exploration of the real meaning and possibilities of the community school is the great debate that never took place in Irish education. David Hargreaves argues that a community school worthy of the name should have four characteristics: first of all, there is the promotion of democracy within the school community itself – a greater sharing in decision-making between teachers and pupils alike; secondly, a greater participation in the affairs of the school by people from outside – parents, employers, local residents and people from all walks of life; thirdly, the multi-purpose use of school buildings by adults and pupils alike – the school could even be part of a community centre, open every day and providing a wide range of educational and recreational facilities; and lastly, the idea of a community-oriented curriculum where a major part of the school's work is organised around community themes, interests and needs (1982: 114–7). Of the four characteristics, the last according to Hargreaves is the most important and most difficult to achieve.

From my own experience in Ballyfermot, I would agree with him. A community-oriented curriculum will find itself at odds with conformity. If the curriculum is to relate meaningfully to the needs of its students, there will have to be differences between one school and another. We are talking here about differences of approach, not differences in standards. We all want to uphold standards but not by imposing a grey uniformity or, as Patrick Pearse once said, by having all the students of Ireland read the same textbooks each night. The ideal of the community school, as we pointed out earlier, is now giving way to the marketplace image of the school, and aspirations towards social solidarity and the common good are regarded as utopian.

My hope is that more schools today would fashion themselves into communities, where the students feel at home. At the end of the nineteenth century, John Dewey wanted schools to revive some of the traditional crafts that were disappearing from the American home. A century later another American educationalist Jane Roland Martin argued that the home itself is now under threat and the school should come to the rescue by cultivating the traditional domestic virtues of care, concern and connection (Mulcahy 2002). I think she is right. We are educating young people for a world that is rapidly changing, using structures that themselves have not changed for generations. We are pouring new wine into old wine-skins. Jerome Bruner, after many years of pioneering work, once remarked: 'If I had it all to do over again, and if I knew how, I would put my energies into re-examining how the schools express the agenda of society, and how that agenda is formulated and translated by the schools. That, it seems to me, would be the properly subversive way to proceed' (1983: 198).

LEADERSHIP AS SERVICE

I once spent a year teaching in a school recognised by the Headmasters' Conference in England as a public school. This meant that the school, although not in England itself, belonged to the prestigious inner ring that included Eton, Harrow, Winchester and the like. My time there was not a happy one and I was glad in the end to escape. Looking back on the experience now, I realise that the main reason for my unhappiness was the elitist notion of leadership that the school was trying to foster in its students, a colonial model fitted for the training of military officers and administrative mandarins. No wonder my rebellious Irish instincts were aroused.

This is not to say that leadership is not an important issue in education, but much depends on the way we define it. Leadership is a worthy ideal provided we move on from elitist ideas to a wider, more inclusive understanding of the term that fits in better with our modern concept of democracy. In Chapter 1 we saw how John Dewey built his theory of education around his concern for democracy. He knew what would happen if education failed to uphold our democratic way of life: we would be left with the shadow not the substance of democracy. Today we may be nearer to Dewey's prediction than we care to admit. Abraham Lincoln's aspiration of a government of and for and by the people is far from being realised. What passes for democracy is often no more than the control of the electorate through a subtle manipulation of the media, not far short of propaganda. Plato's conception of a society based on few leaders and many followers is now a reality.

On one occasion in my time in Ballyfermot, I invited a local clergyman to visit the school and see for himself how we were implementing our comprehensive education programme. He was a kind man and took the invitation seriously. I asked various members of the staff to make presentations about their work, to which our visitor listened patiently. At the end of the proceedings he thanked us and then gave his parting shot: 'It's all very fine, but where are the hewers of wood and drawers of water?' In a way, he was right: we had not clarified our minds about the vital issues of class and power in society – who would become the leaders and who were destined to remain followers.

For years afterwards I pondered this question and now at the end of my life as an active educator I am proposing a tentative solution. The kind of leadership that we should foster in our students should have nothing to do with elitism – it should be for everybody. But we have to think out its meaning. I would now rather call it a personal commitment to use our gifts and resources to help make this world a better place to live in. Such a commitment does not happen overnight; it has to be cultivated carefully over time like one of the classical virtues. And virtue, we should remember, was defined by the Greeks as the ability to perform a good action continuously with ease and grace.

For us, 'action' should be the operative word. Education is not solely about thinking and feeling, it is also about doing. The various curriculum initiatives we discussed in previous chapters, like saving the environment, caring for the deprived and striving for peace and reconciliation, would all be meaningless without an action-oriented dimension. Thinking and doing should complement one another: we should think out our action and act out our thought. Our aim as educators should be to invite everybody, young and not so young, to develop their individual talents with two things in mind: to fulfil themselves as persons and help other people do the same. That is the kind of leadership we need today, where people are encouraged to fulfil their potential, pursue their aspirations and follow their convictions in the service of others. It will demand courage, persistence and belief in ourselves. It will also mean the readiness to stand on our own feet, have a go and lead through example. At the end of the day, leadership is a moral quality not a management strategy. No amount of management on its own will ever solve the problems our society is now grappling with. Leadership must always have a vision of what people are capable of achieving through discovering their own talents and abilities. Irenaeus of Lyons, one of the fathers of the early Christian Church, put it very well many centuries ago: 'The glory of God is a human being fully alive.'

HOPE FOR THE FUTURE?

Up to comparatively modern times, western society transmitted its values through what were traditionally called the virtues. The virtues have a long history, going back as far as the epics of heroic society as portrayed for example in Homer and the old Irish sagas. They were refined in the classical period of ancient Greece, particularly by Plato and Aristotle and by dramatists like Sophocles, Aeschylus and Euripides. They were later modified by the influence of Christian theology and moral philosophy. The tradition of the virtues has lasted down to our day but is now greatly weakened, if not in decline. Since the time of the Enlightenment in the eighteenth century, the broad moral consensus in Western culture about the nature of the virtues has broken down and now we have reached a stage where ethical standards are more or less relative.

This predicament presents teachers with a dilemma. They are expected to play a major role in transmitting values to the next generation, but there is no agreement any more on what these values are.

'Teachers', Alasdair MacIntyre remarks, 'are the forlorn hope of the culture of western modernity' (1987: 16). They are like an advance party sent on a dangerous mission whose success we have to depend on but which we know in our hearts is bound to fail. The reason for the failure, MacIntyre argues, is the fatal breakdown in the continuity of the moral tradition of the West. There is no longer agreement about the fundamental nature of a human being or what human happiness consists of. There is no basis any more for practising the virtues.

In the past the crucial point about the virtues was that they required a social context in which to practise them. Homer portrayed the virtues against the background of a warrior society which demanded qualities like strength, courage and loyalty to one's friends. Aristotle painted a picture of the Athenian gentleman, magnanimous, restrained, knowledgeable and with a clear conception of what was his due in the Greek city state of the fourth century BC. Aquinas described the virtues in the context of medieval Christendom, with the theological virtues of faith, hope and charity at the apex. But, in today's world, where can we find a social context and a moral consensus that is sufficiently coherent to act as a suitable medium for the transmission of values? The family is under siege, the churches are in retreat and the modern state is at best an uneasy accommodation of adversarial interests.

Do teachers and schools give us any hope that values can be passed on in a meaningful manner from one generation to the next or must we share MacIntyre's pessimism? MacIntyre himself, despite his despondency, sounds a faint note of hope. In an earlier work (1981), he pointed out that ours is not the only age that has had to face a break in its cultural and moral traditions with a consequent crisis in its value system. In the fifth century AD, when the Roman Empire was crumbling and the Dark Ages were casting their shadow on Europe, men and women were forced to look elsewhere for the continuation of civilisation and a moral tradition:

What they set themselves to achieve instead, often not recognising fully what they were doing, was the construction of new forms of community within which the moral life could be sustained, so that both morality and civility might survive the coming ages of barbarism and darkness. If my account of our moral condition is correct, we ought also to conclude that for some time now we too have reached that turning point. What matters at this stage is the construction of local forms of community within which civility and the intellectual and moral life can be sustained through the new dark ages which are already upon us. (1981: 244–5)

MacIntyre was referring to the rise of the Christian monastic movement which helped to preserve European civilisation after the fall of the Roman Empire. The situation today is just as grave, although the danger is less obvious:

This time, however, the barbarians are not waiting beyond the frontiers; they have already been governing us for quite some time. And it is our lack of consciousness of this that constitutes part of our predicament. We are not waiting for a Godot, but for another – doubtless very different – St Benedict. (McIntyre 1981: 245)

Can our schools and colleges today be communities within which civility and the intellectual and moral life can be sustained? My hope is they can, but first of all teachers will have to recover the sense of their own professionalism. Teachers like to think of themselves as professionals and sometimes envy the status, power and wealth of the 'strong' professions like medicine and law. But the essence of a profession, as the original meaning of the word indicates, is a pledge to serve people in need. True professionals are able to transcend considerations of personal gain and prestige in the interests of people who need them most. It is not altogether surprising to find that some of our best teachers are working in disadvantaged situations where money and prestige are not the motivating force.

A professional is also characterised by two other things: specialist knowledge and skill, and autonomy of judgement and action. In the teacher's case, the three characteristics of a professional find their focus in the understanding and operation of the curriculum. The essence of the curriculum, as this book has tried to show, is that it represents our attempt to understand the world we live in. Ultimately we depend on teachers to make education relevant to the needs of the people they profess to serve and to change the curriculum when these needs are being neglected. That is the only hope we have, forlorn or otherwise. We have to trust our teachers, engage with them as human beings, encourage them to take risks, rejoice in their successes, sympathise with their failures, help them renew their energies and inspiration and reassure them of the worth of their calling. To paraphrase Lawrence Stenhouse, it is teachers who in the end will transform the world by helping their students to understand it.

Bibliography

Adler, M. (1982), *The Paideia Proposal: An Educational Manifesto*, London: Collier MacMillan.

Akenson, D.H. (1975), *A Mirror to Kathleen's Face: Education in Independent Ireland*, London: McGill: Queen's University Press.

Arendt, H. (1977), *Between Past and Future*, London: Penguin.

Aristotle, *Ethics* (translated by J.A.K. Thompson, 1955), Harmondsworth: Penguin Classics.

Assessment Reform Group (1999), *Assessment for Learning*, Cambridge: University of Cambridge School of Education.

Augustine of Hippo, *Confessions* (translated by R.S. Pine-Coffin, 1961), Harmondsworth: Penguin Classics.

Barber, N. (1989), *Comprehensive Schooling in Ireland*, Dublin: Economic and Social Research Institute.

Black, P. and D. Wiliam (1998), *Inside the Black Box: Raising Standards through Classroom Assessment*, London: School of Education, King's College.

Black, P., C. Harrison, C. Lee, B. Marshall and D. Wiliam (2003), *Assessment for Learning: Putting it into Practice*, Maidenhead: Open University Press.

Brenan, M. (1941), 'The Vocational Schools', *Irish Ecclesiastical Record*, 5th series, vol. 57: 113–27.

Brennan, N. (1987), 'Conference Overview' in T. Crooks and D. Stokes (eds.), *Disadvantage, Learning and Young People*, Dublin: Curriculum Development Unit.

Bruner, J. (1966), *Towards a Theory of Instruction*, Massachusetts: Harvard University Press.

Bruner, J. (1977), *The Process of Education,* Cambridge, Massachusetts: Harvard University Press.

Bruner, J. (1983), *In Search of Mind: Essays in Autobiography,* London: Harper Colophon Books.

Bruner, J. (1996), *The Culture of Education,* Massachusetts: Harvard University Press.

Burke, E. (1974), 'A Study of an Educational Programme for Young Offenders, Undertaken at St Patrick's Institution, Dublin', unpublished M.Litt. dissertation, Trinity College, University of Dublin.

Butterfield, H. (1949), *Christianity and History,* London: Bell.

Callan, J. (1974), 'Behavioural Objectives and Curriculum Planning', unpublished M. Ed. dissertation, NUI Maynooth.

Callan, J. and E. Hillard (1984), 'Final Report from External Evaluation on the Early School Leavers Project, Dublin 1979–1982' in *Preparation of Young People for Work and Facilitation of their Transition from Education to Working Life,* Dublin: Department of Education.

Carroll, D. (1987), *Towards a Story of the Earth: Essays in the Theology of Creation,* Dublin: Dominican Publications.

Carson, R. (1965), *Silent Spring,* Harmondsworth: Penguin.

Casey, M. (1982), 'North Inner City Community College', unpublished document, Dublin Inner City Education Papers, Curriculum Development Unit Archives.

Cassidy, A. (1997), 'The Junior Certificate Elementary Programme: A Framework for Change in the Junior Cycle', *Issues in Education: ASTI Education Journal,* vol. 2: 155–62.

Castiello, J. (1962), *A Humane Psychology of Education,* New York: Loyola University Press.

Central Advisory Council for Education, England (1963), *Half our Future,* London: HMSO.

CDVEC Board of Studies (1969), 'Minutes of Meeting 28 March, 1969', unpublished document, CDVEC Head Office, Ballsbridge, Dublin.

CDVEC Board of Studies (1971), 'Report of the Sub-Committee on the Intermediate and Group Certificate', unpublished document,

Steering Committee Papers, Curriculum Development Unit Archives.

CDVEC (1979), 'Report of Subcommittee on Inner City Education and Training', unpublished document, Dublin Inner City Education Project Papers, Curriculum Development Unit Archives.

CDVEC (1982), 'Minutes of CDVEC Meeting 15 April 1982', unpublished document, CDVEC Head Office, Ballsbridge, Dublin.

Colley, G (1966a), 'The Comprehensive School', *Sunday Press,* 9 January 1966.

Colley. G. (1966b), 'Aspects of Comprehensive Education', Address to the Carlow Group of Pax Romana in the Crofton Hotel, Carlow, 10 March 1966, unpublished text, Ballyfermot Papers, Curriculum Development Unit Archives.

Colley, G (1966c), 'Education Today and in 1916', *Irish Press,* 15 April 1966.

Colley, G (1966d), 'Statement to the Authorities of Secondary and Vocational Schools', in OECD (1969), *Reviews of National Policies for Education: Ireland,* Paris: OECD.

Collingwood, R.G. (1939), *An Autobiography,* London: Oxford University Press.

Collingwood, R.G. (1961), *The Idea of History,* London: Oxford Paperback.

Collins, E. (1978), Parliamentary Speech, *Dáil Éireann Official Reports,* vol. 307, no. 3, cols. 385–407, Dublin: Stationery Office.

Commission of the European Communities (1976), 'From Education to Working Life', *Bulletin of the European Communities; Supplement 12/76,* Brussels: European Commission.

Commission on Technical Education (1928), *Report,* Dublin: Stationery Office.

Commoner, B. (1972), *The Closing Circle: Man, Nature and Technology,* London: Cape.

Connolly, P. and M. Keenan (2000), *Racial Attitudes and Prejudice in Northern Ireland,* Belfast: Northern Ireland Statistics and Research Agency.

Coolahan, J. (1981), *Irish Education: Its History and Structure*, Dublin: Institute of Public Administration.

Craft, M. (1973), 'Economy, Ideology and Educational Development in Ireland' in R. Bell and K. Jones (eds.), *Education, Economy and Politics: Case Studies – Parts 3 and 4*, Milton Keynes: Open University Press.

Cronbach, L. and Associates (1980), *Towards Reform of Program Evaluation,* San Francisco: Fossey-Bass.

Crooks, J.A. (1978), 'A Participant Observation Study of the Factors Which Influenced the Development of the City of Dublin Humanities Curriculum 1972–1976', unpublished Ph.D. dissertation, Trinity College, University of Dublin.

Crooks, J.A. (1987), 'Overcoming Disadvantage: the Educational Response', in T. Crooks and D. Stokes (eds.), *Disadvantage, Learning and Young People,* Dublin: Curriculum Development Unit.

Crotty, R. (1986), *Ireland in Crisis,* Dingle: Brandon.

Curriculum Development Unit, *Annual Reports* (1972–2005), Dublin: Curriculum Development Unit.

Curriculum Development Unit (1979), *Life and Environment,* Dublin: O'Brien Educational.

Curriculum Development Unit (1994), *Environment and Schools Initiative in Ireland: European Action for the Environment,* Dublin: Curriculum Development Unit.

Curriculum Development Unit (1998), *Linking Environmental Education and Community Enterprise: Project Report,* Dublin: Curriculum Development Unit.

Curtis, S.J. and M.E. Boultwood (1961), *A Short History of Educational Ideas*, London: University Tutorial Press.

Dalin, P. (1973), *Case Studies of Educational Innovation: Vol. 4, Strategies for Innovation in Education,* Paris: OECD.

Darling, J. (1994), *Child-Centred Learning and Its Critics*, London: Chapman.

Department of Education (1942), *Memorandum V 40: Organisation of Wholetime Continuation Courses in Borough, Urban and County Areas*, Dublin: Stationery Office.

Department of Education (1962), *Report of the Council of Education in the Curriculum of the Secondary School,* Dublin: Stationery Office.

Department of Education (1970), 'Community Schools', *Studies: An Irish Quarterly Review,* vol. 59, no. 236: 341–4.

Department of Education (1971), *Curaclam na Bunscoile – Primary School Curriculum: Teacher's Handbook, Parts 1 and 2,* Dublin: Browne and Nolan.

Department of Education (1974), 'Report of Working Group on Field Studies and Outdoor Pursuits', Dublin: Department of Education.

Department of Education (1978), *Cúrsaí Reamh-Fhostaíochta (Pre-employment Courses),* Dublin: Department of Education.

Dewey, J. (1916), *Democracy and Education,* New York: Macmillan.

Dewey, J. (1963), *Experience and Education,* London: Collier Macmillan.

Dewey, J. (1965), 'My Pedagogic Creed' in R. Ulich (ed.), *Three Thousand Years of Educational Wisdom,* Cambridge MA: Harvard University Press.

Donoghue, D. (1986), *We Irish: The Selected Essays of Denis Donoghue,* Brighton: Harvester Press.

Dunne, J. (1995), 'What's the Good of Education?' in P. Hogan (ed.), *Partnership and the Benefits of Learning: A Symposium on Philosophical Issues in Educational Policy,* Maynooth: Educational Studies Association of Ireland.

Edwards, R.D. (1977), *Patrick Pearse: The Triumph of Failure,* London: Gollancz.

Eisner, E. (1985), *The Art of Educational Evaluation: A Personal View,* London: Falmer.

European Commission (1997), *Accomplishing Europe through Education and Training: Report of Study Group,* Luxembourg: Office of Official Publications of the European Communities.

Environmental News: European Action for the Environment/ OECD Environment and Schools Initiative Bulletin, Dublin: Curriculum Development Unit.

Farren, S. and R. Mulvilhill (2000), *Paths to Settlement in Northern Ireland,* Gerrard's Cross, Buckinghamshire: Colin Smyth.

Ferguson, M. (1987), *The Aquarian Conspiracy: Personal and Social Transformation in Our Time,* Los Angeles: Tarcher.

Fisher, H.A.L. (1960), *A History of Europe,* London: Fontana.

Fletcher, B. (1971), *The Challenge of Outward Bound,* London: Heinemann.

Fogarty, C. and T. Crooks (1987), *Undertaking School Review: A Discussion Paper,* Dublin: CDVEC Curriculum Development Unit.

Fullan, M. (1991), *The New Meaning of Educational Change,* London: Cassel.

Gallagher, D. and I. Gallagher (eds.) (1976), *The Education of Man: the Educational Philosophy of Jacques Maritain,* Westport, Connecticut: Greenwood Press.

Gerlach, L. and V. Hine (1973), *Lifeway Leap: The Dynamics of Change in America,* Minneapolis: University of Minneapolis.

Gibbon, E. (1899), *The Decline and Fall of the Roman Empire,* New York: Collier.

Gill, B., A. Clifford, S. McCarthy, K. O'Shea and A. Trant (1999), *Education for Reconciliation: A Curriculum Investigation,* Dublin: CDVEC Curriculum Development Unit.

Gleeson, J. (1992), 'A Common Core Curriculum: What Must We Cover?' *Compass: Journal of the Irish Association for Curriculum Development,* vol. 20, no. 2, 7–33.

Goldsmith, E., R. Allen, M. Allaby, J. Davoll and S. Lawrence (1972), 'Blueprint for Survival', *The Ecologist,* vol. 2, no.1.

Goodson, I. (1983), *School Subjects and Curriculum Change,* London: Croom Helm.

Goodson, I. (ed.) (1985), *Social Histories of the Secondary Curriculum: Subjects for Study,* London: Falmer Press.

Goodson, I. (1994), *Studying Curriculum,* Buckingham: Open University Press.

Granville, G. (1982), 'The Work of the Early School Leavers' Project', *Compass: Journal of the Irish Association for Curriculum Development,* vol. ll, no. 1, 21–8.

Hadden, T. and K. Boyle (1989), *The Anglo-Irish Agreement*: *Commentary, Text and Official Review*, London: Edwin Higel and Sweet and Maxwell.

Hamilton, D. (1990), *Learning about Education*: *An Unfinished Curriculum*, Milton Keynes: Open University Press.

Hannan, D. (1987), 'Goals and Objectives of Educational Interventions' in T. Crooks and D. Stokes (eds.), *Disadvantage, Learning and Young People*, Dublin: Curriculum Development Unit.

Hargreaves, D. (1982), *The Challenge for the Comprehensive School*: *Culture, Curriculum and Community*, London: Routledge and Kegan Paul.

Hargreaves, A. (1994), *Changing Teachers, Changing Times*, London: Cassell.

Harlen, W. (1976), 'Change and Development in Evaluation Strategy' in D. Tawney (ed.) *Curriculum Evaluation Today*: *Trends and Implications*, London: Macmillan Education.

Harris, J. (1989), 'The Policy-Making Role of the Department of Education', in D.G. Mulcahy and D. O'Sullivan (eds.), *Irish Educational Policy*: *Process and Substance*, Dublin: Institute of Public Administration.

Havelock, R.G. (1970), *Guide to Innovation in Education*, Anne Arbor, Michigan: University of Michigan.

Healy, L. (1972), 'The Integration of the School with the Community', unpublished Higher Diploma in Education dissertation, School of Education, Trinity College, Dublin, 1972.

Hillery, P. J. (1963), 'Post- Primary Education' in OECD (1969), *Reviews of National Policies for Education: Ireland*, Paris: OECD.

Hirst, P.H. (1974), *Knowledge and the Curriculum*, London: Routledge and Kegan Paul.

Hirst, P.H. (1993), 'The Foundations of the National Curriculum: Why Subjects?' in P. O'Hear and J. White (eds.), *Assessing the National Curriculum*, London: Paul Chapman.

Hirst, P.H. and R.S. Peters (1970), *The Logic of Education*, London: Routledge and Kegan Paul.

Hogan, J.M. (1968), *Impelled into Experiences,* London: Educational Productions.

Holland, J. (1979), *Rutland Street,* Dublin: Van Leer Foundation.

Horgan, J. (1978), Parliamentary Speech, *Dáil Éireann Official Reports,* vol. 307, no. 3, cols. 464–481, Dublin: Stationery Office.

Hughes, J.C and C. Donnelly (2002), *Analysis of the Community Relations Module Included in the 2001 Northern Ireland Life and Times Survey,* Jordenstown: University of Ulster School of Policy Studies.

Hurley, K. (1977), 'Primary School: Whither the Curriculum', *Compass: Journal of the Irish Association of Curriculum Development,* vol. 6, no. 2, 15–25.

Hyland, A. (1993), 'Address to the First Meeting of the Teachers Involved in the Pilot Scheme for the Introduction of Civic, Social and Political Education at Junior Cycle Level', paper delivered to the joint NCCA/Department of Education in-service course in Dublin Castle, 9 December, 1993.

Hyland, A. (ed.) (1998), *Innovations in Assessment in Irish Education,* Cork: Education Department, NUI Cork.

ICE Report (1975), *Final Report of the Committee on the Form and Function of the Intermediate Certificate Examination,* Dublin: Stationery Office.

International Fund for Ireland (1987), *Annual Report 1986/87,* Belfast and Dublin: International Fund for Ireland.

Ireland (1999), *Primary School Curriculum: Introduction,* Dublin: Stationery Office.

IUCN – International Union for the Conservation of Nature and Natural Resources (1970), *Final Report of International Working Meeting on Environmental Education in the School Curriculum,* Morges: IUCN.

Jenkins, D. (1980), 'Man: A Course of Study' in L. Stenhouse (ed.), *Curriculum Research and Development in Action,* London: Heinemann Educational.

Kelleher, M. J. (1998), 'Suicide in Schools' in B. Farrell (ed.), *Issues in Education – Changing Education, Changing Society: ASTI Education Journal, vol 3,* 105–10.

Kelly, A. (1999), *The Curriculum: Theory and Practice,* London: Chapman.

King, A.R. and J.A. Brownell (1966), *The Curriculum and the Disciplines of Knowledge: A Theory of Curriculum Practice,* New York: Wiley.

Larkin Community College (2005), *Damburst and Dreams: A Learning through Arts Secondary School Experience,* Dublin: Larkin Community College.

Lawton, D. (1984), 'Curriculum and Culture' in M. Skilbeck (ed.), *Readings in School-Based Curriculum Development,* London: Harper and Row.

Lawton, D. (1996), *Beyond the National Curriculum: Teacher Professionalism and Empowerment,* Sevenoaks: Hodder and Stoughton.

Lawton, D. and P. Gordon (1996), *Dictionary of Education,* Sevenoaks: Hodder and Stoughton.

Lawton, D. and P. Gordon (2002), *A History of Western Educational Ideas,* London: Woburn Press.

Lee, J.J. (1979), 'Seán Lemass' in J.J. Lee (ed.), *Ireland 1945–70,* Dublin: Gill and Macmillan.

Lipnack, J. and J. Stamps (1986), *The Networking Book,* London: Routledge and Kegan Paul.

Lyons, E (1987), *Partnership in Parish: A Vision for Parish Life, Mission and Ministry,* Dublin: Columban Press.

Lyons, F.S.L. (1973*a*), *Ireland Since the Famine,* London: Collins/Fontana.

Lyons, F.S.L. (1973*b*), 'The Meaning of Independence' in B. Farrell (ed.), *The Irish Parliamentary Tradition,* Dublin: Gill and Macmillan.

Lyons, F.S.L. (1979), *Culture and Anarchy in Ireland,* Oxford: Oxford University Press.

Lynch, P. (1966), 'The Social Revolution That Never Was' in T.D. Williams (ed.), *The Irish Struggle 1916–1926,* London: Routledge and Kegan Paul.

McCormick, J. (1985), *The User's Guide to the Environment,* London: Kogan Page.

McDonagh, S. (2004), *The Death of Life: The Horror of Extinction,* Dublin: Columba Press.

MacDonald, B. (1976), 'Evaluation and the Control of Education' in D. Tawney (ed.), *Curriculum Evaluation Today: Trends and Implications,* London: Macmillan.

MacDonald, B. (1991), 'Critical Introduction' in J. Rudduck, *Innovation and Change,* Milton Keynes: Open University Press.

McDowell, R.B. and D.A. Webb, (1982), *Trinity College Dublin 1592–1952: An Academic History,* Cambridge: Cambridge University Press.

McElligott, T.J. (1955), 'Some Thoughts on our Educational Discontents', *University Review,* vol.1, no. 5, 27–36.

McElligott, T.J. (1966), *Education in Ireland,* Dublin: Institute of Public Administration.

McGlynn, F. (1976), 'Focus on Glencree', Dublin: Curriculum Development Unit.

MacGréil, M. (1974), *Educational Opportunity in Dublin,* Dublin: Catholic Communications Institute of Ireland, Research and Development Unit.

MacGréil, M. (1996), *Prejudice in Ireland Revisited,* Maynooth: St Patrick's College, Survey and Research Unit.

MacIntyre, A. (1981), *After Virtue: A Study in Moral Theory,* London: Duckworth.

MacIntyre, A. (1987), 'The Idea of an Educated Public', in G. Haydon (ed.), *Education and Values,* London: Institute of Education.

McQuaid, J.C. (1946), Address on the occasion of the official opening of Cabra Vocational School, reported in *Irish Press,* 3 December 1946.

MacSuibhne, T., A. Ó Ceallaigh, C. Ó Dálaigh and J. S. Walshe (1983), 'A Review of Four Innovative Programmes in the Senior Cycle of Post-Primary Schools', Dublin: Curriculum Unit, Department of Education.

Malone, R. (1987), 'An Approach to Integrated Science', *Compass: Journal of the Irish Association for Curriculum Development,* vol. 16, no. 2, 57–71.

Maritain, J. (1945), *Christianity and Democracy*, London: Geoffrey Bles.

Maritain, J. (1960), *Education at the Crossroads,* New Haven, Connecticut: Yale University Press.

Martin, J.R. (1992), *The Schoolhome: Rethinking Schools for Changing Families,* Cambridge MA: Harvard University Press.

Martin, J.R. (1994), *Changing the Educational Landscape: Philosophy, Women and Curriculum*, New York: Routledge.

Meadows, D.H., D.J. Meadows, J. Randers, and W.W. Behrens, (1972), *The Limits to Growth,* New York: Signet.

Miles, M. (ed.) (1964), *Innovation in Education*, New York: Columbia Teachers' College.

Milieu: Newsletter of the European Community Environmental Network, Dublin: Curriculum Development Unit.

Ministry of Education (1963), *Half Our Future: A Report of the Central Advisory Council for Education (England),* London: HMSO.

Ministry of Education, (1964), *Report of the Working Party on the Schools – Curriculum and Examinations,* London: HMSO.

Mulcahy, D. (1981), *Curriculum and Policy in Irish Post-Primary Education,* Dublin: Institute of Public Administration.

Mulcahy, D. (2002), *Knowledge, Gender and Schooling: the Feminist Educational thought of Jane Roland Martin*, Westport, Connecticut: Bergin and Garvey.

Naisbitt, J. (1984), *Megatrends: Ten New Directions Transforming Our Lives,* London: Futura.

National Council for Curriculum and Assessment (1999), *The Junior Cycle Review: Progress Report – Issues and Options for Development,* Dublin: NCCA.

National Council for Curriculum and Assessment (2005), 'Assessment for Learning: Report on Stage 2 of the Development Initiative', Dublin: NCCA.

National Council for Vocational Awards (1994), *Annual Report 1993/94*, Dublin: NCVA.

National Economic and Social Council (1985), *Manpower Policy in Ireland,* Dublin: National Economic and Social Council.

Ó Buachalla, S. (1980), *A Significant Irish Educationalist: The Educational Writings of P.H. Pearse,* Dublin: Mercier Press.

Ó Buachalla, S. (1988), *Education Policy in Twentieth Century Ireland,* Dublin: Wolfhound Press.

O'Connor, S. (1986), *A Troubled Sky: Reflections on the Irish Educational Scene* 1957–1968, Dublin: Educational Research Centre, St. Patrick's College.

Ó Donnabháin, D. (1998), 'The Work-Related Curriculum' in A. Trant, D. Ó Donnabháin, D. Lawton and T. O'Connor, *The Future of the Curriculum,* Dublin: CDVEC Curriculum Development Unit.

OECD (1969), *Reviews of National Policies for Education: Ireland,* Paris: OECD.

OECD (1980), *School and Community,* Paris: OECD.

O'Gorman, E. (1998), 'Profiling in the Junior Certificate School Programme' in A. Hyland (ed.), *Innovations in Assessment in Irish Education,* Cork: Education Department, University College, Cork.

Ó Máirtín, G and A. Ó Ceallaigh (1981), 'An Evaluation of the Humanities Programme of the City of Dublin Vocational Education Committee', An tAonad Curaclaim, Department of Education, Dublin.

O'Sullivan, P. (1974), 'The Aran Islands: A Contrast Study', *Compass: Journal of Irish Association for Curriculum Development,* vol. 3, no. 2, 19.

Ó Tuathaigh, G. (1972), *Ireland before the Famine* 1798–1848, Dublin: Gill and Macmillan.

Parlett, M. and D. Hamilton, (1976), 'Evaluation as Illumination' in D. Tawney (ed.), *Curriculum Evaluation Today: Trends and Implications,* London: Macmillan.

Peters, R.S. (1966), *Ethics and Education,* London: Allen and Unwin.

Pius XI, *The Christian Education of Youth,* (translated by the Catholic Truth Society, 1961), London: Catholic Truth Society.

Plato, *The Republic* (translated by F.M. Cornford, 1941), London: Oxford University Press.

Plato, *The Laws* (translated by T. Saunders, 1970), Harmondsworth: Penguin Classics.

Plowden Report (1967), *Children and their Primary Schools*, London: HMSO.

Plunkett, H. (1905), *Ireland in the New Century*, London: Murray.

Pring, R. (1995), *Closing the Gap*: *Liberal Education and Vocational Preparation,* London: Hodder and Staughton.

Randles, E. (1975), *Post-Primary Education in Ireland 1957–1970*, Dublin: Veritas.

Reynolds, J. and M. Skilbeck (1976), *Culture and the Classroom*, London: Open Books.

Roberts, K., G. White and H. Parker (1974), *The Character Training Industry*, Newton Abbot: David and Charles.

Rosen, H. (n.d.), *Stories and Meanings,* Sheffield: National Association for the Teaching of English.

Rossiter, S. and A. Trant, (1971), 'The Concept of a Major Regional School: Memorandum on the Future Development of Clogher Road and Ballyfermot', March 1971, Ballyfermot Papers, Curriculum Development Unit Archives.

Rousseau, Jean Jacques, *Émile* (translated by Barbara Foxley, 1911), London: Dent.

Ruddock, J. (1991), *Innovation and Change,* Milton Keynes: Open University Press.

Ruddock, J. (1996), 'Students' Voices: What can they tell us as Partners in Change?', Address to the Fifth BEMAS Research Conference, 'Partners in Change: Shaping the Future', 25–27 March 1996, Robinson College, Cambridge.

Ryan, L. (1984), 'The Changing Face of Irish Values' in M. Fogarty, L. Ryan and J. Lee, *Irish Values and Attitudes,* Dublin: Dominican Publications.

Ryan, R. (1978), Parliamentary Question, *Dáil Éireann Official Reports,* vol. 307, no. 12, cols. 1913–1914, Dublin: Stationery Office.

Sarason, S. (1990), *The Predictable Failure of Educational Reform*, San Francisco: Jossey Bass.

Schools Council (1965), *Raising the School-Leaving Age: A Cooperative Programme of Research and Development,* London: HMSO.

Schools Council/Nuffield Foundation (1970), *The Humanities Curriculum Project: an Introduction, London*: Heinemann Educational.

Scully, D. (1998), *Bare Boards and a Passion: Drama in Post-Primary Schools,* Dublin: CDVEC Curriculum Development Unit.

Sheehan, J.P. (1972*a*), 'Proposal for Joint Curriculum Development Project for Junior Cycle Post-Primary Courses', unpublished document, Steering Committee Papers, Curriculum Development Unit Archives.

Sheehan, J.P. (1972*b*), 'Correspondence with Seán O'Connor', Department of Education, September 1972 to March 1973, Curriculum Development Unit Archives.

Sisson, E. (2004), *Pearse's Patriots: St Enda's and the Cult of Boyhood,* Cork: Cork University Press.

Skilbeck, M. (1974), 'Proposal for an Enquiry by a New University of Ulster Consultancy Team into the Work of the Dublin Vocational Education Committee's Curriculum Development Unit', unpublished document, Coleraine Evaluation Papers, Curriculum Development Unit Archives.

Skilbeck, M (1975*a*), 'Curriculum Development Unit: Report by the Evaluation Team', unpublished document, Coleraine Evaluation Papers, Curriculum Development Unit Archives.

Skilbeck, M (1975*b*), letter to A. Trant 8 September, 1975, Coleraine Evaluation Papers, Curriculum Development Unit Archives.

Skilbeck, M. (1976), 'Ideologies and Values', Unit 3 of Course E203, *Curriculum, Design and Development,* Milton Keynes: Open University.

Skilbeck, M. (1982*a*), 'Reflections on School-Work Transition: An Overview Paper in Response to Seminar Proceedings' in *Educational Achievement and Youth Employment: The Proceedings of the Dissemination Seminar of the Early School Leavers Project,* Dublin: Curriculum Development Unit.

Skilbeck, M. (1982*b*), *A Core Curriculum for the Common School*, London: University of London Institute of Education.

Skilbeck, M. (1984*a*), *Evaluating the Curriculum in the Eighties*, London: Hodder and Stoughton.

Skilbeck, M. (1984*b*), *School-Based Curriculum Development*, London: Harper and Row.

Skilbeck, M. (1990), *Curriculum Reform: An Overview of Trends*, Paris: OECD.

Skildelski, R. (1969), *English Progressive Schools*, London: Penquin.

Solzhenitsyn, A. (1972), *One Word of Truth: The Nobel Speech on Literature, 1970*, London: Bodley Head.

Stake, R. (1995), *The Art of Case Study Research*, London: Sage Publications.

Stearn, G. (1968), *McLuhan: Hot and Cold*, Harmondsworth: Penguin.

Stenhouse, L (1975), *An Introduction to Curriculum Research and Development*, London: Heinemann.

Stenhouse, L (ed.) (1980), *Curriculum Research and Development in Action*, London: Heinemann Educational Books.

Stokes, D. (1988), *Beyond School,* Dublin: Curriculum Development Unit.

Sugrue, C. (2004), *Curriculum and Ideology: Irish Experiences, International Perspectives*, Dublin: Liffey Press.

Thomson, D. (1976), *Woodbrook*, Harmondsworth: Penguin.

Trant, A. (1967), 'The Idea of Comprehensive Education', unpublished brochure for the official opening of the Emmet Building, Vocational School Ballyfermot, 5 January 1967, Ballyfermot Papers, Curriculum Development Unit Archives.

Trant, A. (1972), 'Memorandum on Curriculum Development in the City of Dublin VEC', unpublished document, Steering Committee Papers, Curriculum Development Unit Archives.

Trant, A. (1974), 'A Proposal for a Project in Outdoor Education for the School Year 1974/75', unpublished document, Outdoor Education Papers, Curriculum Development Unit Archives.

Trant, A. (1978), *Environmental Education in the Age Group 9–14 Years in the European Communities*, Brussels/Luxembourg: Commission of the European Communities.

Trant, A. (1982), 'New Schools for Old: The Experience of a Curriculum Development Project' in *Educational Achievement and Youth Employment: The Proceedings of the Dissemination Seminar of the Early School Leavers Project*, Dublin: Curriculum Development Unit.

Trant, A. (1986), 'The Secondary Network: An Overview', ECEEN Papers, Curriculum Development Unit Archives.

Trant, A. (1989), 'Adventure Sports in Education: the Next Twenty Years', Paper read at the Annual Conference of the Association for Adventure Sports, 28 January 1989, Outdoor Education Papers, Curriculum Development Unit Archives.

Trant, A. (1992), 'The Power of the Provisional: The Curriculum Development Unit – A Case Study in Innovation in Modern Irish Education', unpublished Ph.D. dissertation, Institute of Education, University of London.

Trant, A. (ed.) (1999), *Reconciling Liberal and Vocational Education*, Dublin: Curriculum Development Unit.

Trant, A. and E. McSkeane (1994), 'An Evaluation of Wider Horizons', unpublished document, Curriculum Development Unit Archives.

Trant, A., D. Ó Donnabháin, D. Lawton and T. O'Connor (1998), *The Future of the Curriculum,* Dublin: Curriculum Development Unit.

Trant, A., S. Trant, D. Fitzpatrick and J. Medlycott (2002), *Evaluation of the Wider Horizons Programme of the International Fund for Ireland,* Dublin: Curriculum Development Unit.

Trant, M.L. (2002), 'The Quest for a Liberal Vocationalism: The Experience of the National Council for Vocational Awards', unpublished Ph.D. dissertation, Institute of Education, University of London.

Tyler, R. (1949), *Basic Principles of Curriculum and Assessment,* Chicago: University of Chicago Press.

Ulich, R. (ed.) (1965), *Three Thousand Years of Educational Wisdom*, Cambridge MA: Harvard University Press.

UNESCO (1978), *Intergovernmental Conference on Environmental Education: Final Report*, Paris: UNESCO.

UNESCO (1996), *Learning: The Treasure Within*, Paris: UNESCO.

United Nations (1972), 'Conference Document A/Conf.48PC, United Nations Conference on the Human Environment', unpublished text, UNESCO House, Paris.

Vocational Educational Act (1930), Dublin: Stationery Office.

Walker, D. and J. Soltis (1997), *Curriculum and Aims*, New York: Teachers College.

Walsh, P. (1993), *Education and Meaning: Philosophy in Practice*, London: Cassell.

Walsh, P. (1997), *The Curriculum: Context, Design and Development*, London: University of London.

Weil, S. (1959), *Waiting on God*, London: Collins/Fontana.

White, L. (1967), 'The Historical Roots of Our Ecologic Crisis', *Science*, 155, 1203–7.

White, V. (1947), *How to Study*, London: Aquin Press.

Whitehead, A.N. (1970), *The Aims of Education and Other Essays*, London: Ernest Benn.

Whyte, J.H. (1980), *Church and State in Modern Ireland 1923–1979*, Dublin: Gill and Macmillan.

Whyte, J.H. (1990), *Interpreting Northern Ireland*, Oxford: Oxford University Press.

Wilson, J. (1978*a*), Parliamentary Speech, *Dáil Éireann Official Reports*, vol. 307, no. 9, cols. 1411–1414, Dublin: Stationery Office.

Wilson, I. (1978*b*), Parliamentary Speech, *Dáil Éireann Official Reports*, vol. 307, no.12, col. 1914, Dublin: Stationery Office.

Index